Women Poets in
Ancient Greece
and Rome

Women Poets in
Ancient Greece
and Rome

Edited by
Ellen Greene

UNIVERSITY OF OKLAHOMA PRESS : NORMAN

Also by Ellen Greene

Reading Sappho: Contemporary Approaches (Berkeley, 1996)
(ed.) *Re-reading Sappho: Reception and Transmission* (Berkeley, 1996)
The Erotics of Domination: Male Desire and the Mistress in Latin Love Poetry
  (Baltimore, 1998)

Library of Congress Cataloging-in-Publication Data

Women poets in ancient Greece and Rome / edited by Ellen Greene.
    p. cm.
    Includes bibliographical references (p.   ) and index.
    ISBN 0–8061–3663–4 (alk. paper)—ISBN 0–8061–3664–2 (pbk. : alk.
paper)
      1. Greek poetry—Women authors—History and criticism. 2. Latin
poetry—Women authors—History and criticism. 3. Women—Greece—
Intellectual life. 4. Women—Rome—Intellectual life. 5. Women and
literature—Greece. 6. Women and literature—Rome. 7. Women in
literature. I. Greene, Ellen, 1950–

PA3067.W66 2005
880'.09—dc22

                                                                    2004062023

1 2 3 4 5 6 7 8 9 10

For my sister
DEBRA

Contents

Acknowledgments

This book was a long time coming. I first had the idea for it in 1996 while I was working on my two Sappho volumes. It was then that I became committed to making a contribution to the small but growing body of scholarship on Greek and women poets. I am extremely grateful to John Drayton, Director of the University of Oklahoma Press, for his unwavering enthusiasm and support. Jennifer Cunningham and Julie Shilling, Associate Editors at the Press, have been very helpful as well. I also want to thank Paul Allen Miller and David Larmour for their belief in this project in its early stages. Professor Miller's insights and unfailingly perceptive readings helped to make this a better book. I owe a deep dept to Marilyn Skinner, whose pioneering work on women poets in Ancient Greece has inspired much of my own interest in the poets represented in this volume.

I could not have completed the work for this project without the help of the University of Oklahoma. The Department of Classics and Letters, the College of Arts and Sciences, and the Office of Research Administration provided invaluable moral and financial support. In particular, I am grateful to my department chair, John S. Catlin, for always supporting my professional endeavors.

On a more personal note, I am deeply appreciative of the constancy, affection, and lively companionship of my partner, Jim. This book is dedicated to Debra—my sister, best friend, and the mother of my beloved nephew, Justin.

Introduction

Ellen Greene

The interpretation of women's literature in Greek and Roman antiquity is a notoriously challenging enterprise. To be sure, the relative
obscurity of historical knowledge surrounding Greco-Roman texts in
general invites a higher degree of speculation than modern literary
texts generally do. Yet the texts of women authors in ancient Greece
and Rome present especially difficult challenges. Most obvious, the
fragmentary condition of much of extant women's writing in Greco-
Roman antiquity makes it particularly susceptible to ambiguity. More
important, women's status in antiquity—the constraints on their
legal and political rights, their limited educations, and the extreme
restrictions placed on their involvement in the public sphere—renders
knowledge about the conditions attendant on women's literary productions especially obscure. In addition, much of what we "know" of
ancient women has come down to us through the images created of
them in male-authored texts. While women's own writing might
seem to make the possibilities of ancient female subjectivity accessible
to us, we cannot be certain about the effects of male constraints on
female agency within the performative contexts of women's poetry in
the male-dominated societies of Greece and Rome. Indeed, classical
scholars over the years have often lamented the extreme paucity of
extant women's writing.[1] On the other hand, we have to wonder how
women in Greece and Rome wrote and performed their poems at all,

considering their apparent marginality within the cultures in which they lived and wrote.

While the women poets of Greece and Rome have at times fascinated modern scholars, much of the scholarship until recently has been either mildly dismissive or openly denigrating. Early twentieth-century scholars often focused on women's biographies, assuming that there was little poetic artistry to unearth and that women would naturally be concerned exclusively with the "trivialities" of their private lives.[2] Even scholars who wrote admiringly of Sappho's poems, for example, emphasized aspects of her work they perceived to be expressive of purely personal emotions.[3] On the less positive end of this continuum we find scholars such as Devereux and Marcovich, who characterized the seemingly "confessional" quality in Sappho's poems as hysterical and neurotic.[4] Overall, the emphasis on women's biographies and on the seemingly "personal" nature of their literary achievements has occluded the highly intricate and complex character of ancient women's relationships not only to their largely patriarchal societies but also to literary traditions overwhelmingly dominated by male voices.

While it is certainly true that for the most part Greek and Roman women occupied marginal positions in society, there is much evidence to suggest that in certain periods women had at least some exposure to male literary culture. Even in archaic and early classical Greece, where adult women were segregated from the larger public sphere except on ritual occasions, there are indications that women might have produced their own discourses in isolation. The world Sappho inhabited, for example, as represented in her poems seems to be comprised of a community of women within a socially segregated society—a society that appears detached from male "public" arenas.[5] Overall, in spite of the formal exclusion of women from the public domain in both Greek and Roman culture, women poets clearly had some familiarity with literary culture as well as with traditionally masculine forms of public and political expression. The references in Greek and Roman (male) texts to women as practitioners of literature strongly suggest that a tradition of female authorship flourished from the Archaic Age (ca. 700 BCE) into the Hellenistic and Roman periods. A canonical roster of women poets was first compiled by the learned scholars of Alexandria and was in circulation by the time of Augustus in imperial Rome. Sappho was not only the earliest but by all accounts the most highly regarded woman poet in Greek and Roman antiquity. Both classical and Hellenistic women writers looked back to Sappho as their exemplar. While Sappho's work has received considerable scholarly attention in recent years (as have the representations of women in male-authored texts), there are currently no published collections that examine a women's poetic tradition in Greece and Rome or even focus exclusively on women's own voices in Greek and Roman literature.[6] The nine essays collected here treat nearly all of the surviving poetry written by Greek and Roman women.

During the last two decades feminist approaches in classical scholarship have examined the extent to which Sappho's poems and those of her literary successors present a woman-specific discourse that secures a female perspective within male-dominated discursive systems. While the relationship between public and private spheres in the lives of ancient women is a complex one, it is clear that the female voice in ancient lyric reflects the marginal status of women in Greek and Roman societies (see Cantarella 1987). One of the unifying themes of this collection is the investigation of the intricate relationship between "public" and "private" discourses in the poetry of ancient Greek and Roman women. Many of the authors in this volume interrogate the bilingual nature of women's poetic discourses, that is, the ability of women poets to speak in the languages of both the male public arena and the excluded female minority.[7] Perhaps the most pressing concern for scholars working on women's poetic texts is how to situate women poets within a dominant male literary tradition. A central issue in the majority of the essays here concerns questions about the extent to which women's poetry in Greece and Rome may be characterized as distinctly "feminine" or at least as "woman-identified," to use Diane Rayor's term (1993). Some of the essays in this collection also raise questions about the relationship between female-authored poetry and traditional female speech genres. Other essays focus more on how female poets deviate from their male counterparts.

More generally, the collection as a whole addresses the relationship between gender and genre, sexuality and textuality, and implicitly raises the question as to whether Greek and Roman women may be said to have a poetic tradition of their own—despite the fragmentary nature of their surviving poetic texts. Although I do not think it possible to answer that question definitively given our limited knowledge, I do think the essays here point to a surprising degree of congruity and complementarity among female authors writing during vastly different periods. To be more specific, the women poets treated in this collection represent a body of work that shows an extraordinary awareness of literary tradition while at the same time often revealing concerns that may be described as distinctly feminine. Moreover, many of the essays in this volume show how women poets in Greece and Rome, through their innovative reworkings of myth and appropriations of male literary forms, did not merely imitate the prevailing patriarchy (as some scholars have maintained) but uncovered their own art forms within established literary genres. Although the precise dates for many of the authors treated in the collection are either controversial or uncertain, the essays have been arranged in a loose chronological fashion. While this arrangement by no means assumes a continuous line of historical development, it will nonetheless help to clarify influences where they might exist.

In the opening essay of the collection, "Sappho's Public World," Holt Parker argues against the view common in recent scholarship that Sappho's poetry is concerned exclusively with private matters such as weddings and love affairs. Parker cautions, rightly, about the dangers of projecting onto Sappho notions about an "essentialized" image of woman. While he acknowledges that what remains of Sappho's poetry is primarily concerned with traditionally "feminine" concerns, he argues that Sappho's references and allusions to public and political life ought to be taken into account within the context of her body of work. Parker points out that Sappho's concern with defining the noble man, and with ethics in general, reflects the degree to which the public world of aristocratic values and friendship is an important component of her poetry.

Like many of the authors in this volume, Parker has clearly benefited from critical approaches that tend to privilege the feminine in the texts of Greek and Roman women poets. His essay, however, reflects recent trends in scholarship that emphasize the interplay in those texts between the public and the private, the traditional and the innovative. David Larmour's essay on Corinna, "Corinna's Poetic *Metis* and the Epinikian Tradition," also addresses the issue of how Greek women poets appropriate and ultimately transform aspects of male literary form and conventions. His essay explores how Corinna's mythological narratives refashion male traditions of choral lyric—and diverge from or even react against the poetic mode of Pindar's Panhellenic epinikians—as Corinna reworks a Panhellenic perspective, subsuming it within the local raw material of her poems. Yet Larmour argues that Corinna's use of irony and incongruity in her treatment of mythological narrative serves to challenge, albeit subtly, the conventions of the epinikian mode. Examining Corinna's two main fragments—the singing contest of Cithaeron, and Acraephen's reply to Asopus about his daughters—Larmour shows how Corinna's inventive reworking of these narratives foregrounds female figures and experiences, suggesting that her poems were composed primarily for female audiences. By analyzing the two fragments as a single unit of signification, he draws together their shared motifs of secrecy and disclosure. In addition, he evaluates the tradition of the rivalry between Corinna and Pindar within the broader agonistic context of athletic competition and epinikian poetry. While Larmour acknowledges that Corinna works within a patriarchal tradition, he concludes that her "woman-identified" perspective subjects elements of that tradition to scrutiny.

The longest portion of this collection treats the Hellenistic women poets, whose work represents the largest and most diverse surviving body of women's poetry from Greek and Roman antiquity. During the Hellenistic period women were offered new opportunities for education, women poets were revered as never before, and were rewarded for their talents with prizes, state decrees, and even political rights. Some scholars have argued, however, that as Hellenistic women gained greater literacy, women poets produced poems for a predominantly male audience, trading the woman-specific poetic discourse of earlier eras for an aping of patriarchal values and modes of speech. In various ways, however, the authors of essays in this collection on Anyte, Erinna, Moero, and Nossis challenge this position. While the focus on women's lives and community and the resonances of Sappho as a literary exemplar may identify the poetic voices of Hellenistic women poets as peculiarly feminine, the interaction between their woman-identified art and the established male literary culture and convention often results in highly innovative forms of poetic discourse.

Diane Rayor's essay focuses on the power of memory in Erinna's poetry. While Rayor situates Erinna's epigrams within the Sapphic tradition, she points out how the changes in the performative context from the seventh to the fourth centuries BCE suggest that Erinna's epigrams cannot, like Sappho's poetry, encompass a communal audience of women with a shared memory. Rayor shows, however, how the memory of a beloved woman in both Sappho and Erinna functions as a vehicle of poetic inspiration and creation. As Rayor demonstrates, Sappho recalls the beloved woman in part to provoke ongoing communication within a living community of women. Sappho's songs therefore serve to heal the grief brought on by the absence of a woman linked through bonds of affection with both the female narrator and the *hetairia*, the community of female companions. Erinna's poems, on the other hand, express grief for a friend whose absence was caused by her death. While Erinna's epigrams invoke the memory of the beloved friend and commemorate the shared activities of women's lives, they cannot stimulate an ongoing connection, a "continuing conversation" within a community of women. Thus, Rayor argues, memory in Sappho's poems functions as a tool of invocation and epiphany, whereas in Erinna's epigrams it serves to bring forth a written memorial of the past, an expression of lament that gives testimony to the finality of death. Rayor shows that both Sappho and Erinna focus on women's experiences. Yet the shift from song to written text, while signaling the loss of the power of memory as a living link among women, potentially connects the woman poet to the wider community, beyond the limitations of song performance.

Like Rayor, Elizabeth Manwell shows how the absence of the beloved in Erinna activates poetic voice. Rayor emphasizes the ways in which Erinna's epigrams lack the power to connect the dead with the living because epigram's inscribed form can only "recall the dead without connection to community." Manwell instead focuses on the techniques Erinna uses to fashion a poetic identity of her own. While Manwell acknowledges the sense of absolute loss expressed by Erinna in the *Distaff* poem, she also emphasizes how the experience of loss is an essential component in the process of ego formation and individuation. Further, Manwell points out that Erinna's lament for Baucis has both a private and a public dimension. In order for Erinna's lament to have relevance for an audience, it must express emotions that have both personal and universal appeal. Indeed Manwell argues that Erinna is able to manifest and create her identity as a female poet only through a confluence of public statement and the expression of private emotion. In *The Distaff* and in her epigrams Erinna both "laments" and "shouts loudly"; the death of the beloved affords the opportunity for the poetic articulation of loss. Manwell also points to the transgressive character of the female poetic voice. In one of two of Erinna's epigrams that mourn the death of Baucis, (*AP* 7.710), Erinna explicitly identifies Baucis' voice with those of the Sirens and (Manwell argues), implicitly with the narrator's own voice. Manwell demonstrates that the conflation of the voices of Erinna as narrator, of the

Sirens, and of Baucis suggests that female vocalization—the vehicle for realizing the self, in Manwell's view—is always potentially dangerous.

Like Erinna's epigrams, Nossis' poetry also offers a distinctly feminine perspective. As Marilyn Skinner argues, not only does Nossis explicitly identify herself with Sappho but her poetry also focuses on the world of women, addressing an audience of female companions, emphasizing their domestic concerns, and suggesting a cultural environment set apart from the male-dominated social order. Skinner demonstrates that the bulk of Nossis' surviving poetry—dedicatory epigrams that honor gifts made by women to goddesses—often expresses warm personal emotions for the dedicant, which run counter to the "public" and impersonal character of the genre. Discussing those epigrams in which the dedicants are thought to be courtesans, Skinner argues that Nossis not only praises their beauty and elegance but also implicitly rectifies patriarchal literary tradition by expressing nonjudgmental, positive attitudes toward their sexuality and by revising notions of what constitutes respectability. Skinner's analysis of Nossis' ecphrastic epigrams, poems that verbally reproduce artistic works, shows that Nossis wrote her poems with the assumption that she was speaking to an exclusively female audience. Skinner argues that Nossis' tracing of her ancestry to her female line and her use of a "gender-linked form of speech" typical in women's private quarters reveal her attempt to express a commonality in women's experiences and modes of expression. As Skinner points out, Nossis identifies Sappho as her literary model. But, ironically, Nossis also distances herself from Sappho by asserting in her more "public" poems, poems that assume a readership beyond Nossis' female companions, that *eros* can offer unmitigated pleasure and that Nossis envisions herself as creatively isolated, separated by time and space from her literary "mother."

Skinner's essay on Moero's poetry picks up on earlier themes in this volume. In discussing Moero's longest-surviving poem, a ten-line fragment of her epic *Mnemosyne*, Skinner shows how Moero, like Corinna, reworks Hesiod's creation myth in order to accentuate female heroism and Zeus' powerlessness. Skinner also draws comparisons between Moero's *Mnemosyne* and the didactic poem *Phaenomena* of the Hellenistic poet Aratus. Given that Aratus was probably a contemporary of Moero's, Skinner suggests that the echoes of Aratus, along with reminiscences of Hesiod and Corinna in Moero's poetry, show her to be an astute practitioner of poetic allusion, a poet keenly aware of literary predecessors as well as literary contemporaries. Thus Skinner proposes that the title *Mnemosyne* might very well refer both to the mother of the Muses and to the memory of the poet herself. Skinner discusses Moero's two ecphrastic epigrams, taking issue with the common view of modern scholars that Moero's poetic style is affected and excessive. Skinner argues that Moero's anthropomorphizing of entities in nature—portraying the vine as a bereaved mother, for example—conveys a parodic quality that may be paralleled with Anyte's animal epigrams. In the cases of both Anyte and Moero, Skinner suggests that the element of parody issues from the incongruity attendant on taking the commemoration of plants and dead animals to absurd lengths. By pointing up the subtle and artful poetic strategies at work in Moero's surviving texts, Skinner's analysis offers an alternative to the mostly negative critical assessments of Moero's poetry by modern readers.[8]

My own essay on Anyte focuses on a number of themes treated in many of the essays in this volume. I consider the ways in which Anyte introduces innovative approaches to conventional literary genres, specifically examining her transposition of Homeric vocabulary to the personal and domestic sphere. I argue that Anyte's laments and her epitaphs for pets do not merely imitate either the tradition of women's lament or the traditions of masculine epic. Rather, Anyte's epigrams create an innovative blending of "high" and "low" art, a complex intertwining of modes of expression associated with epic, public funerary speech, and women's lament. Anyte commemorates the lives of women through a rich tissue of allusion. She often combines numerous references to heroic lament in Homer with images drawn from the domestic lives of women. One of the most striking features of Anyte's version of epigram is the way in which the mourner frequently evokes the emotional engagement and intensity characteristic of traditional women's lament and, at the same time, takes on the impersonal voice of the epic poet in conferring glory on the deceased. Praise and pathos are mixed very cleverly. This is also true of Anyte's pet epitaphs. Like Skinner, I point to some of the parodic qualities in Anyte's animal epitaphs. In addition, I emphasize that her use of Homeric references and her witty wordplay suggest an ironic stance toward male heroic tradition. Anyte's ability to intermingle traditionally masculine and feminine forms of expression constitutes a significant innovation within the genre of traditional epigram.

The final two essays of this collection focus on the Roman poet Sulpicia. Ironically, even though Roman women generally had greater social status and enjoyed more freedoms than Greek women did, it appears that Roman society did not give rise to the rich literary heritage we have for women in ancient Greece. We do know that Roman women wrote letters and possibly orations and autobiographies, but there is scant evidence of women as authors of imaginative literature. The six extant elegies of Sulpicia, who wrote during the Augustan Age, represent much, if not all, of surviving women's literature in ancient Rome.[9] Thus, two essays in this collection are devoted to Sulpicia's poetry. Until relatively recently, scholars have generally regarded Sulpicia's poetry as amateurish and naive. The two essays on Sulpicia in this volume reflect more current views that regard her poetry as sophisticated and original. More than that, scholars have recently acknowledged that the study of Sulpician elegy offers the possibility of gaining insight into women's perspectives on love and sexuality in ancient Rome.[10]

Carol Merriam's essay focuses on Sulpicia's innovative use of literary allusion, arguing against the widespread view that Sulpicia's poems are simply expressions of girlish emotions rather than artistically wrought literary productions. Merriam shows how Sulpicia, like her fellow elegists, makes abundant use of mythological allusion. Merriam specifically points out allusions to the *Iliad*, examining parallels between Sulpicia's use of the figure of Venus as a facilitator of desire and Homer's demonstrations of Aphrodite's power in rescuing her favorites on the battlefield. Merriam suggests links between Sulpicia and Helen and between her beloved Cerinthus and both Paris and Aeneas. Merriam argues that both Venus and her son Amor are typically portrayed in Roman elegy as beneficent toward women in love, but capricious and vindictive toward male lovers. Merriam also notes similarities between Sulpicia's allusions to Venus and Sappho's close identification with Aphrodite. Both Sulpicia and Sappho express confidence in Venus' protection and assistance in helping them fulfill their desires. Merriam suggests that Sulpicia may be placing herself within a female literary tradition, yet at the same time showing that she is as conversant with the art of allusion as her male counterparts.

In her essay on Sulpicia, Barbara Flaschenriem also addresses, albeit implicitly, the dismissive strain in critical responses to Sulpicia's elegies. Flaschenriem argues that through a rhetoric of disclosure the Sulpician narrator subverts elegiac convention and presents a new, artful presentation of self. As Flaschenriem points out, Roman women would potentially subject themselves to disgrace if they spoke openly, particularly about matters relating to love and sexuality. Sulpicia's apparently flagrant openness about her desires has often led readers to assume that she simply flouts social convention and expresses no compunctions about adopting the self-revealing postures of the elegiac lover. Yet Flaschenriem demonstrates that, despite Sulpicia's unabashed self-revelations, her diction suggests a strategy of self-protection. While the Sulpician speaker avowedly desires poetic renown, she also mediates her public speech with a reticence that may protect her from censure. Further, although the speaker in Sulpicia's elegies wants to celebrate her love affair with Cerinthus, she devises a self-protective rhetoric in order to mitigate perceptions of immodesty. Flaschenriem argues that Sulpicia embraces the contradictions inherent in her public and private personas. The act of writing for Sulpicia, as a woman, produces a sense of fragmentation as a result of an inherent lack of congruence with both literary and cultural convention. But ultimately, as Flaschenriem points out, by openly claiming a literary and erotic identity for herself Sulpicia overturns the elegiac tradition of portraying the woman as the "eroticized other." Sulpicia finally gives up her reserve and fully acknowledges herself as both the subject of her own desires and an active discursive agent. Flaschenriem shows that, in the body of her surviving work, Sulpicia achieves a masterly elegiac rhetoric while maintaining a degree of privacy, thus epitomizing the elegiac image of the partially clothed woman.

It is my hope that the essays in this collection will give readers a glimpse of the rich literary tradition that may be claimed for ancient Greek and Roman women writers. Although so much of ancient literature in general has not survived, it seems especially important to recover and acknowledge women's writing in antiquity—given how difficult it was for Greek and Roman women to be "heard" and also given the restricted role of women in public discourse. Classical scholars are generally in the business of piecing together bits of evidence in their efforts to better comprehend the ancient world. That task is especially daunting to those interested in discovering what the place of women in ancient societies might have been and how their contributions to Greco-Roman literary tradition can be evaluated. As the authors in this volume often emphasize, the written evidence we have for women's own poetic

voices suggests a dynamic relationship between women's poetry and established literary tradition, a relationship that clearly involves both appropriation and invention.

NOTES

1. Antipater of Thessalonika, writing in 20 CE, named nine women poets as earthly Muses: Praxilla, Moero, Anyte, Myrtis, Erinna, Telesilla, Corinna, Nossis, and Sappho. Since then we have come to know of about ninety additional Greek and Roman women poets. Of these, the work of only about fifty has survived, much of it fragmentary. See Plant 2004.

2. See Lefkowitz's groundbreaking 1973 article. Lefkowitz's critique of biographical approaches to Sappho's poetry may be fruitfully applied to criticism on classical women's poetry in general. Specifically, Lefkowitz takes issue with the tendency of male critics to assume that the work of women writers in Greece and Rome lacks artistry and merely constitutes personal, emotional outpourings.

3. Gordon Kirkwood, Bruno Snell, and C. M. Bowra, for example, write about Sappho's poetry as expressive of intimacy and candour, reflecting Sappho's personal confessions. Their attitudes toward Sappho's poems are representative of general attitudes among classical scholars (until recently) toward women poets in Greece and Rome.

4. Devereux 1970 and Marcovich 1972.

5. For discussions of Sappho's "society," see especially Calame 2001, Lardinois 1994, and Parker 1993.

6. Snyder 1989 provides a solid introduction to and translations of women's poetry in Greece and Rome.

7. See John Winkler's essay "Double Consciousness in Sappho's Lyrics" (Winkler 1990, 162–87). Winkler characterizes Sappho's poetry as "bilingual." This characterization can be usefully applied to other classical women poets as well.

8. Although there is evidence that Moero was praised in antiquity, modern readers have not generally praised her work.

9. In addition to Sulpicia, brief works have survived from several other women poets of ancient Rome, including a two-line fragment of Sulpicia the Satirist who lived during the reign of Domitian (81–96 CE), a few graffitti written by Julia Balbilla of Egypt (c. 130 CE), two poems of the Christian author Proba (fourth century CE), and one poem written by the empress Eudocia (c. 400 CE). See Josephine Balmer's translations (1996) of these and other women poets from antiquity.

10. See especially Keith 1997.

Women Poets in
Ancient Greece
and Rome

1   Sappho's Public World

Holt Parker

πόλεμος δὲ γυναιξὶ μελήσει.
War will be the concern of *women*.
—Aristophanes, *Lysistrata* 538

Every age creates its own Sappho.[1] At the moment our own dominant image of Sappho is a private, and often explicitly Romantic/romantic one. Sappho is a locus where, oddly enough, the prejudices of the past and the projections of the present become bedfellows. Add to this an explicit or implicit contrast with her island fellow, Alcaeus, and the result is our standard view of Sappho: off by herself with a coterie of girls, divorced from any involvement in public affairs.

First, the view of a purely private Sappho accords far too well with the traditional idea of what a woman poet and a woman's poetry should be (Lefkowitz 1973). Women write about love, not politics.[2] As Susan Friedman notes (1975, 807): "The short, passionate lyric has conventionally been thought appropriate for women poets if they insist on writing, while the longer more philosophical epic belongs to the real (male) poet."[3] This idea has contributed in part to Sappho 44 ("The Marriage of Hector and Andromache") being labeled as "abnormal" (and not for reasons of dialect alone) and to the attempts to force it to be an epithalamium, whether it will or no.[4] At the same time, since 44 is less girly than some would like, there have been recurrent attempts to claim that it is not by Sappho after all.[5] To turn to the opposite end of the political spectrum, a private Sappho also accords far too well with certain ideas of *écriture féminine* of what a woman poet and a woman's poetry should be.[6]

The most common image—that of Sappho running, if not a girls' school on Lesbos, then at least an all-girl coterie—also fits all too well into some our own private concerns.[7] A separate world—apart from men, war, politics—is very attractive. Sappho is often placed in a landscape, both literal and emotional, that combines all the best features of Arcadia and Academe. There seems to be a certain element of wish fulfillment in this picture. Further, the private Sappho lends herself so very easily to certain ideas much discussed in feminist poetics and politics: a woman-centered poetry, a female-only poetic tradition, and so on. Elsewhere, the image of Sappho Schoolmistress has been invoked as a model for various kinds of lesbian separatism.

The third factor in creating an image of a purely private Sappho, the contrast with Alcaeus, is natural. For example, one article contrasts "Romantic and Classical Strains in Lesbian Lyric" (Race 1989). No points for guessing who is which. Further, the contrast seems to have antique precedence.[8] For example, the Cologne commentary on Sappho (dating to the second century CE) begins with a ὁ μὲν (but he) and continues with ἡ δ' ἐφ' ἡσυχία[ς] (while she in peace) apparently contrasting Sappho's quiet life with Alcaeus' stormy life in politics.[9] This has become standard in the literature. So Lefkowitz (1981, 36): "Politics and conflict are missing entirely from Sappho's biography." As we will see in a moment this is not the case. So too Campbell (1983, 107): "The violent political life of Mytilene is hardly reflected at all in the fragments of Alcaeus' contemporary, Sappho." The most recent survey (Tsomis 2001, 168) flatly states: "Alkaios was primarily a political poet," a conclusion that Horace for one did not agree with, and continues "All three poets concerned themselves with invective as a literary form, but in contrast to Alkaios, Sappho and Anakreon did not write invective based on political grounds."[10]

Page was more cautious (1955, 130–31): "First, it is noticeable that whereas Alcaeus has much to tell of the political revolutions which Mytilene underwent in his and Sappho's lifetimes; and although it is attested that Sappho herself suffered in those stormy days, yet there are very few allusions to these great affairs in Sappho's verse."[11] It is to these "few allusions" that I wish to turn.

To a large measure, however, I think, this picture is correct. Sappho's poetry does indeed, at least in the wretched fragments we possess, seem to depict a separate world, a world apart from men and their concerns. My title alludes to Eva Stehle's outstanding 1981 article, "Sappho's Private World."[12] John Winkler's article of the same year, "Gardens of Nymphs: Public and Private in Sappho's Lyrics," in turn alludes to Demetrius' famous summary of "the whole of Sappho's poetry" as "gardens of nymphs, wedding-songs, love-affairs."[13] My only point is that these do not, in fact, comprise the *whole* of Sappho's poetry. What I want to do is sound a bit of warning that, when our standard view of Sappho begins to replicate too closely certain old-fashioned notions about the essential nature of women (private, passionate, sex-obsessed) and at the same time takes on aspects of projection of our own ideas of a lost golden age of poetry and power, it is time, perhaps, to examine our views carefully.

We tend to limit Sappho. She is discussed as "love poet," a "woman poet," a "lesbian poet," rather than as a poet. This is a failure even of the best-disposed of critics. As Dolores Klaitch was forced to write in *Woman + Woman* (1974, 160): "Sappho was a poet who loved women. She was not a lesbian who wrote poetry." In order to counter this tendency, I wish to raise the possibility of "reading otherwise" (Felman 1982, Ender 1993). I want to look for Sappho's Public World.

First, we can note that there is considerable clear evidence for Sappho's involvement in and making songs about public matters. Second, if we reexamine the corpus, actively presupposing that Sappho, like any other Greek poet, might have written about politics (by which I mean nothing more and nothing less than matters of importance to her polis), we can view a number of neglected poems in a new and interesting light. We have always approached Sappho looking for traces of her private life (in more senses than one). I simply want to see what happens if we read with an eye open for traces of her public life.

A Sappho intimately involved in political affairs and making public utterances emerges clearly from the texts. First, of course, the Parian Marble tells us of her exile—exile (φυγοῦσα), not a "voyage to Sicily" (Page 1955, 226): Sappho was not on a cruise.[14] Exile is the fate of the losing side in a civil war, as Alcaeus tells us. This event, almost certainly one of her adulthood, is consistently played down and indeed belittled, as though exile to Sappho meant nothing more than the inability to shop for the latest hats.[15] The background to Sappho's life is the background to her poetry; the two cannot be separated. That background is the same for Alcaeus' life and poetry: the overthrow of the aristocrats and the rise of the newly wealthy, all that we call The Age of the Tyrants.[16]

So just like Alcaeus, Sappho attacked the rival aristocratic families of Mytilene. She was manifestly a member of *exactly* the same aristocratic circle as Alcaeus. Her enemies were his enemies. Campbell (1983, 132) rightly says that "Sappho made hostile political comments on women or girls of her acquaintance." She attacked a certain Mica, whom she calls κα[κό]τροπ' (evil doer) because she chose "the friendship of the women of the Penthilidae," the former royal family of Mytilene (71).[17] Alcaeus also attacks the Penthilidae (70, 75). She attacked the Cleanactidae, the family of the treacherous Myrsilus (98b).[18] The Cologne commentary mentions attacks on women of an uncertain noble house, and attacks specifically on a daughter of Cleanax or his family.[19]

> οὕ[τως ἀπο]φαίνει τὰς ἐπὶ [βασ]λικὸν οἶκον φοι[τώσ]ας καὶ περὶ πολ[λοῦ π]οιουμένας [περιεν]εχθῆναι καὶ . . .
>
> This is how she portrays the women who visit the royal house and consider it very important to be spoken of and . . .

The papyrus continues:

> τω[ν   ]νακτιδω[ν   ] Κλεανακ[τος] ἡ παῖς κ[   ]ρους με [   ] καὶ ὠνει[δι-] προς μα[   ] εὐγενεια [
>
> . . . of the [   ]nactidae . . . of Cleanax . . . the daughter . . . and (she) blamed (?) . . . nobility of birth . . .

Alcaeus also attacks the Cleanactidae.[20] The first house mentioned in the commentary might be the Cleanactidae, the Archeanactidae, or the Polyanactidae.[21] For the first family, Sappho mentions an Archeanassa as the "yokemate" of Gorgo (213; cf. 214):

> σε εμα κ' Αρχεάνα[σ-
> σα Γόργω< ι> σύνδυγο(ς)·
> . . . my . . . Archeanassa the yokemate of Gorgo

The commentary explains:

> ἀντὶ τοῦ σ[ύν]ζυξ· ἡ Πλειστοδίκη [τ]ῆι Γ[ο]ργοῖ σύνζυξ μετόα τ[ῆς] Γογγύλης ὀν[ο]μασθήσετ[αι· κ]οινὸν γὰρ τὸ ὄνομ[α δ]έδοται ἢ κατὰ τῆσ[ ] α[   ] Πλ[ε]ιστοδίκη[ ] ν [ὀνομ]ασθησετ[αι] κυ[ρι-
>
> *sundugos* [is the Aeolic form] for *sunzux* ("yokemate"): Pleistodica will be named Gorgo's yokemate along with Gongyla. For the common

name has been given rather than the one deriving from [her family name?] . . . Pleistodica . . . will be named (her) proper (name?) . . .[22]

Gentili seems to think σύνζυξ (Attic σύζυξ, σύζυγος) an "official" term, "referring to the actual bond of marriage," between the women (1988, 76).[23] Gentili, however, ignores the fact that Gorgo is a hated enemy and the phrase is extremely likely to be insulting, not because Sappho is doing anything so anachronistic as calling Archeanassa a "dyke," but because Sappho disliked Gorgo and therefore attacked Gorgo's friends and henchwomen.[24] Pleistodica seems to the enemy woman's proper name, while "Archeanassa" is derived from her family, the Archeanactidae, who were the family of Pittacus, the tyrant and eventual winner in the civil war.[25] Sappho was attacking Pittacus' family in the female line. Alcaeus also attacked Pittacus (112).

Sappho attacks another aristocratic family, the Polyanactidae (99, 155, 213Ab), whom we know of only from her. She specifically mocks a daughter of the house in 155:

πόλλα μοι τὰν Πωλυανάκτιδα παῖδα χαίρην
[I say] a fond farewell from me to the daughter of the Polyanactidae.[26]

A similar phrase in found in 213A(b).9 (*SLG* 273.9), preceded by a mention of gold (4: χρύσωι):

]παῖ Πολυα[νακτι-
O child of the Polya[nactidae[27]

And in 99 the notorious *olisbos* occurs, if indeed it does.

] . γα . πεδὰ βαῖο[   ] . α
.[ ]οῖ Πωλυανακτ[ίδ]αις
. αισ σαμιασι . ιε . [ ]τοισ . . . . [.] [ ]
χόρδαισι διακρεκην
ολισβ . δοκοις περκαθ . ενος   5
. . ου . [.]σι φιλοφ[ρό]νως
] . . . . δε . ἐλελίσδ[ε]ται πρ . τανεως
] . . οσδεδιο[.]ω .
] . υαλωδ' . [.] . . . ενητε[.] . χ . .

. . . after a short while (?) . . . the Polyanactidae . . . Samian . . . to strike the strings, dildo-takers . . . kind-minded . . . is made to vibrate . . .

We cannot know for certain whether the poem is by Sappho or by Alcaeus, and that is precisely the point. Lobel, the first editor was cautious: "Aeolic verse in stanzas of three lines are naturally attributed to Sappho, since we know of no poems of Alcaeus so composed, but too little is legible of what was contained in the papyrus here published for the hypothesis to be either confirmed or disproved."[28] Others have said that the poem(s) is (are) by Alcaeus.[29] The reasons themselves, seldom explicit, are a nice matter of sexual/textual politics. Snell said the matter was uncertain, but a prayer to Apollo and above all the mention of the Polyanactidae pointed to Alcaeus (1953a, 118). Gomme argued that "it is more likely that Alkaios would use ὀλισβο- (ὀλισβοδόκοισι ?), if either of them did," and the mention of the Polyanactidae "looks much more like his work than Sappho's, even though she is said to have reproached a girl from this family for deserting her (fr. 155)."[30] Meyerhoff is the most explicit (1984, 184): "For Sappho the goddess is Aphrodite, while Apollo as addressee makes one think more of Alkaios as composer. Above all, the attack against the Polyanactidae with the vehemence of the foregoing verses is only thinkable for Alkaios," though he, too, has to admit that Sappho did address a female member of the family. None of these arguments is of any value. Sappho, of course, addresses Apollo elsewhere (fr. 44A).[31] Himerius' testimony is explicit (Sappho 208): "Sappho and Pindar, adorning him in song with golden hair and lyres, send him borne by swans to Helicon to dance with the Muses and Graces."[32] As for the second point, what is odd is that the Polyanactidae, supposedly the mark of Alcaeus, in fact are mentioned *only* by Sappho and never by Alcaeus (at least in the surviving fragments and testimonia).

The poems are better attributed to Sappho. Both mention the Polyanactidae. In the first Sappho talks about ὀλισβοδόκοισι (dildo receivers)[33] presumably an insult to the women of the family.[34] The second poem (99b) begins

Λάτως] τε καὶ Δί[ος] πάϊ[
O child (of Leto) and of Zeus

and continues

δειχνυσ[ ]ε δηὖτε Πωλυανακτίδαν   23
τὸν μάργον ὄνδειξαι θέλω

. . . showing . . . once again I wish to put on display the madman of the Polyanactidae.[35]

The evidence is unequivocal: Sappho declares herself an aristocrat, waging the same kind of war against rival clans that we see Alcaeus waging. Especially interesting here is the prevalence of attacks on the women of the families. Alcaeus, too, attacks Pittacus' mother (72; see below). However, Sappho 99b.14–15 (99.23–24) shows a willingness to hold up even the men of the family to public scorn. Attacks on, and control of the women of noble families were a prominent feature of the politics of archaic Greece. Two examples from Athens may serve to illustrate this trend. Megacles changed his political alliances when Pisistratus insulted his daughter by using her "not according to custom" in order to avoid having children (Herodotus 1.61). In the next generation, the proximate cause of the assassination of Pisistratus' son Hipparchus was not the love affair of Harmodius and Aristogeiton but Hipparchus' insult to Harmodius' sister (Thucydides 6.56). Further, the women of the aristocratic clans were the venue for competitive consumption. Sumptuary legislation, directed specifically at women, was a prominent feature of the program of social control by many of the tyrants.[36]

Kirkwood (1974, 100–101) shows an interesting mixture of commonplaces and insight. He begins with the received contrast of Alcaeus and Sappho.

> Alcaeus and Sappho are alike in the apparent intensity of their involvement in much of what they write about and in many external features of poetic form, but they are utterly different in the subject matter of their poetry and in outlook. Alcaeus is political and moral, Sappho apolitical, and her primary concern with human emotions and the activities that express them gives moral judgment only an incidental place.

I will return to Sappho's moral judgment. Kirkwood, after citing fr. 71, 98b, and 213, continues:

> There is enough in these slight indications to suggest that Sappho was in the same political group as Alcaeus. We do not know whether she was exiled simply because she was by family a member of this group, or because her expressions of dislike of members of politically powerful families were enough to bring punishment. She may have written much more than we have evidence of in this vein, but it is unlikely: Sappho was much talked about in antiquity, but never for this, so far as we know.

Williamson (1995, 72) makes much the same argument: "Although references to comptemporary politics are not completely absent from Sappho's poetry, they are far fewer and less direct." We need to be on guard against exactly this type of argumentum ex silentio and we can turn to Alcaeus to see why. Time has dealt harshly with the lyric poets, and the papyri are not a representative cross-section (random survival is not random selection). There are lies (the handbooks), damned lies (the ancient biographies), and statistics. Were it not for a single passage in Horace and a passing mention in Quintilian, we would never know that Alcaeus had written love poetry.[37] A poet may have been much talked about in antiquity, but it was usually for the same old things and seldom for anything true.[38]

Against this undoubtedly public and even political background, we can argue for the possibility at least of a political interpretation of many overlooked fragments. One extremely important, though neglected, fact is that Sappho wrote both iambics and elegiacs, none of which survive.[39] These are not what we think of when we think of Sappho. Elegy is associated with the symposium (Archilochus and Mimnermus), with military and political themes (Callinus, Tyrtaeus, Mimnermus, Solon), and iambics are the medium for satire and invective. These are meters for public matters.[40] Sappho was not all sweetness and light. Philodemus commented on her tone: "Even Sappho writes some things iambically."[41] Burnett rightly says this "refers to the temper, not the metre of certain songs," as the context shows, but that in itself is significant.[42] It is this iambic tone that causes Horace to compare Sappho and Alcaeus to Archilochus in a much-misunderstood line (Epist. 1.19.28–29): *temperat Archilochi Musam pede mascula Sappho, / temperat Alcaeus, sed rebus et ordine dispar* (Manly Sappho tempers the Muse of Archilochus in her verse / so does Alcaeus, but different in subject matter and order).[43] Critics leap on *mascula* with but one thought and ignore Archilochus.[44] Sappho is *mascula* not because she he has sex like a man but because she writes poetry (*pede*) like a man, in fact like the manly man Archilochus. Sappho and Alcaeus are both invective poets, says Horace, they're just not as vicious as Archilochus.

In the surviving poetry, once we read with a eye to Sappho's Public World, one dominant theme appears. In a manner recalling Theognis, Archilochos, Anacreon, and Alcaeus, Sappho is concerned with the proper definition of the noble man, the *kalokagathos,* by which she means, just as they do, the man who upholds the old aristocratic values against the tide of new wealth. So Sappho 148, defining *arete,* could have come from the mouth of Alcaeus (cf. 360, 364) or Theognis (cf. 46, 119–24, 183–86):

ὁ πλοῦτος ἄνευ ἀρέτας οὐκ ἀσίνης πάροικος,
ἀ δ' ἀμφοτέρων κρᾶσις †εὐδαιμονίας ἔχει τὸ ἄκρον†

4

Wealth without virtue is not a harmless neighbor.
The mixing of them both is the height of good fortune.[45]

So too in the same papyrus that contains a mention of the Polyanactidae, 213A(g).9–11 (*SLG* 276(1) col. ii.9–11):

ειγι[ ]ṿ ν[ ]σων πέ-
φυκ[ ] πλοῦ[τ]ο[ν] θέοι δίδοι-   10
σιν[ ]οιν [ ]ε[ ] σιν· λέ-
. . . grew . . . the gods give wealth . . .[46]

Sappho's reference to gold as not corrupted by rust (204) perhaps came from such a context.[47] Poem 3 has not been discussed in the literature, in part because of its fragmentary nature, but it is filled with the social language of nobility and baseness.[48]

]δώσην

κλ]ύτων μέντ' ἐπ[
[κ] άλων κάσλων, σ[
τοὶς φί]λοις, λύπηις τέμ[
]μ' ὄνειδος

]οιδήσαις ἐπιτ [
]΄ αν, ἄσαιο τὸ γὰρ [
]μον οὐκ οὔτω μ[
] διάκηται,

]μηδ[ ] αζε, [
]χις, συνίημ[
] ης κακότατο[ς
]μεν

]ν ἀτέραις με[
]η φρένας, εὖ[
]ατοις μάκα[ρας

. . . to give . . . of the famous . . . of the beautiful and good . . . friends, and you grieve me . . . shame . . . having become swollen . . . you might be disgusted by . . . for my mind not thus . . . is disposed . . . I understand . . . of baseness . . . others . . . minds . . . well-[. . . the blessed ones . . .

Sappho speaks here specifically of the *kalokagathos* ([κ]άλων κάσλων) and in the same terms that Alcaeus uses. So Alcaeus 6.13–14:

καὶ μὴ καταισχύνωμεν [ἀνανδρίαι
ἔσλοις τόκηας γᾶς ὕπα κε[ιμένοις

Let us not disgrace by cowardice our noble begetters lying under the earth.

And his attack on Pittacus' family (72):[49]

σὺ δὴ τεαύτας ἐκγεγόνων ἔχηις
τὰν δόξαν οἴαν ἄνδρες ἐλεύθεροι
ἔσλων ἔοντες ἐκ τοκήων

Do you then, born from such a woman, have the sort of reputation that free men have who are from noble parents?

Using the same vocabulary of aristocratic social relations, Sappho 50 examines true beauty, playing on the senses of κάλος:

ὁ μὲν γὰρ κάλος ὄσσον ἴδην πέλεται <κάλος>,
ὁ δὲ κἄγαθος αὔτικα καὶ κάλος ἔσσεται.

For the beautiful man is beautiful only to look at, but the good man will become instantly beautiful as well.

This is not a matter of erotics, it is a matter of ethics.[50] This is not Sappho the solo aesthete; this is Sappho publicly declaring what is important to her and defining κάλος in moral terms. The proper comparison here is not Sappho 16 ("Some say an army of horsemen") but rather Archilochus 60 ("I don't love a big general"). A beautiful exterior may mask a treacherous interior.

I believe we may be able to catch glimpses of the same conflict of the older aristocratic families against the new and vulgar rich, specifically their women, in several other poems. So Sappho 55:

κατθάνοισα δὲ κείσηι οὐδέ ποτα μναμοσύνα σέθεν
ἔσσετ' οὐδὲ πόθα εἰς ὕστερον· οὐ γὰρ πεδέχηις βρόδων
τῶν ἐκ Πιερίας· ἀλλ' ἀφάνης κἀν Ἀίδα δόμωι
φοιτάσηις πεδ' ἀμαύρων νεκύων ἐκπεποταμένα.

You will lie there dead and there will be no memory of you ever in later times. For you have no part in the roses from Pieria. Invisible in the house of Hades too, you will flit about among the shadowy dead when you have flown away.

Plutarch says in one place that this was addressed to one of the uncultured and unlearned women and in another place that it was addressed to a rich woman.[51] The woman was apparently both. Sappho's immortality through poetry is contrasted with the woman's ignorance, Sappho's true riches with the woman's false wealth. Was Sappho's insult literary or political? And is there a difference? The wealthy uneducated woman has no share in the roses of Pieria. Wealth does not make the man, or the woman either; aristocratic culture does.[52] As Williamson preceptively notes (1995, 86): "If poetic skill was a badge of social accomplishment for aristocratic women as it certainly was for men, then this poem may be as intimately bound up in the politics of Lesbos as any of Alcaeus' tirades, pitting aristocratic culture against mere wealth." Sappho's disdain recalls similar attacks on the newly powerful, newly rich such as Anacreon's picture of Artemon (388). In fr. 90 (part of a commentary), in what appears to be a discussion of the relation between beauty (κάλλος) and virtue (ἀρετή), the scholiast tells us Sappho applied the adjective ἀγέρωχος (proud, arrogant) to "women who have too much privilege" (ἀγε]ρώχου[ς τὰς ἄγαν ἐχού]σας γέρας). She accuses someone (7.4) of arrogance (ἀγερωχία).[53] Alcaeus (206) and Archilochus (261) use the same word of boastful men. All these poets are condemning upstarts who do not know their place.

Likewise 57, which attacks Andromeda for loving a rustic, dressed in rustic clothes, may have more to do with class than erotics.[54]

τίς δ᾽ ἀγροΐωτις θέλγει νόον . . .
ἀγροΐωτιν ἐπεμμένα σπόλαν . . .
οὐκ ἐπισταμένα τὰ βράκε᾽ ἔλκην ἐπὶ τῶν σφύρων;

> What country woman bewitches your mind . . . dressed in a country stola . . . not knowing how to draw the rags over her ankles?

Sappho speaks several times about clothing (22, 39, 98, 100; perhaps 152). This is usually treated dismissively as "girl-talk" and mined for details about the curriculum at Sappho's boarding school.[55] Such an attitude is naive and ignores the important fact that male poets, too, talk about dress.[56] Theognis (55-59) and Anacreon (388) both mock the new rich for the rags they once wore and their bad taste in clothing now. Clothes are more than a sign of adolescent narcissism (Burnett 1983, 213); they are signs of status, a semiotic system.[57] Sappho uses clothes in 57 to contrast one who recognizes class, in its literal sense, with one who does not.

In the same vein, when Sappho rebukes one of her brothers for his public behavior (5), she reveals an aristocratic self-presentation where her public status is bound up with family honor:

Κύπρι καὶ] Νηρήιδες ἀβλάβη[ν μοι
τὸν κασί]γνητον δ[ό]τε τυίδ᾽ ἴκεσθα[ι
κὤσσα ϝ]οι θύμωι κε θέληι γένεσθαι
ὔόπάντα τε]λέσθην,

ὄσσα δὲ πρ]όσθ᾽ ἄμβροτε πάντα λῦσα[ι   5
καὶ φίλοισ]ι ϝοῖσι χάραν γένεσθαι
κὠνίαν ἔ]χθροισι, γένοιτο δ᾽ ἄμμι
πῆμ᾽ ἔτι μ]ηδ᾽ εἶς·

τὰν κασιγ]νήταν δὲ θέλοι πόησθαι
[ἔμμορον] τίμας, [ὀν]ίαν δὲ λύγραν   10
           ]οτοισι π[ά]ροιθ᾽ ἀχεύων
           ]˳να

           ]˳ εισαΐω[ν] τὸ κέγχρω
           ]λ᾽ ἐπαγ[ορί]αι πολίταν
           . . .

   Cyrpis and the Nereids, grant that my brother arrive here
unharmed and that whatever he wishes for in his heart, all be fulfilled
and that whatever mistakes he has made, he atone for them all, and
that he be a joy to friends and a pain to enemies, and may no one still
be a grief to us. Rather may he wish to make his sister share in honor,
but sad pain . . . sorrowing before (masc.) . . . hearing the . . .(than) a
millet seed . . . the accusations of the citizens . . . .[58]

   Joel B. Lidov (2002) has convincingly disposed of our assumption that this poem (or 15) has anything to do with the famous story
of her brother Charaxus' love for Rhodopis (who then mysteriously
gets named Doricha), and has traced that tale back (like so much else
in Sappho) to Old Comedy. What remains is an emphasis throughout
on τιμή (reputation). Williamson rightly observes (1995. 86):

   Elsewhere she expresses concern for family honor in a poem (5) about
   her brother Charaxus [though perhaps not him]. Praying that he will
   redeem former mistakes, she sets out a model of behavior that any aristocrat from Homer on would recognize: he should be a joy to his
   friends and a band to his enemies. That this is a public aspiration, and
   not one peculiar to Sappho, is suggested both by the mention of citizens later in the poem (though in a context too damaged for precise
   interpretation) and by the very fact that the poem was composed for
   performance.

Later Williamson notes (1995, 138–39):

> The poem does not say what Charaxus' misdemeanors were, but its
> talk of friends, honor, and crimes or mistakes indicates that they may
> arise from the complex maneuverings of Lesbian politics . . . Charaxus
> was probably caught up in the turmoil described by Alcaeus, and it is
> not impossible that his return is longed for because, like both Alcaeus
> and Sappho, he has suffered exile.[59]

The same concern with reputation before the citizens motivates, for
example, Theognis (453–56) and Archilochus' attack on Lykambes
(172). Sappho upholds, through the person of her brother, the masculine code of the aristocratic warrior. Campbell (1967, 269; 1983,
120–21, 123) rightly compares the same wish by Archilochus,
Solon, and Theognis.[60] Sappho, too, wishes to help her friends and
harm her enemies.[61]

We can see in Sappho the same theme of betrayal by friends
that is so prominent in Alcaeus and Theognis. Several well known
poems of Sappho have always been assumed to refer to betrayal in
love. It is not so clear that betrayal in private life can be separated
from betrayal in public life. The Greek definition of friendship did
not allow so sharp a distinction and no one would think of applying
it to the male poets. Theognis considers his lovers, his companions
at the symposium, and his political allies all to be friends, all to
come from the same circle, and betrayal in any sphere is betrayal in
all (31–38, 61–68, etc.). As Campbell rightly says (1983, 121):
"All these poets [Archilochus, Solon, Sappho] saw the world in
black and white, making a clear-cut distinction since prestige, secu-
rity and welfare depended on one's 'friends'." So too Gentili
(1988, 81):

> Unfortunately, our limited information does not allow us to recon-
> struct the actual episodes in the interplay or erotic and political motives
> that must have been behind the tension within Sappho's group and
> her open expression of jealousy toward her rivals. Certain institutional
> differences notwithstanding, the uniformity of the linguistic code per-
> taining to crisis, exile, and lovers' wrongs suggests that, like the male
> clubs that provide Alcaeus and Theognis with their subject matter, the
> female communities of archaic Lesbos were familiar with the way
> erotic relationships and political orientation can influence and interfere
> with each other.

For Sappho, 131 has traditionally been read as defection to a rival lover or a rival finishing school (Kirkwood 1974, 125; Campbell 1983, 133):

Ἄτθι, σοὶ δ᾽ ἔμεθεν μὲν ἀπήχθετο
φροντίσδην, ἐπὶ δ᾽ Ἀνδρομέδαν πότηι
O Atthis, to think of me was hateful to you and you fly to Andromeda.

The situation, however, might be similar to 71 where Mica chose the friendship of the daughters of the house of Penthilus. Atthis may be hanging around with the wrong faction, not merely the wrong lover.[62] Similarly, 26.2–4:

ὅ]ττινα[ς γὰρ
εὖ θέω, κῆνοί με μά]λιστα πά[ντων
δηὖτε σίνοντα]ι
For whomever I treat well, these (again ?) hurt me most of all.[63]

and 37b:

τὸν δ᾽ ἐπιπλάζοντ᾽ ἄνεμοι φέροιεν
καὶ μελέδωναι.
May winds and sorrows carry off the one who rebukes me

These fit best into a context of public discourse, recalling similar complaints about criticism and humiliation by Theognis (367–70) and others.[64] Likewise, 120 is a claim to impartiality:

ἀλλά τις οὐκ ἔμμι παλιγκότων
ὄργαν, ἀλλ᾽ ἀβάκην τὰν φρέν᾽ ἔχω ...
But I am not one of those who fester in anger, but I have a quiet heart.

Here Sappho says that she does not attack her enemies merely from spite; she is simply giving good advice. The language recalls Theognis' claims to impartially and straight speech (219–20, 331–32, 335–36, 851–52) and Ancreon's hatred for the sullen and love for those who are quiet (416).[65] When Sappho defends her friends and attacks her enemies, she is not acting like a bitch; she's acting like an Alcaeus.

Finally, even the poems which we label the most "private" may well have carried a "public" agenda. Arthur (1973, 38–40) well describes the elegant world in which Sappho wrote:

The works of these aristocratic poets [Alcaeus, Sappho, Ibycus, and Anacreon] are especially distinguished by their portrayal of a world of youthfulness, beauty and grace, peopled by gods, heroes, or luxuriating aristocrats, and characterized especially by the absence of conflict. There are hymns to deities, stories of the old heroes, celebrations of the pleasure of love and wine. It is a world, and a way of life, which contrasts quite strikingly with the struggle—social, political and economic—that was going on all around these poets, and as such it represents something of an anachronism. For it looks back to an era when aristocratic manners dominated the culture, and when the aristocratic class ruled society. . . . The pursuit of love by these poets is equally refined and voluptuous. . . . The love-affairs of these poets, whether heterosexual or homosexual, are invariably pursued in cultivated gardens of rural sanctuaries, in an atmosphere of refined beauty and elegance.

Sappho is suffused with this shared aristocratic nostalgia, which is especially prominent in fr. 98. Nagy (1990, 285) notes "Sappho's theme of luxuriance": "This inherent sensuality, even eroticism, of *habros* and its derivatives [in Pindar] is most vividly attested in the compositions of Sappho," citing fr. 2.13–16, 58.25–26, 128, 140. Thus even Sappho's most private world, her "gardens of nymphs, wedding-songs, love-affairs," may be seen also as a public celebration of a world of aristocratic values in opposition to the squalid and rustic world of the rising bourgeoisie. Her descriptions of perfect symposia, festivals, and feasts (frs. 2, 9, 19, 40, 94)—no less than the symposia, festivals, and feasts of Xenophanes, Anacreon, Ibycus, Theognis, and Alcaeus—are also part of a public (and defiant) world of aristocratic values and friendships.[66]

I would like to end with a thought experiment as a way of seeing how partial our reading of Sappho may be. Here is the fragmentary Sappho 20:

>]επιθεσμα[
>]ε, γάνος δὲ και [
>]
> τ]ύχαι σὺν ἔσλαι
> λί]μενος κρέτησαι   5
>   γ]ᾶς μελαίνας
>   ]
> οὐκ εθ]έλοισι ναῦται
>] μεγάλαις ἀήται[ς
>]α κἀπὶ χέρσω   10
>]
>]μοθεν πλέοι [

]δε τὰ φόρτι᾽ εἰκ[
]νατιμ᾽ ἐπεὶ κ [
]   15
]ρέοντι πόλλαι[
     ]αιδέκα[
     ]ει
]
]ιν ἔργα   20
] χέρσω [

. . . gladness (of wine ?) . . . with good luck . . . to gain the harbor
. . . of the black earth . . . the sailors (unwilling ?) . . . great winds . . .
and upon the dry land . . . from somewhere they may sail . . the cargo
. . . flowing many . . . to receive (?) . . . works . . . dry land . . .

Let me ask: If this poem had been assigned to Alcaeus, would it
not unhesitatingly have been labeled a metaphor for the ship of state?

NOTES

1. See especially Andreadis 1996, Prins 1999, DeJean 1989, 1996. The
text of Sappho and Alcaeus used here is based on Voigt 1971, but I have incorporated various supplements as indicated in Voigt's apparatus criticus, in *PLF*
(Lobel and Page 1963), and Campbell 1982. It is not possible here to give a full
treatment of all the issues involved, for which the reader must consult the original publications and relevant editions. Abbreviations follow the conventions of
the *Oxford Classical Dictionary*. Translations of the original languages are mine.
2. For example, Klinck (1994, 14) gives this as a definition of *Frauenlieder*, into which category she places Sappho's songs as part of a "probably universal phenomenon" (15–19): "1. the femininity lies in voice rather than
authorship; 2. the utterance is perceived as in some way contrastive to male-voice
song; 3. the language and style are simple, or affect simplicity; 4. the subject is
the loves, loyalties, and longings of the speaker." See Greer 1995, ch. 2 "Poet,
Poetaster, Poetess," for survey of attitudes to English women poets.
3. See also Ostriker 1985, 322. See Prins 1999, ch. 4, for an analysis of
how this notion was applied to Sappho in the nineteenth century.
4. Page (1955, 65), of course, used the term "abnormal" purely to indicate a departure from poetic Aeolic. For Sappho 44 as an epithalamium, see
Wilamowitz 1914, 229; Snell 1931, 73; Page 1955, 71–74; Saake 1971, 156;
Fränkel 1973, 174; Rösler 1975; Campbell 1983, 167–68. Page makes the best
case that can be made (most others simply follow him), but it is a silly idea and
needs to be dropped. Two questions will suffice: (1) Is there any other epithala-
mion/hymenaion known, Greek or Latin, with any narrative at all, mythological, epic, or otherwise? The closest approach, Aristophanes *Birds* 1731–45,
shows the difference. (2) Is Catullus 64, therefore, an epithalamium, intended
to be sung at an actual wedding?

5. Wilamowitz 1914, 230; Schadewaldt 1950, 48–49 (with a telling remark: "It lacks the magic of her simplicity"); Treu 1963, 197 (lacks "self-expression").

6. Cixous (1986, 309, 310, 312, 313): "I, too, overflow; my desires have invented new desires, my body knows unheard-of songs. . . . I write woman: women must write women; and man, man. . . . Write your self. Your body must be heard. . . . Text: my body—shot through with streams of song," etc. For two feminist critiques of *écriture féminine*, see Jones 1985, Minogue 1990.

7. Parker 1996. The idea is ineradicable. A few recent examples: Lardinois (1994, 1996, 2001) wishes to turn Sappho into a choral poet, despite a total lack of evidence (Page 1955, 72, 119, 126; Parker 1996, 168–70), apparently on the hopeful theory that if chorus, then *khorodidaskalos*; if *khorodidaskalos*, then *didaskalos*. A widely used textbook, Fantham et al. (1994, 12) states that she was "an initiator of young women . . . . [T]he poets [Alcman and Sappho] show a close association between young women on the verge of marriage and more mature women who served as mentors and, it appears, often as lovers to the initiates." *Der Neue Pauly* does not in fact contain anything new (11 [2001] 47): Wilamowitz's picture of her as "a type of teacher" with students who leave for marriage, is called "still essentially plausible" despite the criticisms of "English-language scholarship." Sharrock and Ash (2002, 26) write: "It is very likely that many of her poems are written for choruses of girls, both in ritual and less formal situations, and that the girls learned music and dancing as well as aristocratic socialisation and preparation for marriage, from their association with Sappho."

8. So Calame (2001, 211 n. 15): "The use of this term [*hetairai*] has led some interpreters to compare Sappho's group with the political *hetaireia* Alcaeus was creating at the same time at Mytilene [Trumpf 1973 and Burnett 1983, 209]. This hypothesis has now been put forward by Parker [1993]. But Sappho's dancing companions are not represented as revelers at the banquet!" [his exclamation point]. In fact, they are. Calame simply assumes that they cannot be. But Athenaeus (11.463a–c) quotes Sappho 2 as part of a series of descriptions of the features of a perfect symposium, beside Xenophanes' famous description (1), as well as Anacreon *eleg.* 2 West (96 D), Ion 27, Theophrastus fr. 120 (Wimmer), and Alexis *Tarentinoi* (222 KA). The clear evidence for Sappho and her companions as precisely "revelers at the banquet" is given by Page 1955, 43 and Parker 1996, 179–82.

9. Sappho 214b V = S 261a *SLG* = *P. Colon.* 5860. So Gronewald 1974, 114. Contra Burnett (1983, 210 n. 4) who translates ἐφ' ἡσυχίας as "at her leisure," commenting, "surely ἐφ' ἡσυχίας must mean that Sappho acted as a private citizen, not as a priestess or the appointed leader of an initiation group." While I agree with her conclusion, the contrast of ἡσυχία here following a reference to κρατοῦσι is with war (cf. Thuc. 3.12), not with public status.

10. For politics in Anacreon, see below.

11. For others, see Fränkel 1973, 188: Alcaeus' life "in complete contrast to Sappho's, was directed to activities and objectives alien to poetry." I do not think a Greek would have considered politics and beautiful boys alien to poetry.

12. So too Snyder 1991 emphasizes certain secluded and private aspects of Sappho's poetry.

13. Demetrius *Eloc.* 132 (T 45 Campbell): νυμφαῖοι κῆποι, ὑμέναιοι, ἔρωτες.

14. Parian marble: between 605/4 and 595/4. Suda: γεγονεῖα in 612–608, almost certainly her *floruit* (Page 1955, 225 n. 4), that is, roughly *aetate sua* 25–35. Burnett 1983, 214 n. 13 is rightly skeptical of using Sappho 98 for historical reconstruction.

15. Page 1955, 97–102, 131: "cut off from her customary luxuries and pleasures"; Burn 1960, 227. Tsagarakis 1977, 70 n. 5: "She was exiled . . . but the thiasos interested her more than partisan politics."

16. Andrewes 1963, 92–99; Murray 1993, 155–58; Dubois 1995, 5–6.

17. φιλότ[ατ'] ἥλεο Πενθιλήαν[. See Tsomis 2001, 212.

18. Burnett (1983, 212 n. 13), though she trivializes the poem, has a good survey of the various reconstructions, of which Page (1955, 102) remains the most sensible. Tsomis (2001, 201) calls this "the only fragment that alludes to a political situation" and dismisses out of hand any "direct political invective."

19. *SLG* 261A = 214B Campbell. Supplements by Gronewald (1974) incorporating those of Lobel. The correction in the papyrus points to Κλεανακ[τος rather than Κλεανακ[ιδ- . For the Cleanactidae, see Strabo 13.2.3 (T 1 Campbell); as the family of Myrsilus: Alcaeus 112.23–24 and *SLG* 263. See Podlecki 1984, 65–66.

20. Strabo 13.2.3, Heraclit. *Alleg. hom.* 5 (4 Buffière) ad fr. 208; frgs. 70, 112; and all the references to Myrsilus himself: 70, 129, 332; in the scholiasts: 6, 60(a), 70.4 ("tyrant"), 114, 241, 259(a), 302(a), 305(b).8, 306(a).13, 306B.11–12, 306C(c).3; possibly in 63.3 (suppl. Treu).

21. For the Polyanactidae, "Children of Great Lord," see Sappho 155, and 99.2, 23 discussed below.

22. The futures are puzzling and may refer to something in the poem itself.

23. Attic σύζυξ, σύζυγος (yoked together, coupled) *can* of course be applied to humans and to a married couple (A. *Ch.* 599; Eur. *Alc.* 314, 343, 921), but it is used equally of (male) comrades (Eur. *IT* 250, Ar. *Pl.* 955, etc.), and brothers (Eur. *Tr.* 1001). It is interesting to watch Gentili's language—as he convinces himself of this notion—progress from "so to speak official unions" to "which did not exclude a genuine rapport with the matrimonial type" to "the concrete bond of matrimony" in a single paragraph: (1995, 122; unaltered from the 1984 ed.). Calame is also quick to believe (1996, 115; 2001, 212).

24. Page (1955, 145), though his comment "the judgement passed by the ancients on the women of Lesbos will now appear easily intelligible" seems to ignore Ar. *Lys.* 109, etc. (οὐκ εἶδον οὐδ' ὄλισβον ὀκτωδάκτυλον, said by a comic Athenian wife) as well as what λεσβιάζω actually meant (Henderson 1991, 183–84). For Gorgo, see Sappho 144: μάλα δὴ κεκορημένοις / Γόργως (for those who have had their fill of Gorgo); Max. Tyr. 18.9a–d (T 20 Campbell): καὶ ὅ τι περ Σωκράτει οἱ ἀντίτεχνοι Πρόδικος καὶ Γοργίας καὶ Θρασύμαχος καὶ Πρωταγόρας, τοῦτο τῇ Σαπφοῖ Γοργὼ καὶ ᾿Ανδρομέδα· νῦν μὲν ἐπιτιμᾷ ταύταις, νῦν δὲ ἐλέγχει καὶ εἰρωνεύεται αὐτὰ ἐκεῖνα τὰ Σωκράτους (And what the rival craftsmen Prodicus and Gorgias and Thrasymachus were to Socrates, Gorgo and Andromeda were to Sappho. Sometimes she upbraids them, sometimes she refutes them and uses irony, just like Socrates). For the interpretation of this gobbet, see Page 1955, 145; Parker 1996, 154–55.

25. Alcaeus 112, with scholiast; Strabo 599. See Page 1955, 174–75.

26. The context, judging from Max. Tyr. 18.9d (so far as one can trust him), is one of ironical dismissal, see Page 1955, 135. Snyder (1997, 114) and Tsomis (2001, 210) point out the alliteration of *p*-. The meter is uncertain (see Voigt for possibilities), and the text may have been adapted to indirect discourse. For the ethical dative μοι, cf. Eur. *Ba.* 1378 χαῖρε, πάτερ, μοι.

27. Not necessarily female.

28. Lobel, *POxy* 2291, p. 10. The top of the column seems to be in two-line stanzas (paragraphoi after 3 and 5, the latter oddly missing in Lobel and Page 1963), the bottom is marked in three. However, the scribe has made several errors in the placing of the paragraphoi and whether 99 should be divided, and if so where, is very uncertain. Voigt's presentation makes it difficult to reconstruct the layout of the papyrus, and one should consult Lobel and Page 1963 and Lobel's original publication of *POxy* 2291. The best reading is that 99a is in two-line stanzas (telesillean + a longer line) and ends at 9. A new poem in three-line stanzas (ia2 + a longer line ending in a glyconic + ia2) begins in line 10 and continues beyond the end of column ii (despite the scribe having added a coronis and in the wrong place).

It is now claimed that there *is* one poem by Alcaeus in three-line stanzas. Voigt divided Alcaeus 130 into 130a (five stanzas of three lines each) and 130b (six stanzas of the standard four lines). In this, she is followed by Meyerhoff (1984, 184) and Campbell 1983. However, the papyrus (*POxy* 2135) shows no paragraphoi but marks the beginning and end of 130 with a coronis. The balance of evidence points to 130b as a new poem (Page 1955, 200–201), but with a line missing in 130a (probably a glyconic between 10 and 11). Voigt's metrical analysis of 130a is uncertain. See Lobel on *POxy* 2165, Lobel and Page 1963, 130 (G2), and Page 1955, 198–201 for a full discussion.

29. Snell 1953a; Gallavotti 1953, 163 (nothing more helpful than "it makes one think of Alcaeus"); Merkelbach 1958, 91; Gomme 1957, 260; Voigt 1971 (no. 303A); Rösler 1980, 38 n. 36; Burnett 1983, 122; Meyerhoff 1984, 184; Tsomis 2001, 55–56.

30. Gomme 1957, 261. Notice "girl" and "deserting."

31. Though this too has been attributed to Alcaeus (Lobel and Page 1952; Lobel and Page 1963, 304, Page 1955, 261: "There is no evidence that Sappho wrote poems of this general type"). For Sappho's authorship, see Treu 1963, 161–64; Voigt 1971; Kirkwood 1974, 145–47; Burnett 1983, 217. One notices an interesting circularity of argument: 99 and 44A are by Alcaeus because Sappho never mentions Apollo (a curious thing for a lyric poet); 99 and 44A mention Apollo and therefore cannot be by Sappho. Sappho never wrote this type of poem; therefore, this type of poem is not by Sappho.

32. Sappho also mentions Artemis (84) and wrote hymns to her (Philostr. *Vit. Apoll.* 1.30 = T 21 Campbell).

33. For this type of compound in Sappho, see Hamm (Voigt) 1957, 99, 104. The form is better read as dative; there is space for the final <ι>, which gives an opening of $\times - \smile\smile - \smile$. West, who assigned the poem to Sappho, suggested (1970, 324), "prima facie the word agrees with χόρδαισι, which would mean that ὄλισβος was once a synonymn of πλῆκτρον," and translates (1993, 44), "to strum across the plectrum welcoming strings." However, the next line seems to begin with τεουτ[αι]σι or τεουτ[οι]σι for a nice dative plural and

ὄλισβος only ever means "dildo" in its attestations; nor does the notion receive any support from its etymology (probably from the same root seen in ὀλισθός, ὀλισθηρός, "slippery," hence "the slider"; see Chantraine 1968–1980, s.v.).

34. Page 1955, 135, 145; West 1970, 234; Dover 1978, 176 n. 9. Giangrande's comment (1980, 250) that the papyrus "leaves us in no doubt as to what Sappho and her companions were up to," merely shows that he has not understood the context. A reference to the men of the Polyanaxidae is not unthinkable, but dildos are attributed only to women and satyrs in literature and the visual arts, and even κίναιδοι are not so attacked as far as I know. See Dover 1978, 102, 132; Henderson 1991, 221–22; and the Boeotian BF vase, Berlin 3364 (Dover's BB 24).

35. West 1993 rightly takes this last group as a single phrase. ὄνδειξαι = Attic ἀναδεῖξαι.

36. See especially Andrewes 1956, 51, 97; Arthur 1973, 35, 39.

37. Horace Odes 1.32.9–12: Liberum et Musas Veneremque et illi / semper haerentem puerum canebat / et Lycum nigris oculis nigroque / crine decorum (who used to sing of Liber and the Muses and Venus and the boy who always clings to her and Lycus beautiful with his black eyes and black locks). Contrast Odes 2.13.27–28, where Alcaeus' subjects are summed up as dura navis / dura fugae mala, dura belli (the hardships of his boat, of exile, of war). Quintilian 10.1.63: sed et lusit et in amores descendit, maioribus aptior (but he played around and stooped to love affairs, even though he was better fitted for greater subjects), a good example of what gets quoted and why.

38. Kirkwood (1974, 102, 138), for example, rightly points out that the marriage poems of Sappho are given an illusory prominence in both ancient citations and modern scholarship simply because the separate ninth book of epithalamia "made a convenient quarry for ancient scholars in search of metrical examples." See also Page 1955, 112–15.

39. The testimony of Julian, who had the full text of Sappho before him, is unmistakable for the iambics: Letter 10 (403d = 13.5 Bidez-Cumoz). The Oxyrhynchus commentary (POxy 1800 = T1 Campbell) mentions one book of elegies (and other meters?); see Page 1955, 114. Suda Σ 107 (4.322 Adler = T2 Campbell) mentions "epigrams, elegiacs, iambics, and monodies." While the Suda's "epigrams" may be Hellenistic poems under Sappho's name (three in Anth. Pal. 6.269, 7.489, 7.505), the elegiacs and iambics cannot be so explained.

40. West 1974, 32–37; Campbell 1983, 127, 129; Herington 1985, 32–39; Bowie 1986, 13–21; Gentili 1988, 32–35; Bartol 1992; Stehle 1997, 215–22.

41. οἱ γ[ὰρ ἰ]αμβοποιοὶ τραγικὰ ποιοῦσιν, καὶ οἱ τραγῳδοποιοὶ πάλιν ἰαμβικά, καὶ Σαπφώ τινα ἰαμβικῶς ποιεῖ, καὶ Ἀρχίλοχος οὐκ ἰαμβικῶς (The iambic poets write tragic things, and the tragedians write iambic things, and even Sappho writes iambically, and Archilochus not iambically): de poem. fr. 117 (p. 330 Janko = fr. 29, p. 252 Hausrath).

42. Burnett 1983, 212 n. 11; so too Tsomis 2001, 213 n. 220.

43. Does the dispar apply only to Alcaeus?

44. Beginning with Porphyrio ad loc.

45. The textual and metrical uncertainties arise from the problem of disentangling Sappho's words from the paraphrase of the scholiasts on Pindar.

46. Treu (1966, 18) proposed πλοῦ[τ]ο[ν] <τε> θέοι δίδοισιν / [το]ῖσιν [θ]έλ[ο]υσιν of which one can say only that it is not impossible as to the general sense.

47. Cf. for example, Ananius 2–3 or Pythermus 910.

48. Since the poem is in Sapphics, we can be a little more confident in some of the supplements.

49. See Page 1955, 172–73 on context.

50. Contra Gentili 1988, 91. See the discussions of Bowra 1961, 223, and Wilson 1996, 170–71.

51. *Quest. conv.* 646e–f: πρός τινα τῶν ἀμούσων καὶ ἀμαθῶν γυναικῶν; *Conj. praec.* 145f–146a: πρός τινα πλουσίαν; Stob. 3.4.12: πρὸς ἀπαίδευτον γυναῖκα.

52. Cf. the reminiscence (Sappho 193) by Aelius Aristides: "I think you have heard Sappho boasting to some of the women who seemed to be prosperous/happy (εὐδαιμόνων) and saying that the Muses made her rich (ὀλβίαν) in reality and to be envied and that there will be no forgetfulness of her even when she was dead." See Dubois 1995, 5–6.

53. Lidov (2002, 223–24) rightly points out that the traces are too exiguous to restore Δωρί]χαϲ (in as Voigt 1971) with any confidence.

54. For the difficulties of the composite text, see Voigt 1971 and Tsomis 2001, 206–208 (though I disagree with his conclusions). Misread by Calame 2001, 232. Gerber 1997, 156–57: "She mentions the exile of Cleonactids in fr. 98b, the family to which Myrsilus belonged, suggesting that she was not unaware of the clan feuds in Mytilene (cf. the reference to the Penthilid clan in fr. 71). Indeed, the tension underlying remarks about her poetic rivals such as Andromeda in fr. 130.3–4 or Gorgo in fr. 144, may have political underpinnings: Andromeda and Gorgo both belonged to the Polyanactid clan, treated unkindly by Sappho in fr. 155. We possess little else in the way of evidence about Sappho's rôle in the politics of Lesbos during her lifetime." Generally speaking correct, but it is nice to know that Sappho was "not unaware of" her own exile. That either Andromeda or Gorgo or both were Polyanactidae is the logical inference from the way Max. Tyr. cites 155. In 213 Gorgo is the "yoke-mate" of Archeanassa (Pleistodica).

55. See Burnett 1983, 212, for example. There is an assumption that women everywhere and at all times have been obsessed with clothes. An important fact about the social construction of the "female" is concealed here, but any Elizabethan or Wodabe man can disabuse us of the notion that clothes are an exclusively female concern.

56. As shown by Athenaeus (21c–d) who writes, "They were careful to arrange their clothes beautifully and mock those who did not do this," and goes on to quote Plato (*Theat.* 175e), Sappho 57.1, 3, Philetaerus (18 KA), Hermippus (FHG 3.51), Kallistratus (the grammarian, PW 38), and Alexis (265 KA). So too Max. Tyr. 18.9 (18.254 Trapp) compares Socrates mocking the dress and dinner deportment of a sophist (cf. *Protag.* 314e).

57. Alcaeus 77A, for example, uses rough clothing apparently to indicate a change of fortune.

58. Despite the suggestion (Lidov 2002, 226 n. 51, by an anonymous reader) that τὸν κασί]γνητον of line 2 might instead reflect a proper name in -γνητος (and so the whole poem has nothing to do with *any* brother), I still feel confident about the restoration, based on ἄμμι "to us" (7); so too for τὰν κασιγ]νήταν (7). Page's alternative suggestion (1955, 47) αἰν]ήταν δὲ θέλοι πόησθαι τὰν τότ᾽ ἠ]τίμασ᾽ (may he wish to make her praised whom once he dis-

honored) is attractive, "if the gap at the beginning of v. 9 could be suitably filled"; but αἰνητός is extremely rare, and as the only use before Hellenistic poetry shows (Pi. N. 8.39: αἰνέων αἰνητά) the meaning is more "praiseworthy" than "praised" (both possible for -τός past participles, of course) and "making someone praiseworthy" seems to be a job more suitable for a poet.

59. See also Wilson 1996, 172–85. Page's omission of the final fragmentary lines in his translation (1955, 46) has caused others to misread this poem.

60. Arch. 23.14–16, 126, to which add 66; Solon 13.5–6; Theog. 871–72.

61. Sappho's lines demonstrate neither her Victorian moral uprightness (that is, shock at her brother's mistress: rightly Page 1955, 50–51), nor her sisterly shrewishness (wrongly Page ibid.). Homer had already paved the way for women's participation in this code of honor in Odysseus' speech to Nausicaa (Od. 6.184–85): ἀνὴρ ἠδὲ γυνή· πόλλ᾽ ἄλγεα δυσμενέεσσι, / χάρματα δ᾽ εὐμενέτῃσι, μάλιστα δέ τ᾽ ἔκλυον αὐτοί (man and wife: many pains to their evil-wishers, but a joy to their well-wishers; and most of all they gain glory).

62. For Andromeda, see 57 (65.2 ?), 68a, 90, 133, and Max. Tyr. 18.9 (T 20 Campbell). Page (1955, 134): "'Andromeda is properly paid out' [133]: perhaps she in turn has lost a lover to Sappho, or one of her own captives has done her injury. The outlines are unmistakable, the details seldom or never clear."

63. Gentili 1988, 257 n. 39. For text see Voigt 1971, Lobel and Page 1963.

64. The gender in both cases is masculine, but since ὅ]ττινα[ς is indefinite and τὸν δ᾽ ἐπιπλάζοντ᾽ may be, we do not know for certain that Sappho is speaking of men. She is in any case not speaking about specific women. The verb ἐπι-πλάζω (= ἐπι-πλήσσω) refers to public reproof and humiliation.

65. Sappho's and Anacreon's lines are preserved in the same glosses on ἀβακής in Etym. Magn. 2.43–47.

66. Parker 1996, 179–83.

2

Corinna's Poetic *Metis* and the Epinikian Tradition

David H. J. Larmour

for George Huxley

Our assessment of Corinna depends principally on the two long fragments (654.i.12–34, and iii.12–51 *PMG*) in the 2nd-century Berlin papyrus from Hermopolis (284), one containing the singing contest of Cithaeron and Helicon and the other Acraephen's reply to Asopus about the fate of his daughters.[1] Although they presumably come from two separate poems, these fragments are closely connected by their proximity in the papyrus and, we may assume, by the circumstances of their composition and performance. What those circumstances were remains a matter of debate and uncertainty.[2] There has been much discussion about the audience of Corinna's poems; it seems likely that some of her works were performed before both men and women, and that some of them may have been specifically intended for a female audience.[3] Either or both fragments could well be from poems composed in connection with the major cult of Hera in Plataea.[4] Although it is clear that the poetry all too briefly visible within these fragments was inscribed within the patriarchal tradition, the style, content, and tone give sufficient indication of an attempt to strike a divergent note; it may not be going too far, in other words, to characterize Corinna's poetry as significantly "woman-identified," to use Rayor's term.[5] The anecdotal tradition of Corinna's rivalry with Pindar, even if not always reliable in its details, is nonetheless indicative of some area of dispute between them, or at least of notable differences between the two poets that were detected, and viewed as significant, by ancient critics.[6] In some important ways, Corinna's Boeotian-oriented narratives of myths diverge from, and perhaps even react against, the poetic mode of Pindar's Panhellenic epinikians.[7] It is the purpose of this investigation to examine that reaction in order to recover, so far as the fragmentary evidence allows us to, the distinctive voice that speaks in the poetic narratives about the mountains Cithaeron and Helicon and the river Asopus. The investigation begins with a close reading of each fragment, with particular reference to the motifs of deception, violence, revelation, and loss, which link them together and which may, in fact, constitute a thematic model that Corinna followed in her other narratives. There follows an examination of the cult of Hera at Plataea, especially the Daedala festival, as possible occasions for the performance of the two poems under discussion. Finally, we move to Corinna's relationship to Pindar in general, and then to an examination of one particular epinikian, *Pythian* 9, in connection with the two surviving fragments. By deploying incongruity and irony in her own deft fashion, Corinna appears to blur boundaries between Panhellenic and local, human and divine, truth and falsehood, in a manner that subtly challenges the conventions of the epinikian mode.[8]

THE SONG CONTEST OF CITHAERON AND HELICON

The fragment from the contest of Cithaeron and Helicon begins as one of the competitors is completing his song. This song ends with Rhea hiding the baby Zeus and thereby gaining great honor (τιμή) from the gods:[9]

```
]Κώρει-                                                    12
τες ἔκρου]ψαν δάθιο[ν θι]ᾶς
βρέφο]ς ἄντροι, λαθρά[δα]ν ἀγ-
κο]υλομείταο Κρόνω, τα-
νίκά νιν κλέψε μάκηρα 'Ρεία
───────
μεγ]άλαν τ' [ἀ]θανάτων ἔσ-                                 17
ς] ἔλε τιμάν· τάδ' ἔμελψεμ·
μάκαρας δ' αὐτίκα Μώση
φ]ερέμεν ψᾶφον ἔ[τ]αττον
κρ]ουφίαν κάλπιδας ἐν χρου-
```

σοφαῖς· τὺ δ' ἅμα πάντε[ς] ὦρθεν·

πλίονας δ' εἷλε Κιθηρών·   23
τάχα δ' Ἑρμᾶς ἀνέφαν[έν
νι]ν ἀούσας ἐρατὰν ὡς
ἔ]λε νίκαν στεφάνυσιν
...]..ατώ.ανεκόσμιον
μάκα]ρες· τῶ δὲ νόος γεγάθι·

ὁ δὲ λο]ύπησι κά[θ]εκτος   29
χαλεπ]ῆσιν ϝελι[κ]ὼν ἐ-
.....] λιττάδα [π]έτραν
.....]κεν δ' ὄ[ρο]ς· ὑκτρῶς
.....]ων οὐψ[ό]θεν εἴρι-
σέ νιν ἐ]μ μου[ρι]άδεσσι λάυς·

"the Couretes hid the goddess's holy infant in a cave, secretly from crooked-minded Cronus, when blessed Rhea stole him and great was the honor she got from the Immortals." This he sang. At once the Muses ordered the blessed gods to bring their secret ballot stone to the gold-gleaming urns; they all got up together. Cithaeron got more votes; quickly Hermes proclaimed with a shout that he [cithaeron] had won a lovely victory, and with wreaths . . . the blessed gods crowned him, and his mind rejoiced. But, filled with harsh griefs, Helicon [ripped out] a bare rock . . . and the mountain . . . groaning pitifully he hurled it from on high into a myriad stones.

Let us look first at the way Rhea is presented. Zeus is not mentioned by name and hence it is likely, as Rayor argues, that Corinna gave more attention to the role of Rhea than Hesiod did in the *Theogony* passage (453–506) on which her poem is apparently modeled.[10] It is indeed probable that a song concluding with Rhea's hiding of Zeus as a baby—rather than with, say, his reappearance when grown or his triumph over his father Cronus, would have focused on the heroic actions of this goddess. Corinna may have portrayed Rhea as a resourceful female, who manages to outwit a powerful and very cunning male deity by her own devices (Rayor 1993, 226–27). In Hesiod's *Theogony* (469–71), she asks Gaea and Ouranos to devise a plan for her. It could be argued that it is risky to read so much into such a brief narrative, especially one almost devoid of tropes. Certain critics have, in fact, censured Corinna for her lack of embellishment, including a lack of novelty in adjectives.[11] But this is to misunderstand the way a deliberately spare narrative of this kind contrives its effects: because of the generally uncluttered mode of expression, any particularly descriptive or polyvalent word draws attention to itself.[12] It is clear from other fragments, such as 655 and 674 *PMG*, that Corinna uses epithets with more inventiveness and frequency when she wants to: in 674 Thespia is described as καλλιγένεθλε φιλόξενε μωσοφίλειτε (of beautiful offspring, loving strangers, loving the Muses). Thus ἀγκυλομήτης (used in *Theogony* 473 and 495) here in the song-contest fragment is not just a conventional epithet: it serves to emphasize Rhea's intellectual supremacy by reminding us of the formidable abilities of her adversary. Harvey, in his detailed survey of the lyric poets, notes that "ornamental Homeric epithets were not used indiscriminately" and that Corinna's diction "shows the same sort of discrimination in the use of Homeric epithets that characterizes archaic lyric . . . the work has been done by a singularly delicate and well-trained hand."[13] The word ἀγκυλομήτης also inevitably evokes the world of Homeric epic; for Rhea the act of taking or stealing is concomitant with the getting of τιμή and this is reminiscent of male heroes seeking τιμή by violent physical action. Such juxtaposing of male and female figures and qualities we may designate a defining characteristic of Corinna's method: in another fragment (664B), she claims that she recounts the arete of both heroes and heroines (εἰρώων ἀρετὰς χειρωάδων). In another of her poems, Corinna is said to have told of the "impetuous shield" (θοῦριν ἀσπίδα) of the goddess Athena (667 *PMG*). Such a poem might have recounted Athena's exploits as a warrior or strategist and relied upon the same collocation of traditionally "masculine" and "feminine" features. A similar promotion of the female role or feminine cleverness is perhaps indicated by Plutarch's statement (*De Musica* 1136B) that "Corinna says Apollo was taught to play the aulos by Athena"; this goes against the popular tradition that Athena threw away the aulos in disgust, preserved in Athenaeus 616E.[14]

If we focus now on the song as a whole, we see that its content is appropriate for a mountain because Rhea's concealment of Zeus took place in another mountain locale, usually said to be Mt. Ida.[15] It is the second entry in the contest and is sung either by Cithaeron or by Helicon; the preponderance of scholarly opinion to date has favored Cithaeron for two main reasons. First, the prominence given to geographical locations in the poem invites an aetiological interpretation and there was a well-known cult of Zeus on Mt. Cithaeron (Paus. 9.3.1–2). Given that Cithaeron wins the contest, it would be fitting that he do so with a song about Rhea and Zeus.[16] Against this, however, the singing contest and its outcome could easily be connected with the cult of the Muses on Helicon.[17] The second argument for assigning the song about Rhea to Cithaeron is that the winning song usually comes second in such contexts.[18] However, in view of Corinna's penchant—visible even in these meagre fragments—for surprising details and for reworking the tradition, it is unsafe to assume that the song is Cithaeron's simply on the basis of what might be "expected" from looking at the available evidence for song contests in Greece. One could reasonably make an argument based on the power of tradition with regard to mythical content and say that to have Helicon lose the contest would be at least very unexpected and perhaps even inappropriate, but this is what Corinna does.[19]

Far more important than the identity of the singer, however, is the artful manner in which the song is linked to the remainder of the fragment. Most obviously there is the striking repetition of forms of αἱρέω in lines 18, 23, and 26: Rhea *seized* honor from the gods, Cithaeron *seized* more votes, and Hermes proclaims that Cithaeron has *seized* a "lovely victory."[20] Three other elements serve to connect the song with what we have of the narrative: first, there is the motif of secrecy: the Curetes hid the baby in a cave (ἔκρου]ψαν)[21] when Rhea stole him (κλέψε) from Cronus. As Snyder puts it, "the secrecy surrounding Zeus' whereabouts at the end of the second contestant's song is echoed in the ensuing description of the secret ballots used by the Muses."[22] The Muses themselves are the daughters of Zeus and Mnemosyne who, like Rhea, is a Titan daughter of Ouranos and Gaea.[23] They are heavily associated with notions of uncovering and secrecy, since they can both recover the past and can leave things hidden in it.[24] What Segal terms the "precise dicaeastic particularity" of the voting scene draws attention to, among other things, the secrecy of the process.[25]

Second, the presence of Hermes—broadly associated with both contests and trickery, as well as theft—also ties the two parts together. Hermes is said to have performed the first song in the *Homeric Hymn to Hermes* (425–33). He was an important deity in Corinna's vicinity: Pausanias mentions Hermes in Tanagra at 9.22.1–2, just before he describes the famous painting in the gymnasium there of Corinna tying on her victory wreath after defeating Pindar "at

Thebes with a poem."[26] The verb Corinna uses to describe Hermes' announcement, ἀναφαίνω, means literally "make bright," "shed light upon," or "bring to light"; the suggestion of uncovering something hidden or throwing light upon something hitherto unremarkable is particularly significant here.[27] The uncovering of the pebbles in the contest parallels the eventual uncovering of Rhea's stone and the emergence of Zeus from the cave in the myth; although this was apparently not related in the song, it is clearly implied by the statement that Rhea "won great honour from the gods" and was so well known that audiences would not fail to recall it.[28]

Third, the stones: Helicon throws down part of himself, a boulder, which breaks into thousands of tiny stones, and these, as Snyder says (1984, 128), "are reminiscent of the very instrument of his defeat, the voting pebbles cast by the Muses." But the pebbles, and more especially the boulder from which they come, are also reminiscent of the stone Rhea substituted for the baby Zeus, part of herself so to speak, and which was then swallowed by Cronus.[29] Eventually, the stone was to be vomited up (after Metis' emetic, according to Apollodorus 1.2.1), and its reappearance marks the moment when Cronus is displaced by Zeus. The unexpected and distressing outcome of the contest for Helicon is thereby likened to Cronus' discovery that Zeus has survived and that he is being thrust from power by his son. The vomited up stone reveals to Cronus that Zeus is alive and he has been deceived by Rhea; the counted up small stones reveal to Helicon that Cithaeron's song about Zeus has won and he has been cheated of the victory he desired and expected. The large stone tumbling down the mountainside and shattering into thousands of pieces, together with the adverb ὐκτρῶς (pitifully), succinctly expresses Helicon's chagrin at his defeat and loss of preeminence in singing. The presence of Rhea and Hermes, and the implied reference to Metis' role later, may also suggest that Cithaeron's victory was achieved by trickery and that Helicon's rage is in that sense motivated or justified. It is also possible that the victory of Cithaeron over Helicon is to be seen as analogous to the displacement of Cronus or the older generation of gods by Zeus or the younger generation. In this case, we might see the voting as a manifestation of the *dike* of Olympian rule, and Helicon's outburst as an instance of that hubris which it replaces.

The two narratives contained within this first fragment, then, both move from an initial situation marked by seizure, secrecy, and deception to a moment of the revelation of what has occurred. This is followed by an effective encapsulation of the pain of loss and defeat, together with a sense of the inevitability and finality of the train of events. The poem as a whole appears to be framed around issues of generational conflict, or at any rate, the shifting dynamic between old and young. It also rests upon the encounter between the male and the female, an encounter marked by both conflict and cooperation. The action moves swiftly and is punctuated by acts of violence.[30]

THE DAUGHTERS OF ASOPUS

This same combination of features is found in the second fragment, in which the prophet Acraephen reveals to Asopus what has happened to his daughters.[31] The piece should be read with a mind to the content of the first poem because of their proximity in the papyrus and the fact that they were in all likelihood arranged together in a collection of poems united by form, theme, and occasion of performance:

τᾶν δὲ πήδω[ν τρῖς μ]ὲν ἔχι
Δεὺς παπεὶ[ρ πάντω]ν βασιλεύς,
τρῖς δὲ πόντ[ω γᾶμε] μέδων
Π[οτιδάων, τ]ᾶν δὲ δουῖν
Φῦβος λέκτ[ρα] κρατούνι,   5

τὰν δ᾽ ἴαν Μή[ας] ἀγαθὸς
πῆς Ἑρμᾶς· οὔ[τ]ω γὰρ Ἔρως
κὴ Κούπρις πιθέταν, τιὼς
ἐν δόμως βάντας κρουφάδαν
κώρας ἐννί᾽ ἐλέσθη·   10

τή ποκ᾽ εἰρώων γενέθλαν
ἐσγεννάσονθ᾽ εἰμ[ιθί]ων
κἄσσονθη π[ο]λου[σπ]ερίες
τ᾽ ἀγείρω τ᾽, ἐς [μ]α[ντοσ]ούνω
τρίποδος ὤιτ[......]   15

τόδε γέρας κ[..........]ν
ἐς πεντείκο[ντα] κρατερῶν
ὁμήμων πέρ[οχο]ς προφά-

τας σεμνῶν [ἀδο]ύτων λαχὼν
ἀψεύδιαν Ἀκ[ρη]φείν·　　　　　　　　　　　　　　　20

πράτοι [μὲν] γὰ[ρ Λατ]οίδας
δῶκ᾽ Εὐωνούμοι τριπόδων
ἐsw ἰῶν [χρε]ισμῶς ἐνέπειν,
τὸν δ᾽ ἐς γᾶς βαλὼν Οὐριεὺς
τιμὰ[ν] δεύτερος ἴσχεν,　　　　　　　　　　　　25

πῆς [Ποτ]ιδάωνος· ἔπι-
τ᾽ Ὠα[ρί]ων ἁμὸς γενέτωρ
γῆα[ν ϝ]ὰν ἀππασάμενος·
χὼ μὲν ὡραν[ὸ]ν ἀμφέπι,
τιμὰν δ᾽[......]ν οὕταν.　　　　　　　　　　　30

τώνεκ[.......]ν ἐνέπω
τ᾽ ἀτ[ρ]έκ[ιαν χρει]σμολόγον·
τοῦ δέ [νου ϝῖκέ τ᾽ ἀ]θανάτυς
κὴ λού[........] φρένας
δημόν[... ἐκου]ρεύων·　　　　　　　　　　　35

ὡς ἔφα [μάντις] π[ε]ράγεις·
τὸν δ᾽ Ἀ[σωπὸς ἀσ]πασίως
δεξιᾶς ἐ[φαψάμ]ενος
δάκρού τ᾽ [ὀκτάλ]λων προβαλ[ὼν
ὦδ᾽ ἀμίψ[ατο φ]ωνῆ·　　　　　　　　　　　　40

"Of your daughters, Zeus, Father and King of all, possesses three;
Poseidon, Lord of the Ocean, took three as wives; Phoebus rules the
beds of two; and Hermes, the noble son of Maia, has one. For thus
Eros and Cypris ordained that the gods, going secretly into your
house, should seize for themselves your nine daughters. And hereafter
they shall give birth to a race of half-divine heroes, and they shall be
fecund and ageless, [this I learned] from the oracular tripod . . . to me,
Acraephen, alone of fifty mighty brothers, sublime prophet of the holy
sanctuary, has been given this honor of the truth. For first the son of
Leto granted to Euonymus to utter oracles from his tripod, but
Hyrieus threw him out of the land and held the honor second, the son
of Poseidon. Then Orion, my father, after he regained his own land;
and now he dwells in the sky and this honor has come to me. Therefore . . . I tell the truth from the oracle. But you, now yield to the

Immortals and free your heart [from sorrow], father-in-law to the gods." Thus spoke the aged prophet. And Asopus, gladly touching him by the right hand, and shedding a tear from his eyes, replied as follows:

The initial situation, we may note, is characterized by deception and seizure: the gods came "in secret" (κρουφάδαν)—paralleling λαθρά[δα]ν of Rhea's actions—to Asopus' house, having been persuaded by Eros and Aphrodite to "seize for themselves" (ἐλέσθη) his nine daughters. These daughters various gods now rule over (κρατούνι). These are the facts of a hitherto unclear situation laid bare, very much akin to the revelation of the numbers of pebbles in the voting urns in the other poem; Corinna then deftly conveys the emotional reaction of Asopus to his loss, just as she went on to encapsulate Helicon's reaction to his defeat in the contest. West (1970b, 287) finds hints in column ii of the papyrus that Asopus "goes out to his watery haunts" (26), that he is grieving over the loss of his daughters (32) and is "baffled" (43) until he meets the prophet of Apollo.[32] In the readable part of the poem in column iii, considerable emphasis is placed on the truthfulness of the revelation (ἀψεύδιαν, 31; ἀτ[ρ]έκ[ιαν χρει]μολόγον, 43) that comes from the oracle, probably of Apollo Ptoios.[33] The oracle does not lie—just like the voting pebbles—and the result is incontestable.

Once again, there are obvious connections with a local cult and geographical features. We have Acraephen, the eponymous hero of Acraephia, speaking from the tripod on Mt. Ptoios, to the river-god Asopus. The account of his daughters in the missing parts of the poem could also have had a strongly aetiological flavor. We know that Corinna called Tanagra, her hometown, a daughter of Asopus.[34] The aetiological element serves to connect the narrative with the preceding story of the contest between the mountains, and in fact, in the later parts of the Asopus fragment (only barely visible), it seems that the mountain Parnes may have delivered a speech as well. Cithaeron is also named there twice (Page 1953, 27). In each fragment, then, landmarks—mainly Boeotian—feature prominently as anthropomorphized figures in a mythological narrative; the boundary between geographical locations and living human characters is all but erased in this thought-provoking presentation. It is noteworthy that there are nine daughters of Asopus in Corinna's account, paralleling the nine Muses. Other versions give quite different numbers: Apollodorus says twenty (3.12.6), Diodorus has thirteen (4.72.1, 73.1), the scholiast on Pindar *Olympian* 6.144 lists seven.[35] This looks like a deliberate move on Corinna's part, either to make a connection with the other poem, or because the song was performed at a festival in which the Muses featured, such as the Mouseia at Thespia.[36]

Acraephen's account of the succession of Hyrieus and Orion to the oracular tripod harks back to Asopus' situation in various subtle ways. Here, too, it would be a mistake to think that there is no real connection between Acraephen's speech and the rest of the narrative. According to a story preserved in Palaephatos 51 and Ovid, *Fasti* 5.493-536, Hyrieus entertained the gods Zeus, Poseidon, and Hermes,[37] who came disguised to his home one evening, and was rewarded for his hospitality with a wish; being wifeless, he asked for a son and Orion was the result.[38] These are the same gods who steal Asopus' daughters, so that the father's loss of his daughters is paralleled by the childless Hyrieus' acquisition of a son. The throwing of Euonymus out of the land by Hyrieus (line 35) and Orion's regaining of his own land (39) clearly continue the motif of loss and recuperation, although we do not have the precise details; we also know that Orion pined for his lost wife, Side, according to Ovid *Ars Amatoria* 1.731. The repetition of τιμάν in lines 36 and 41, with reference to the holding of the honor of the oracle by Hyrieus and now by Acraephen (τιμὰ[v] δεύτερος ἴσχεν, 36 . . . τιμὰν δ[......]v οὔταν, 41) sets up what was undoubtedly the main thrust of Acraephen's speech, that Asopus too will gain τιμή through his daughters' unions with the various gods; it also echoes Rhea's gaining "great honor" from the gods in lines 17–18 of the song-contest poem. There is a loose connection between Acraephen and Asopus through Hyrieus, according to Apollodorus 3.10.1: Hyrieus was also the grandfather—via Nykteus—of Antiope, who is described in *Odyssey* 11.260–65 as a daughter of Asopus (see Gantz 1993, 215–16, 232); it is unclear whether Corinna knew of this tradition, but if she did, she could have been manipulating it here. The violent displacement of Euonymus by Hyrieus and his replacement by Orion, which may also have been achieved by force, is also vaguely reminiscent of the Zeus/Cronus struggle alluded to in Cithaeron's winning song.

At the end of the fragment (48–51), we are told of Asopus' reaction to the information he has received about his daughters: he takes hold of the prophet's right hand "gladly" (ἀσ]πασίως), dropping a tear from his eyes (δάκρού τ' [ὀκτάλ]λων προβαλ]ών). His reply is lost, but Page (1953, 25) interprets as follows: "He is obviously pleased with what he has heard . . . and will cease to grieve his loss. Indeed he will give something by way of a dowry." Gerber (1977, 220) finds considerably less enthusiasm, merely "a father's reluctant submission." Once again Corinna seems to be developing Hesiodic material in her own way. Her source this time could be the *Catalogue of Women*, in which the daughters of Asopus probably featured (West 1985, 100–103). West suggests that Euripides, who is the earliest author to give the genealogy Hyrieus-Nykteus-Antiope, may have found it in the *Catalogue*. This poem could be one of the "tales of heroines" Corinna mentions in fr. 664B, perhaps a *partheneion* composed for a festival. There is no direct evidence that she wrote these, although in *PMG* 655.1.2–3, Corinna says she sings "fine old tales for the white-robed women of Tanagra" and "adorned stories from our fathers' time for *parthenoi*". She goes on to mention as examples "the leader Cephisus" (the Boeotian river-god), "great Orion," and "the fifty mighty sons" he sired "by mating with nymphs" *PMG* 655.1.12–16; this suggests that the Asopus poem may be typical of this part of Corinna's oeuvre.[40] Stehle (1997, 103–104) points out that stories about sets of daughters are frequent subjects of Corinna's lost poetry (daughters of Orion, Euonymus, and Minyas) and says that, if these were choral pieces, "these paradigmatic or cautionary tales about groups of young women must have seemed directly applicable to the *parthenoi* who performed them."

Skinner (1983, 15) argues that the author "surely intended us to regard her female figures as mere personifications and accept the rape as a standard plot device of aetiological fable" and sees no evidence that Corinna "was treating her subject matter ironically or that she ever questioned the myth's underlying assumptions." Rayor (1993, 228) contends that Acraephen's response is the traditional one—"when gods steal sons or daughters, the parents should feel honored"—and that Corinna moreover gives reason *not* to identify with him: "she presents this character as pompous and self-absorbed, someone who provides factual information but from his own limited perspective."[41] Although neither reading can be securely justified, we may note that it is striking how Acraephen does not name the daughters, only numbering how many were seized by each particular god; in contrast, it looks from the papyrus as if Asopus did name at least some of his daughters later in the poem: Page detects signs of Corcyra, Aegina, Sinope, Thespia, and Plataea (Page 1953, 26–27). There are some other indications that the poem contains at least a whiff of irony at the expense of Asopus and Acraephen: the very suddenness of the change of attitude evinced by Asopus—who, in Skinner's words, "is mollified as soon as he learns that the rapists were gods" (Skinner 1983, 15)—raises suspicion. So does the mention of Orion, who was especially popular in Boeotia (according to *PMG* 673, most authorities say he was from Tanagra):[42] Corinna wrote a *Cataplous* about him (*PMG* 662) and in another fragment she is said to have called him εὐσεβέστατον (most pious) and to have written that he "reclaimed many places, clearing them of wild beasts" (673). It is obvious that Corinna's treatment of this hero may have been quite different from what appeared in the more common myths about him, yet it is difficult to imagine that the name would not have conjured up at least some echoes of his better-known adventures: his love affair with Eos, which ended in death on the point of one of Artemis' arrows when the gods became jealous; his journey to Chios, where after getting drunk he raped Oenopion's daughter Merope and was then blinded and exiled; his hybristic hunting boast on Crete, which caused Gaia to kill him with a giant scorpion; and finally his being placed among the stars by Zeus, as requested by Artemis and Leto (Gantz 1993, 271–73).

As in the first fragment, then, there do appear to be intimations of a "woman-identified" perspective, even if there is no direct contestation of the patriarchal value system. Corinna seems to be engaged in re-forming the mythical tradition, perhaps for a specifically female audience, in a manner that enables her to foreground female figures, actions, and experience. Even though she works within the patriarchal tradition, the deployment of ambiguity and the use of allusion open up some elements of this tradition to ironic scrutiny and problematize those aspects that might be expected to resonate particularly forcefully among female listeners. The motifs of secrecy, deception, and revelation she deploys become a metaphor for her own poetic activity, for this is, in itself, an act of uncovering, of revealing truths that are "hidden" within the standard versions.[43] The same activity is required of the audience of the poems: to appreciate the startling juxtapositions, the unexpected details, the subtle reworkings within what appear to be straightforward narratives of old stories. Behind the surface—as is the case with Rhea— lies complex manipulation.[44] For those who encountered Corinna's poems outside their local setting, for whom the dialect might have been challenging, or who read them in their collected form later, the labor of discovery would have been all the more painstaking.

Perhaps this is what is meant by Statius' reference to "opening up the secrets of subtle Corinna" (*pandere . . . tenuisque arcana Corinnae*, *Silvae* 5.3.158); Corinna comes at the end of a list that includes Callimachus, Lycophron, and Sophron, all of whom are designated obscure or complex.[45]

THE DAEDALA FESTIVAL OF HERA

In what context might these two poems have been performed? They could have been sung at cult celebrations in any of the locations prominent in their verses, and West (1990, 556–57) proposes the Mouseia at Thespia, although this works better with a Hellenistic date for Corinna than a fifth-century one. By far the most intriguing possibility, however, is the one elaborated by Burzacchini: the Daedala in honor of Hera, which was held at Plataea.[46] There are compelling reasons to think that this was the occasion of the Asopus poem and perhaps of the song-contest poem as well. First, the festivities of the Daedala were held in two locations: the river Asopus and Mt. Cithaeron. It began with the ritual bathing of a wooden statue (Daedale, the "fictitious Hera") in the Asopus, and this figure was then carried in a cart to the summit of Mt. Cithaeron, where the sacrifice took place. In the myth, Cithaeron (in either human or mountain form) tells Zeus to make a wooden statue and says that he is celebrating his marriage with Plataea, daughter of Asopus (Paus. 9.3.1).[47] Clark (1998, 25) observes that, "though the ritual itself is heavily dependent on themes from marriage and wedding ritual, the festival also brings together a number of communities to celebrate a deity who has regional importance as a political figure. The myth and ritual relate as much to the early history and identity of Plataia as they do to the wedding of Hera." The name of this town, it will be recalled, seems to appear in the latter part of the papyrus of the Asopus poem (Column iv, line 42).

Second, there are a number of elements in the ritual and the associated myths that could well have inspired the content of Corinna's poems or at least have provided a suitable context for their themes. Significantly, this festival was not a standard representation of the *hieros gamos*, but was primarily a celebration of the reconciliation of Zeus and Hera after a quarrel. Clark (1998, 25) says: "Although there are wedding preparations, there is no point which corresponds to a wedding, and no groom is present. The myth itself makes clear that no wedding takes place because all the preparations are a trick to make Hera jealous," and further, "Though the festival is said to have been founded to celebrate Hera's reconciliation to her husband, both the aetiological myth and the practices of the festival seem to focus on the quarrels of Zeus and Hera." The course of this quarrel is, moreover, pervaded by acts of deception, moments of revelation, and outbursts of anger or jealousy. As Plutarch records it, Hera withdraws after a quarrel, Zeus pretends to marry an image named Daedale made from an oak tree, Hera gets jealous, the trick is revealed, and finally there is a reconciliation, after which Hera burns the wooden image (fr. 157.6, from his treatise *On the Daedala at Plataea*). In Pausanias' version, Zeus is advised by Cithaeron, the ruler of Plataea and described as "second to none in cleverness" (9.3.1) to make a false bride called Daedale and to say that she is the daughter of Asopus (9.3.1–9).

The connection with the Asopus poem is obvious, but the cleverness of Cithaeron in advising Zeus in his quarrel with Hera also parallels Rhea's craftiness in protecting Zeus in her quarrel with Cronus, the subject of Cithaeron's winning song. The fictitious Hera is analogous to Rhea's stone. Nor is it impossible that the contest between Cithaeron and Helicon, with its disputed outcome, could also have been associated with the argument between Zeus and Hera, which formed the basis of the Daedala rituals. Reconciliation between the deities might have been symbolized by a reconciliation between the two mountains—Skinner (1983, 14), for instance, suggests that "in the missing part of the papyrus, the Muses . . . may well have consoled the defeated party by making his own mountain the site of their principal shrine." Moreover, there was a close association between Rhea and Hera at this cult. Pausanias (9.2.7) mentions that on entering the temple of Hera at Plataea, worth seeing for its size and the beauty of its images, one saw Rhea carrying to Cronus the stone, wrapped in swaddling clothes, as if it were the child she had just given birth to. He then describes the huge statue of Hera and says both were made by Praxiteles from Pentelic marble. Some have argued that Hera was an earth goddess, and one Orphic source even suggests that Hera and Rhea are identical.[48]

If Corinna's song-contest poem was written in connection with the cult of Hera, it would have been entirely in keeping with the occasion to include a winning song about Rhea. Plutarch in fr. 157.3 records another story, in which Hera, while still a *parthenos*, was kidnapped by Zeus. Cithaeron—who is either a personification of the mountain or a king of Thebes in Plutarch's account—provided a shady dell as a marriage chamber and prevented Hera's nurse from searching for her there. Hera thus escaped discovery. It is not difficult to see how rituals associated with this story would be suitable occasions for the performance of either the song contest or the Asopus poem. For these reasons, then, it is likely that the two poems of Corinna under discussion were composed for the festival of Hera, or performed at it, or (even more vaguely) written in connection with the rites and myths that formed the basis of the Hera cult in Plataea.

CORINNA AND PINDAR'S EPINIKIANS

The tradition of the rivalry between Corinna and Pindar is a typical "poets' quarrel" and the snippets recorded are of dubious reliability.[49] Nonetheless these stories do represent something important: they are a form of literary criticism before it existed as a separate discipline. Uncertainty about the date of Corinna makes it impossible to say whether their rivalry was actual and personal—that is, that they were contemporaries, performing in the same public arena— or created, either from comments made by Corinna in an attempt to distinguish herself from him, or out of the differences in their techniques that were noticed by later critics.[50] It is known that poets assimilated their personal disputes to quarrels between figures in their poems and this could have inspired allegorical readings of the song contest in terms of the supposed rivalry between Pindar and Corinna (see Clayman 1993, Henderson 1989). One such interpretation of Corinna's song-contest poem has been proposed by Clayman (1993), who likens it to the contest between the olive and the laurel in Callimachus *Iamb* 4 (fr. 194 Pfeiffer), and goes on to read Helicon and Cithaeron as representing Pindar and Corinna respectively: "If Corinna's poem was an allegory like Callimachus', it would begin in a similar fashion, with a brief challenge to Pindar's supremacy in Boeotian poetry. . . . This would be followed by an Aesopic debate, in which Helicon takes the part of Pindar and victorious Cithaeron is Corinna. At the conclusion, Corinna, like Cithaeron, crowns herself victor, and Pindar, like Helicon, is enraged at the sight."[51] It is interesting that Cithaeron is mentioned only once in the extant poetry of Pindar (P.1.77), while there are several references to the Muses as the "Heliconians."[52]

Perhaps Pindar and Corinna assimilated their poetry to these two mountains, which came to symbolize their differences. Bowra (1979) suggests that Cithaeron and Helicon stand for different kinds of poetry. Clayman (1993) transposes this to a Hellenistic setting, amid the self-conscious quarrels between Alexandrian poets; earlier "contests" such as the famous one between Homer and Hesiod represent a more rudimentary version of the same phenomenon perhaps. Even without this kind of systematic allegory, the tradition of the quarrel itself is enough to show that there were significant differences in their approach to poetry, which were apparent to ancient readers (Snyder 1989, 42–44). And, as Rayor (1993, 229) observes: "Even if she did not actually compete with Pindar, her mythological narratives are new versions of traditional tales, which is a form of competition." In the case of Corinna and Pindar, of course, the "competition" or "quarrel" is underpinned by a significant extra element, namely gender difference.[53] Clayman (1993, 641) points out that one of the major elements of Corinna's critical position is "an emergent awareness of the relationship between gender and art. Here, for the first time in the Western tradition, we find a woman considering the issue of how women should write and concluding that the imitation of the best male model is not necessarily a good choice."

In what senses, then, might Corinna be diverging from or challenging the epinikian mode of Pindar's poetry? Most obvious, of course, are the differences in the circumstances of their production and performance: Pindar's epinikians were produced as hymns celebrating an athletic victor, who had won an agon at a Panhellenic festival held in honor of Zeus, Poseidon, or Apollo. The epinikian was the crowning moment of agonistic achievement: it enacted the transformation of the victor from an individual human athlete into the embodiment of aristocratic male arete. Victorious athletes, decorated with sacrificial fillets as the finest human specimens available, acquired a semidivine status or at least were closely associated with the divine, and the epinikian sought to express this in a complex, almost mystical, fusion of words and music.[54] The setting is very much male-dominated and the poem oriented toward a male audience. Athletic contests featured only male competitors, and married women were excluded from the Olympia, on penalty of death (Paus. 5.6.7, 6.7.2), although *parthenoi* may have been permitted to attend as spectators (6.20.8–9). There were running races for women at various festivals, including the Heraea at Olympia, but these were separate events and are not in any meaningful way the equivalent of male agones.[55]

In the epinikian, the individual athletic victor is associated with the heroes of the past, and the present is subsumed under a weighty amount of myth, history, and genealogy. Much of the poem looks back from the perspective of present triumph and the culmination of glory to the past, stressing links with the athlete's father and family line. Corinna's poems are far removed from the realm of the epinikian: many of them appear to have been produced for choruses of young women at local, not Panhellenic, festivals such as the Daedala of Hera. Many were concerned with marriage and women's experience and probably paid more attention to female figures like Rhea and various sets of daughters. The poems are preparatory and anticipatory, looking toward the culmination of marriage rather than back from the moment of victory. There is undoubtedly some common ground: Pindar sheds light on cultural links between the telos of athletic victory and of marriage in *Pythian* 9 and there were running races for *parthenoi* at various festivals, including the Heraea at Olympia, which appear to have been closely connected with marriage.[56] Corinna's poems are quite different in their orientation. So, for instance, Corinna's use of the Asopus myth differs substantially from Pindar's: he refers frequently to one daughter in particular, Aegina, in odes written for victors from that island, such as *Isthmian* 8:

χρὴ δ' ἐν ἑπταπύλοισι Θήβαις τραφέντα
Αἰγίνᾳ Χαρίτων ἄωτον προνέμειν,
πατρὸς οὕνεκα δίδυ-
     μαι γένοιτο θύγατρες Ἀσωπίδων
ὁπλόταται, Ζηνί τε ἅδον βασιλέι.
ὃ τὰν μὲν παρὰ καλλιρόῳ
Δίρκᾳ φιλαρμάτου πόλι-
ος ᾤκισεν ἀγεμόνα·

σὲ δ' ἐς νᾶσον Οἰνοπίαν
     ἐνεγκὼν κοιμᾶτο, δῖον ἔνθα τέκες
Αἰακὸν βαρυσφαράγῳ πατρὶ κεδνότατον
ἐπιχθονίων (16-22)

A man nursed in seven-gated Thebes must present to Aegina the first flower of the Graces, for these were twin daughters of Asopus, the youngest, and they were pleasing to Zeus. One of them he made live by lovely flowing Dirce, as ruler of a chariot-loving city; but you he carried away to the island of Oenopia and bedded, and there you bore divine Aeacus to the loud-thundering father, the most noble of mortals.

There is no hint here of the violent seizure of the girls or of Asopus' distress such as we find in Corinna's piece.

In *Paean* 6.134–37, likewise, Pindar focuses on the beatific nature of the union and its glorious offspring,[57] giving only a brief picture of the moment when Aegina was violently carried off: Κρόνου παῖς. ὑδάτ[εσσ]ι δ' ἐπ' Ἀσ[ω]/που π[οτ' ἀ]πὸ προθύρων/βαθύκολπον ἀνερέψατο παρθένον Αἴγιναν (son of Cronus. Beside the waters of Asopus he once carried off the deep-breasted maiden Aegina).[58] Corinna and Pindar both fuse girl and geographical location in the same way, but it is clear that Corinna's perspective is not male-identified in the same way nor to the same extent as Pindar's. In Pindar there is no suggestion that the "love" does not go smoothly or that it could possibly be viewed as anything other than a great boon; Corinna, by showing us Asopus' initial distress, hints otherwise. She may well have drawn on such accounts as that found in Apollodorus 3.12.6, in which Asopus travels to Corinth in search of Aegina, finds out that the abductor was Zeus, and pursues him until the god drives him back to his waters with his thunderbolts.[59] Perhaps Pindar manipulated the tradition in order to silence these elements.[60] The only details that stand out in his vignette—that Aegina was carried off from the doorstep and that she is "deep-zoned" or "deep-breasted" (βαθύκολπον)—place her outside her father's home rather than inside, which would require Apollo to invade this space (as he and the other gods do in Corinna's presentation)—and emphasize her modesty and fertility.[61] In this version, moreover, it is apparently only Aegina who is carried off by a lone god; in *Isthmian* 8.15–20, Pindar has only the twins Aegina and Thebe, "the youngest daughters" of Asopus, and the violent seizure is erased—they "were pleasing" (ἅδον) to Zeus. Corinna may have chosen to emphasize the violent character of the act of abduction by having nine daughters seized at the same time. In her version it is a planned and collective act of rape.

In Pindar's epinikians, there is always a strong Panhellenic flavor, even in poems with a significant local reference.[62] In *Isthmian* 8.15a–16a, for instance, he says that a man "nursed in Thebes" must sing of Aegina. Corinna is often regarded as firmly local, even parochial, in her themes, and this impression is of course strengthened by her regional dialect. It is worth noting, however, that her narrative of Cronus and Rhea constitutes a significant Panhellenic element, and the subjects of Helicon, Cithaeron, and the daughters of Asopus were certainly not confined to her region. In *Isthmian* 8, it is precisely the connection with Asopus that provides the link between the Theban poet and his Aeginetan subject. It is not so much that Corinna rejects a Panhellenic perspective, rather that she subsumes it into the locally based raw material of her poems. We might say that she inverts Pindar's priorities, which would not be surprising given the fact that her pieces appear to be connected with Boeotian festivals rather than the four great Panhellenic gatherings. By presenting narratives about Cithaeron, Helicon, and Asopus' daughters that were perhaps less well known or indeed her own inventions and by retelling myths from a de-centered position, she seeks to alter the Panhellenic consensus about these figures. Hers is a "clear-sounding" voice from the margins that subtly challenges the content of the Panhellenic chorus.

It would be a simplification to say that Corinna's output was simply "women's poetry," for in many ways she competes with Pindar on his own ground. Corinna appropriates his role at the intersection of agon and poetry. She steps into a male poetic space. This can be gathered also from the painting of Corinna crowning herself victor over Pindar, which was kept in Tanagra's gymnasium, the male preserve par excellence, a space that women were not permitted to enter (Paus. 9.22.3).[63] The epinikian rested upon an equivalence, or at least a close relationship, between the athletic victor and the poet who offers the victory song (Larmour 1999, 41–50), and Corinna insinuates herself into this intersection of patriarchal roles. The song-contest fragment has obvious agonistic features and the voting procedure may reflect actual practice at festival agones (Segal 1975; Henderson 1995, 34–35). Poetic and athletic contests were two sides of the same coin of agonistic worship of divinities, although women could compete in at least some poetic contests against men. The repetition of αἱρέω in Corinna's song-contest poem might be designed to recall athletic victories: Pindar uses the verb in O.8.63–73 (of Alcimedon's thirtieth victory), P.1.106 (of the prizes of good fortune and fame), and P.3.74 (of winning crowns). The adjective ἐρατός is used of contests at the Nemean festival (N.6.12).

Corinna's narrative of the daughters of Asopus also contains some agonistic overtones in the alternating speeches of Acraephen, Asopus, and Parnes, and in the gods competing for the nine girls, who parallel the nine Muses in the song-contest poem. The struggle between Asopus and the gods for his daughters is like one of those running races for suitors of marriageable maidens: such myths often include an unwillingness on the part of the father to let his child go (e.g. Hippodameia) or on the part of the girls themselves to accede to marriage (e.g. Atalanta). Like Cyrene, Atalanta's "masculine" behavior places her in a position of ambiguous gender and, as Scanlon says, "only male trickery can overcome female strength, a complete reversal of the Greek norm" (Scanlon 2002, 175–98, esp. 177–78). In Corinna's poem the male gods use trickery, and the resulting distribution of daughters reflects Olympian hierarchy: Zeus gets three, so does his brother Poseidon; Apollo gets two; Hermes, who is youngest, just one. The first three gods are the patrons of the four Panhellenic athletic festivals, and Hermes had a major role in many athletic contests, especially running races (Larmour 1999, 83–85, 105–106). In *PMG* 666, we find περὶ τεοῦς Ἑρμᾶς ποτ' Ἄρεα/πουκτεύει (for you, Hermes boxes against Ares): περὶ τεοῦς could refer to Tanagra (Page 1953, 37 [fr. 19]). This is the only mention of such a contest (and could be connected with the rivalry between Corinna and Pindar), but at any rate, it offers more evidence of Corinna's agonistic interests. If the Asopus poem was a *partheneion*, it might have included the agonistic elements of strife, blame, and praise similar to those we find in Alcman's (Rayor 1993, 229 n. 34).

Particularly striking is Corinna's appropriation of the procedural accoutrements of agonistic competition: the way the contest of Helicon and Cithaeron is judged and Helicon's violent reaction look like a calculated attempt at undermining some of the most significant elements of the ideology surrounding athletic competition, an ideology promulgated most eloquently by Pindar. In his epinikians, he constantly urges restraint and moderation on the victor; all athletes were supposed to obey the judges of the *agones*, like the Hellanodikai at Olympia, unquestioningly (Larmour 1999, 85). Helicon's outburst of anger after losing the contest is wildly inappropriate in this context, it recalls the outrageous tantrums of athletes like Theagenes of Thasos or Cleomedes of Astypalaea: when the Hellanodikai refused to award Cleomedes the crown, after he had killed his boxing opponent with a foul blow, he went mad and caused the roof of a school building to collapse. Having lost sixty of their children, the irate Astypalaeans stoned Cleomedes, who had to take refuge in the temple of Athena. Such tales about the excesses of athletes became commonplace (Kurke 1991, 149–52; Larmour 1999, 59–60).

The shattering of Helicon's boulder into a thousand pieces could be a parody of the ritual of the *phyllobolia*, in which victorious athletes were showered with flowers or leaves.[64] Cithaeron's victory is marked by stones—strangely appropriate on one level for a contest between two mountains—but the stones are launched in anger, not celebration. The presence of Hermes might suggest some trickery in the process of adjudication, which would further distance the contest from the Pindaric ideal of an *agon*. We may compare Pindar's pointed comments on the votes that cheated Ajax in *Nemean* 8.24–28: ἤ τιν' ἄγλωσσον μέν, ἦτορ δ' ἄλκιμον, λάθα κατέχει / ἐν λυγρῷ νείκει· μέγιστον δ'αἰόλῳ ψεύδει γέρας ἀντέταται. / κρυφίαισι γὰρ ἐν ψάφοις Ὀδυσσῆ Δαναοὶ θεράπευσαν·/ χρυσέων δ' Αἴας στερηθεὶς ὅπλων φόνῳ πάλαισεν (a steadfast heart, if without a ready tongue, lies hidden and forgotten in mischievous strife: the greatest prize is given to the wily liar. For in their secret votes, the Danaans paid court to Odysseus and Ajax, robbed of the golden armor, wrestled with death). Segal (1975, 6) argues that Corinna's words φερέμεν ψᾶφον ἔταττον/ κρουφίαν κάλπιδαςἐν χρου-/ σοφαῖς in 20–22 are in fact a deliberate reworking of Pindar's κρυφίαισι γὰρ ἐν ψάφοις in Nemean 8, line 26. Segal notes that the situations are similar—"a contest of sorts and bitter resentment following"—and contrasts Corinna's mood of "light burlesque" with Pindar's one of "bitter tragedy." Perhaps Corinna's poem was indeed intended to recall Pindar's: it is worth noting that at the center of the ode, just before the account of the awarding of Achilles' arms to Odysseus, Pindar pauses to comment (20–22) on the dangers of trying out new things in poetry because "words are nourishment to the envious," and then the remaining lines are all about envy, injustice, and deception. Corinna speaks of a "secret vote," but Pindar's phrase means a voting process kept secret from Ajax, and it is this hidden act of *phthonos* that causes Pindar's outburst. Trickery and unjust decisions go against the epinikian code, and the elaborate precautions taken against cheating at the *agones* suggest that it was, in fact, a major problem.[65]

If Helicon represents Pindar and his poetry, and Cithaeron stands for Corinna and hers, then the way Helicon reacts turns the epinikian code against Pindar himself, for a violent outburst against the judges' decision is highly inappropriate. Helicon becomes an embodiment of hubris and lack of *sophrosyne*, opposed to the proper

Olympian *dike* symbolized by the orderly voting in the urns. The Ajax/Odysseus rivalry is the archetype on which the Cithaeron/Helicon contest depends, but Corinna makes Helicon grotesque rather than majestic in his anger. Perhaps Pindar's reaction to criticism was grotesquely extreme: the forceful comments in *Nemean* 8 could certainly be read as indicative of such sensitivity, even anxiety (cf. N.7.20–30, I.4.36–40).[66] The contest presents the Muses' rebellion or revenge against Helicon and thereby Corinna's against Pindar. The outcome of the contest is that Helicon is without the charms of the Muses, that is, *a-mouson*, the worst possible insult and a striking notion, since Helicon is normally the Muses' home.

According to Plutarch, this was the term that Corinna used to describe Pindar's early poetry: "when Pindar was still young and prided himself on his use of words, she warned him that his writing was lacking refinement (ἄμουσον)."[67] If the song-contest poem does indeed contain information about Corinna's technique, we may interpret Helicon's shattered boulder in connection with her criticism of Pindar's use of myth: sowing with the whole sack is analogous to taking a boulder, a unified mythical narrative, and shattering it into a thousand disjointed pieces. Corinna's method is more like Rhea's with her stone: she uncovers it at the right time in the right circumstances, to reveal its immense significance. She does so, moreover, in few words. It is worth noting that the passage in Plutarch whence the quotation about the sowing in sack-fulls comes is preceded directly by the argument that "poets consider the subject matter more necessary and vital than the words" (*De Glor. Ath.*, 347F–48A).[68] The information recorded in Plutarch points to a basic distinction between Pindar and Corinna: she warned him that he was ἄμουσον ὄντα καὶ μὴ ποιοῦντα μύθους (unrefined and not making myths), which is what poetry should be about, deploying instead as ἡδύσματα τοῖς πράγμασιν (embellishments of the subject matter), unusual words, catachreseis, paraphrases, lyrics, and rhythms. When he responded with four lines filled with half a dozen mythical references, she laughed, telling him to sow with the hand and not the sack. For, Plutarch says, he had "mixed and jumbled together a seed-mixture of myths" (συγκεράσας καὶ συμφορήσας πανσπερμίαν τινὰ μύθων) and had "poured them out" (ἐξέχεεν) into his poem.

The way Corinna is portrayed in this anecdote—warning, laughing, speaking with authority on what constitutes proper poetry and refinement—indicates either that she had a forceful personality and expressed definite ideas about poetry that were very different from Pindar's, or that ancient writers like Plutarch found such stories credible on the basis of what they knew about Pindar's and Corinna's poetic compositions. It is perhaps in this context that we should read her own praise of her voice as "clear-sounding" or "clear-teasing" (λιγουροκωτίλυς ἐνοπῆς).[69] In contrast to Pindar's complicated and allusive epinikian mode, her poems were straight-forward narratives, her expression spare but effective, and her tone teasingly ironic or subtly humorous, all at the expense of Pindaric complexity, density, and seriousness. Rhea's boulder, in other words, is far more effective than Helicon's thousand pebbles. We may recall that *PMG* 695A, from a late *Life of Pindar*, records that he was "the son, according to Corinna and most poetesses, of Scopelinus, but according to most poets, the son of Daifantos" and that Scopelinus means "man from the mountaintop" and was almost certainly a mocking soubriquet.[70]

In connection with irony and humor, critics have noted Corinna's penchant for the incongruous, and here again we may detect a divergence from the ordered universe of the epinikian mode. The ambiguous nature of the two mountains in the song-contest fragment is potentially an example: they are mountains physically but they behave in very human ways. Corinna may have invented the notion of a singing contest between mountains from the traditional account of the rivalry between the brothers Cithaeron and Helicon in human form: they were rival kings, who fought and killed each other.[71] Segal (1975) regards this as "grotesque anthropomorphiza-tion," but what is grotesque from the modern point of view (and that of just one critical approach) is not necessarily so in the ancient Greek context. Perhaps this sort of thing is more expected in a poet like Ovid, who wittily makes the mountain Tmolus a judge in his *Metamorphoses* 11 (Kirkwood 1974, 189), but it is intrinsically no more grotesque than anthropomorphized rivers, cities, or islands, and we find plenty of those in Pindar. Corinna's use of incongruity lies more in the realm of tampering with tradition and playing with expectation, which is of a different order from Pindar's innovations or deviations in this area. Helicon's outburst is a better example; perhaps the pomposity of Acraephen if we go along with Rayor's reading. The voting system is also a good instance: Segal (1975, 2, 5) is on more secure ground when he suggests that there is humour in "this precise dicaeastic particularity" and that the golden urns "epitomize the incongruity, for on the one hand they are part of the technical apparatus of the law-court, but on the other hand they are 'brilliant with gold' . . . the magical gold which characterizes the gods and their beautiful, timeless, radiant world."[72] And, as we saw above, Corinna may have played with Pindar's phraseology here to create her own ironic twist on her rival's words.

CORINNA AND PINDAR'S *PYTHIAN* NINE

There is another of Pindar's epinikians that has particularly intriguing resonances with Corinna's fragments, namely *Pythian* 9, in honor of Telesicrates of Cyrene.[73] Again we cannot be sure that Corinna had it in mind when she composed her poems, but it is certainly useful as one more demonstration of their differences in approach. This ode treats the legend of Cyrene, a woman noted for the "masculine" features ascribed to her in myth, such as athleticism, who was carried off by a love-struck Apollo. The scholiast (P.9.6a) tells us that Pindar took the story of Cyrene from the Hesiodic *Catalogue of Women*, a source on which Corinna probably also drew. The first part of the poem (5–9) summarizes how Apollo carried off Cyrene: τὰν ὁ . . . Λατοίδας / ἅρπασ', ἔνεικέ τε . . . παρθένον . . . / . . . καὶ πολυκαρποτάτας /. . . οἰκεῖν (Her, the son of Leto carried off, and he took . . . the maiden . . . and placed her to live as mistress of a most fruitful land). Then Pindar recounts in more detail how Apollo falls in love with Cyrene upon his first look at her and goes disingenuously to consult Chiron about her identity. The centaur prophesies that Apollo will take her to Libya and make her ruler of a city, where she will give birth to a son. There are some notable verbal echoes with Corinna's song-contest poem: the adjective ἐρατός appears in P.9.12, of the "modesty" Aphrodite sheds on the union of Apollo and Cyrene, and in P.9.73, Pindar informs us that Telesicrates "shone a light on" or "revealed" the city of Cyrene (i.e., made it conspicuous at Delphi), using the verb ἀναφαίνω.[74] This is a verb Pindar uses only rarely elsewhere, again in connection with Cyrene as a city in P.4.62 (how the Pythia βαιλέ' ἄμφανεν Κυράνᾳ, declared Battus king of Cyrene).[75] Gerber, writing on Corinna's song-contest poem, notes that "the conception of places as mythical personages, of legend as embedded deeply in one specific place, is a feature of Pindar's poetry (one thinks of Cyrene in the Ninth *Pythian*)."[76] Cyrene, like Rhea, is a descendant of Gaea and, as one commentator (Carey 1981, 70) puts it, "was no ordinary woman, but one reared by a

man to masculine arts," evincing "the attitude of the Homeric hero
. . . and of the Pindaric athlete." Possibly, Corinna's collocation of
the capable and resourceful goddess Rhea and the mountain
Cithaeron as the embodiment of her own style of poetry was in
some way connected with Pindar's narrative of Cyrene in *Pythian* 9.
Also, the *phyllobolia*, which was mentioned above as a possible athletic allusion in the image of Helicon throwing down the boulder
that splits into a shower of pebbles, is mentioned by Pindar at the
end of this poem in line 125. This is, significantly, the only place
where Pindar refers to this practice.

The strongest thematic connections, however, are with the
Asopus poem: the seizure of Cyrene (ἅρπασ' P.9.6; cf. Corinna's
ἐλέσθη, 21); the suddenness of Apollo's love and of action generally (αὐτίκα, P.9.29, 57, 114); the fact that Cyrene is the daughter
of Hypseus, son of Peneius, the main river of Thessaly (P.9.13–16);
and the depiction of Libya and Cyrene as both individuals and
places simultaneously.[74] Apollo, love-struck and anxious, gets an
oracular answer from Chiron as to how he will get Cyrene and take
her to Libya, his father's place, for a sexual union; Asopus, the grieving
and confused father, gets an oracle from Apollo via Acraephen about
his daughters' whereabouts and their unions with various gods. In
each case, the response emphasizes the future offspring: Asopus'
daughters in Corinna's poem will give birth to "a race of heroes half-
divine" and they will be "fruitful and ageless" (22–25); Cyrene will
produce Aristaeus, who will be immortal (P.9.63). Zeus, Hermes,
and Aphrodite figure in both poems; in Corinna's version Aphrodite
and Eros brought the gods to Asopus' house (18–19); in *Pythian* 9,
Aphrodite welcomes Apollo and his new bride in Libya (9–12).

We can see areas where Corinna and Pindar strike different
notes. The secrecy and deception to which Asopus falls victim is
paralleled by Chiron's remark in P.9.43, to the effect that Apollo is
being deceitful (παρφάμεν τοῦ-/τον λόγον). In Pindar, this is contrasted, not without a smidgeon of irony, with Apollo's role as god
of prophecy ("who must not by law touch a lie," P.9.42) and Chiron's
point is apparently that Apollo has come as close to lying as he can,
but only under the influence of *eros*.[78] In Corinna, there is a similar
contrast of divine deception with the truthful prophecy (43) given
by Acraephen who tells no lies (31), but the depiction of the distress
of Asopus casts it in a very different light. Pindar (P.9.51–58)
describes Apollo's compensation to Cyrene (she will become "the
leader of cities" and will receive a share of the land to be counted as

her lawful lot) (Kurke 1991, 130). Corinna has the compensation revealed to Asopus, still grieving over his loss. The story of Cyrene is located in an agonistic context: as Carson (1982, 121) puts it, Pindar "proceeds by setting up an analogy between the *telos* of marriage in a female life and the *telos* of athletic victory in a man's life," and here Pindar refers to the race for the forty-eight daughters of Danaus (P.9.112–16), in the context of Antaeus' contest for the suitors of his daughter's hand, which was won by Alexidamus (P.9.105–25). We have already noted the ambiguous aspects of these bridal races. Is Cyrene an unwilling bride? There are only hints of this aspect of the tale, which Pindar buries or conceals under the weight of his own agenda: as Carson (1982, 128) puts it "If the victor's personal value is not mingled with that of his community, it has no life. Correspondingly, however brave and beautiful Kyrene is in lonely contests with lions, nothing can come of this ἀλκά until it is planted and housed in the city of her own name. . . . The moment when a bride is plucked in marriage is a *kairos* analogous to that moment when victory flowers around an athlete." Carson also shows how the three stages of the Greek wedding ritual are followed in this epinikian: betrothal (ἐγγύη), bridal procession (ἀγωγή), and incorporation into the new household (καταχύσματα).

In Corinna's fragment, these three stages are missing or not depicted: there was no betrothal (Asopus did not even know his daughters had gone) or procession, and we are told nothing of the καταχύσματα. If the Asopus poem was indeed presented at a ceremony in connection with Hera or marriage rites, this silence tends to suggest a distinctive, "woman-oriented" type of poetry, which would distinguish Corinna's songs quite dramatically from Pindar's. Clearly, the vantage point from which one reads, or hears, matters a great deal. Some comments by male critics on *Pythian* 9 are instructive in this regard: Kirkwood (1982, 223) notes on line 12 that "the union was no violent or casual divine rape, but a chaste, marital love"; Segal (1986, 170–71) finds that Chiron's bestowal of *metis* on Apollo "inhibits violence against a potential female victim" and that the ode deliberately replaces "the mythical pattern of male violence to ancient female deities . . . with a pattern of persuasive cooperation." If Pindar strives to smooth over the violence of Cyrene's seizure and her enforced removal from a life she enjoys, Corinna prefers to be explicit about the rape of Asopus' nine daughters. The Asopus fragment seems to suggest that in her poems, composed perhaps primarily but not exclusively for female audiences, Corinna sought to disguise neither the necessity of marriage nor its harsh realities for women in a patriarchal culture.[79]

CORINNA AND THE EPINIKIAN TRADITION

What then can we conclude about Corinna's position vis-à-vis Pindar and the epinikian tradition? It is possible that the contest of Cithaeron and Helicon was in some way a comment on the personal rivalry between Corinna and Pindar, or at least on the different kinds of poetry they symbolize. It appears that Corinna echoes some of Pindar's phraseology in *Nemean* 8 and, further, that *Pythian* 9 could have been a source of inspiration for one or even both of the pieces from which we have fragments. In the areas of language and the deployment of myth, Corinna seems to be aiming for something quite different from Pindar, and ancient critics clearly picked up on this. More generally, the occasion and circumstances of performance of Corinna's poems—in all likelihood including the Daedala festival of Hera in Plataea—inevitably distance her from the epinikian tradition, since we are talking about *partheneia* or compositions sung by, or in the presence of, young women, probably in some premarriage ritual. This is reflected in the choice of themes and the perspective from which myths are narrated: to this extent it is legitimate to speak of a "woman-oriented" or "woman-identified" poetic voice. Walker (2000, 158) makes the point that even if lyric poets speak in conventionalized roles as public voices of traditional thought, this does not mean they cannot voice novel or counter-hegemonic views—in fact, given the agonistic character of the culture in general, and the aura of competition that surrounded poetic performance in particular, it seems likely that they often did.

We should then judge Corinna in this light. It is clear that Corinna's output was not simply "women's poetry," for in some significant ways she competes with Pindar on his own ground and resists subordination to him. Corinna daringly appropriates his role at the intersection of agon and poetry and thereby stakes her claim to a piece of what might be considered male territory. She does not reject the Panhellenic in favor of the local, or privilege female experience over male, or seek to produce an "anti-epinikian." Nonetheless, there is a deliberate and systematic blurring of epinikian's clear boundaries, an undermining of its absolutist perspective of *aletheia* (Nagy 1990, 61), a subversion of its conventions and of the agonistic ideology it promulgates. Epinikian was clearly a problematic form, even in Pindar's day, as Burnett observes: "By the time that Pindar and Bacchylides began to compose for choral performances the victory hymn had thus become a highly retrograde and difficult form of song. Its mere multiple performance made it suspect in the eyes both of heaven and earth, and meanwhile its overweening ancient pretensions to truth served to emphasize the present possibility of sordid corruption. Its patrons were at best anachronistic, at worst rich ruffians or overbearing tyrants who were not themselves even victors but only patrons who had paid the cost of a contestant."[80]

Much of Corinna's subversion is achieved through effective use of juxtaposition, which leads to the apprehension by the hearer of incongruity and even irony, aided by a clarity of expression that harks back to Alcman and Sappho rather than Pindar. She carries on a different kind of *eris* with Pindar from the variety for which she criticizes Myrtis. Corinna, who speaks of her own "clear-teasing" voice (λιγουροκωτίλυς ἐνοπῆς) also calls Myrtis "clear-sounding" (λιγουρά): but she tried to imitate him, when the subject matter and style were not suitable for her. Rather than competing directly, Corinna, like Rhea in her poem, deploys her own devices, her poetic *metis*, in order to achieve her poetic telos. The images that recur most noticeably in her poems—as far as we can tell from the fragments—are of sudden violence and rape, of deception and uncovering. She emphasizes the agony of loss from the position of the victim, the ambiguous experience of revelation, and the joy of victory from the point of view of both victor and loser. Helicon's display gives voice to the agony of the defeated, a voice that is all but silenced in Pindar. This may be connected with Corinna's presentation of mythical narratives from the female perspective—being on the receiving end, so to speak, of ideology and its real-life consequences (violence against women, male dominance, desire and rape, victory for the man accompanied by suffering for the woman, the inevitability of marriage and of producing offspring). In a sense, the portrayal of Asopus' grief at the loss of his daughters partakes of this same "receiving end" perspective, even if only momentarily. These are expressions not only of women's lived experience but also of Corinna's poetic stance. In particular, her poetic technique is structured on the oscillation between deception or obscurity and uncovering or revelation. Her language is deceptively simple, yet it is also obscure by virtue of its local dialect, and through it are revealed new perspectives on traditional mythical material and, ultimately, on the institutions of patriarchy by which the lives of Corinna and all her listeners were governed.

NOTES

George Huxley introduced me to the intricacies of Corinna one Saturday morning in Belfast in 1982; it is with fond memories of many such days in what was then the Queen's University Department of Greek—before the arrival of the marketing managers of a barbarous and shameless government—that I dedicate this article to him.

1. For my classical references, I follow the standard abbreviations from the *Oxford Classical Dictionary*. All references to *PMG* are to *Poetae melici graeci* (Page 1962).

2. This is bound up with the question of Corinna's date, on which see Page 1953, 65–84; Allen and Frel 1972; Segal 1975; Snyder 1989, 42–44; Burzacchini 1992; West 1970b and 1990.

3. See especially West 1970b, 280; Skinner 1983, 16–17; Snyder 1984, 132, and 1989, 45, 50–51; Clayman 1993, 639; Rayor 1993, 224; Henderson 1995, 30–31, 35; Stehle 1997, 100–104; Gerber 1997, 216–17.

4. See Burzacchini 1990, 34–35.

5. Rayor 1993; for a contrary view, see Skinner 1983.

6. See especially Clayman 1993; also Snyder 1989, 42–45, 52; Rayor 1993, 228–29; Henderson 1995, 32.

7. Snyder 1989, 44: "what we know of each poet's works indicates a widely discrepant practice in themes and treatment."

8. I am using the term "epinikian" to refer to Pindar's entire oeuvre, not just the victory poems written for winners in events at the four Panhellenic festivals, for many of the features that characterize these pieces are also found in the fragments of his other works. We are dealing with the same "voice" in terms of language and style, the use of myth, and the moral and religious content. On the epinikian in general, see Burnett 1985, 38–47; Hubbard 1988; Nisetich 1989, 27–49; Nagy 1990; Heath and Lefkowitz 1991.

9. If, as is likely, she is the subject of the verb ἕλε; most commentators read it this way, including Campbell 1967, 411, who says Rhea is "more probably" the subject. This fragment comes near the end of a poem that tells the story of a contest between two Boeotian mountains.

10. Rayor 1993, 226–28; Page (1953, 20 n. 5) comments that "Corinna remembers, though she goes beyond, the narrative in the *Theogony*; its influence is clearly visible in her words."

11. See, for instance, Kirkwood 1974, 189: "the style is plain, with just a few rather tame epithets (crooked-counselling Cronus, blessed Rhea) and one fairly rare color word, *chrousophaes* 'gold-shining'"; on 191, he makes similar observations on the Asopus poem. Cf. Page 1953, 75–76: "simile and anything worthy of the name of metaphor are wholly absent."

12. Elsewhere, Corinna describes her own voice as λιγουροκωτίλυς, "clear-sounding" or "clear-teasing" (*PMG* 655.5), and there is a story in Plutarch that she criticized Pindar for "sowing with the whole sack" when it came to myths in his poems (*Mor*alia [*De Gloria Athen*iensium] 347F–48A).

13. Harvey 1957, 222–23; he cites ἀγκυλομείταο Κρόνῳ and μάκηρα Ῥεά as examples in this poem and says that νίκαν ἐρατάν is a favorite *Lieblingswort* of archaic lyric.

14. This is although Athenaeus himself goes on to cite Telestes against the story of Athena's disgust, which he says he found in Melanippides' *Marsyas* (616F–17A).

15. Except by Hesiod, who places it on Mt. Aigaion (*Theog.* 484).

16. Snyder 1984, 128; Page 1953, 20 n. 3.

17. Cf. Skinner 1983, 14; Burzacchini 1990, 32; Henderson 1995, 29–30; Gerber 1997, 218. West (1966b, 174–75, on *Theog.* 54) comments that Hesiod's words mean that Mnemosyne had a cult on Cithaeron and "as she was primarily a goddess of singers, it is not unlikely that a 'school' of poets existed there in Hesiod's time. It is possible that the existence of rival Muse-cults on Helicon and Cithaeron may have some connexion with the legend of the singing contest between the two mountains described by Corinna." Frr. 674 and 676A of Corinna also mention the Muses.

18. Thus Bolling 1956, 283, and Weiler 1974, 82 n. 189; Wilamowitz chose Cithaeron, (Page 1953, 3 n. 3, does not "know why"); Henderson 1995 says "usually presumed to be Cithaeron" (33 and n. 32); Snyder (1989, 46) says "perhaps", (cf. 1984, 128); Gerber (1997, 218) says "probably."

19. Page (1953, 21) notes that the "president Muses might have been expected to favour their familiar Helicon; but in fact it is Cithaeron who has the judges' voice." Henderson (1995, 35) concludes: "Certainly the result is surprising; Corinna seems to be going against traditional attitudes which favoured Helicon."

20. See Snyder 1989, 47; she also notes (1984, 128) that the verbal repetition "may suggest that Hermes is deliberately echoing the language used by the victorious contestant; thus it would seem that the opening lines of the fragment should be assigned to Kithairon."

21. *PMG* reading, followed by Campbell 1967 and most others; Page 1953 reads ἔθρε]ψαν.

22. Snyder 1984, 128; Corinna's word λαθράδαν occurs only here and may indicate some linguistic ingenuity with vocabulary of this type; West (1970b, 284) compares κρουφάδαν in the Asopus poem, line 20; see also Campbell 1967, 411.

23. Hesiod, *Theog.*, 51–60, line 135; Pindar, O.10.96

24. Hesiod, *Theog.*, 26–28; Pratt 1993, 106–113, especially 112: "As the audience to the Muses, we can never be certain when we have been granted insight and when we have been duped. The Muses are consequently dangerous customers, tricksters themselves, and, like Odysseus and Hermes, capable of both harm and good."

25. See Segal 1975, 2: he argues that Corinna adapts Pindar's κρυφίαισι γὰρ ἐν ψάφοις (in their secret votes, N.8.26) into ψᾶφον . . . κρουφίαν. Page (1953, 76) terms the scene Corinna's "one flight of fancy."

26. It has been suggested by Bowra 1953a, 57, that Tanagra was assigned to Hermes in Corinna's poem about the daughters of Asopus (but see Page 1953, 27 n. 1).

27. As it is at Pindar, P.4.62, where the oracle reveals that Battus is the destined king of Cyrene, or N.9.12, where Adrastus is said to have "shed luster"

on Sicyon. See also Sophocles, fr. 432 (from the *Nauplius*), line 7: ἔδειξε κἀνέφηνεν οὐ δεδειγμένα.

28. Hesiod, *Theog.* 468–500; cf. Nagy 1990, 203, on the association of time and poetry: "just as the poet . . . 'wins as prize' [= verb *phero*] for his subject the honor [*time*] as conferred by the words of poetry, thereby 'making great' [= verb *auxo*] both the subject of the poetry and the poetry itself, so also the person who happens to be the subject of the poetry, as a man of the present who has performed a glorious deed, can 'win' the honor conferred by the words of poetry in an unbroken continuum extending from the world of heroes to the world of the here and now."

29. Cf. Hesiod, *Theog.* 485–96; Metis does not appear in his account, Cronus was "beguiled by Gaea."

30. See Snyder 1984, 128: "the recurrence of an adverb of speed (αὐτίκα, line 9, followed by τάχα, line 24), emphasizing the swiftness of the Muses' administering of the voting process and of Hermes' announcement of the result, creates a sense of swift-paced, decisive action that is echoed in the sudden, violent reaction of Helicon upon learning that he has lost the contest."

31. Only the middle part of this fragment survives from a long narrative poem found on the same papyrus as the fragment previously discussed. Line references will be given parenthetically in the text.

32. Fr. 690 *PMG* (cf. Page 1953, 28, fr. 2A) may have dealt with the Trojan Horse: there may be a reference to hiding in line 4 (κρούψε).

33. Guillon (1958, 54–60) connects Corinna and the oracle story with the reorganization of oracles by the Boeotian Confederacy in the latter half of the 3rd century; cf. West 1970b, 286, who argues that Asopus consults not the oracle of Apollo Ptoios but a local oracle in Tanagra. On the cult of Apollo Ptoios, see Schachter 1981–1994, 1:61–64; on Corinna, he comments that "the fact that she went into such detail over the antecedents of her prophet may indicate that she was inventing a new genealogy" (1:62).

34. Page 1953, 26 and n. 6; Paus. 9.20.2.

35. For details and identification of the daughters, see Bowra 1953a; Page 1953, 25–27; Gantz 1993, 219–32; West 1985, 100–104, 162–64. The figure of Asopus represents not only the river in Boeotia but also the Phliasian Asopus in Sicyonia, and there was also, it seems, a smaller river on Aegina that was named or associated with Asopus. Apollodorus makes Asopus the son of Oceanus and Tethys but records other lines of descent, from Poseidon and Pero or Zeus and Eurynome: see Gantz 1993, 219–20.

36. Schachter 1981–1994, 2:147–79, esp. 163–79; *IG* 7.1785, 4240b–c; Paus. 9.27.5. See also Henderson 1995, 29–31, who comments on the song-contest fragment (30) "we are surely justified in linking the text of the poem with the reality of the cult ceremonies in honour of the Muses."

37. Or, in one source, Apollo: Tzetzes, *in Lycophr.* 328. For more details, see Frazer 1973, 58, who notes that although Ovid does not say where this takes place, Strabo (9.2.12, p. 404) locates the story in Tanagra; Pindar puts it in Hyria, a town that belonged to Thebes; Hyginus has Thebes in *Astr.* 2.34, but Thrace in *Fab.* 195. Perhaps we can see traces here of another area of rivalry between Corinna and Pindar or another instance of her local focus: Hyrieus makes a fleeting appearance in *PMG* 655.4, lines 4–6, βάρβαρον κ[. . . βὰς δὲ Οὐριε[ύς . . . ἐσσείλκουσε, see Campbell 1992, 38–39; Hyria is mentioned in *PMG* 669, καλλιχόρω χθονὸς Οὐρίας θουγάτειρ.

38. Gantz 1993, 273; see also Schol. A *Iliad* 18.486; Hyg. *Fab.* 195; *Astr.* 2.34.1

39. See Snyder 1984, 132; Gerber 1997, 217–18; also Stehle 1997, 100–104, who takes the view that Corinna characterizes songs for *parthenoi* as stories from our fathers' time (103).

40. See Snyder 1984, 132; Stehle 1997, 101–104; *PMG* 692 fr. 2a refers to "virgin daughters" and "well-wooded Cephisus": on the matter of authorship, see West 1970b, who argues convincingly for Corinna.

41. Cf. Stehle 1997, 104: "Korinna's may be another, more traditional, way of inhibiting a sense of authority in parthenoi: the young women celebrate patriarchy and male power, specifically sexual power, over women. . . . If she was composing for communal choral performance, she must have had to meet public expectations, both in matters of gender and local focus. One can, indeed, note shifts and exaggerations in her versions of myths that intimate the possibility of another perspective; perhaps her two audiences, Tanagran men and Tanagran women, were meant to hear slightly different messages."

42. See Page 1953, 35, fr. 15; Schol. Nic. *Ther.* 15; Paus. 9.20.3.

43. *PMG* 672 (Page fr. 22) brings Oedipus (uniquely) into connection with the Teumessian fox, which he killed; usually it is Cephalus who performs the deed for Amphitryon, see Page 1953, 38–39.

44. The pattern is an old one, clearly visible in Hesiod: Arthur 1982 (esp. 65, 71–72) discusses violence and concealment in the *Theogony*, Rhea's stone, and the combination of ideas of "hiding, concealing, binding and trickery, and of display, giving, releasing and prophecy" (72).

45. *tu pandere doctus/ carmina Batiadae latebrasque Lycophronis arti/ Sophrona implicitum tenuis arcana Corinnae* (you were skilled at opening up the songs of Battus' son, and the hidden places of straitened Lycophron, tangled Sophron, and the secrets of subtle Corinna). On the interpretation of these lines, see Snyder 1984, 133–34.

46. On this, see Schachter 1981–1994, 1:242–50; Furley 1981, 201–210; Avagianou 1991, 59–68; Burzacchini 1990; Clark 1998, esp. 22–26.

47. See Avagianou 1991, 61–63, 67.

48. See ibid., 66–67.

49. See Henderson 1989, esp. 32–33; Clayman 1993.

50. Allen (Allen and Frel 1972, 28) makes some good points in connection with Paus. 9.22.3, on the painting in the gymnasium at Tanagra, and Plut. *De Glor. Ath.* 4.347, on Corinna's advice to Pindar about using myths: "it is hard to imagine that a curious visitor to the gymnasium came away misinformed on its notable painting. Pausanias' account will reflect current belief at Tanagra. So too will Plutarch's report. He was a native of Boeotia and well acquainted with things Boeotian . . . if the Boeotians erred on Corinna's date, if she really lived only two centuries before Propertius, they did so uncomfortably soon after her death. It is not an easy error to believe in. That it was accepted in Corinna's own Tanagra, that Pindar's Thebes permitted it would be astonishing. The alternative is that there was no error, that Corinna and Pindar were contemporaries." Cf. Burzacchini 1992, who also argues for an early date for Corinna on the basis of Propertius' (2.3.21) and Statius' (*Silv.* 5.3.158) references.

51. Clayman 1993, 636; he adds (638): "it is not inconceivable that Cithaeron's 'Zeus hymn' provided scope for allusion to Pindar's. Alternatively,

the reference to Pindar might have been in a previous 'hymn' sung by Helicon and intended to contrast with Cithaeron's, which reveals its Hesiodic/Callimachean stylistic legacy by giving prominence to the Curetes."

52. See I.2.34; 8.59; *Paean* 7b.16. Other lore about the mountains could of course have featured in such an allegory: Hesiod was initiated on Helicon, which Pausanias describes as "most fertile" (9.28.1–4), but Pausanias also says that the Muses on Cithaeron gave out prophecies (9.3.9).

53. Cf. her remarks on Rayor 1993, 226: "readers who ignore gender codes, such as the context of a female poet repossessing myth for a female audience, miss important feminine discourse. Once the reader knows the gender of the poet, certain expectations arise which can obscure the text itself."

54. See Sansone 1988, 80–82; Nagy 1990, 142–43; Larmour 1999, 44–50, 63–64.

55. On the exclusion of women, see Scanlon 2002, 38–39; he has a bibliography on women and athletics on 377–78.

56. See Kurke 1991, 112–34. Scanlon 2002 discusses races at the Heraea (cf. Paus. 5.16.2–8), held in celebration of Hippodameia's marriage (98–120), the Dionysiades at Sparta (121–38; cf. Paus. 3.13.7), and the chase at the Arkteia (139–74). These races run by girls may have their origins in myths of races held for suitors seeking to win a bride, such as those of Pelops and Hippodameia or Atalanta and Hippomenes: see further Scanlon 2002, 32, 135–36, 175–98, 222–24.

57. As he does in another Aeginetan ode, N.8.6–10.

58. For text and commentary see Rutherford 2001, 301, 306, 324, who sees in the "golden tresses of covering Aegina" (325) a reminiscence of the golden cloud in the "*Dios Apate*" episode of *Iliad* 14.341–60.

59. Cf. the Greek historian Pherecydes 3 fr. 119; Callimachus, *Hec.* 4.77–78; Nonnus, *Dion.* 7.180–83.

60. As he does elsewhere, with Pelops, for example; see Howie 1983.

61. Pindar uses the adjective in only two other places: in P.1.12 of the Muses, and in P.9.101 of the earth. The word means "with deep folds" of clothing, appropriate to the chaste Muses concealing their body, or "with deep, full breasts" suggesting the fertility of the earth.

62. See Walker 2000, 158; cf. Nagy 1990, 60–67, 82–83.

63. See Scanlon 2002, 190–97, 211–19.

64. Larmour 1999, 97–98; Euripides, *Tro.* 573–774 and scholiast.

65. On cheating at the games, see Paus. 5.21.2–4, 24.9–10, 6.3.7; Forbes 1952; Larmour 1999, 85, 143–44.

66. Demand 1982, 105: "Could we perhaps infer that some of the human losers behaved with a similar lack of restraint? It would be interesting to know if a Theban audience heard this and went away chuckling over what was to them a transparent reference to a Great Poet—perhaps even to Pindar himself."

67. The term was bandied about in their "quarrel": Aelian (*Varia Historia* 13.25) reports that Pindar was defeated five times in contests at Thebes, where the audiences were ignorant, so he called Corinna a "sow" as a means of criticizing their ἀμουσία.

68. Henderson 1989, 32: "The criticism is clearly levelled at the young poet's conscious exploitation of *language* at the expense of *content*. . . . It is significant that in the first comment Pindar's phraseology and in the second his

use of myth is under scrutiny: the focus is both on *style and content of the text.* This is good critical reporting on Plutarch's part (whether it really involved Corinna or not)."

69. Segal (1975, 5) translates "clear-coaxing" and says "the verb clearly implies a quality of teasing, intelligence, trickery"; Skinner (1983, 19 n. 11) notes that the verb κωτίλλειν (wheedle, tease) is "definitely associated with feminine guile" (cf. Hesiod, *Works and Days*, 374); West (1970b, 285) cites possible uses in a "complimentary sense."

70. Clayman 1993, 636: "Corinna's name . . . is certainly a humorous patronymic she invented for this context. Although Pindar's biographers failed to understand Corinna's point and soberly listed Scopelinus among Pindar's possible forebears, their certainty about the Pindar/Scopelinus connection indicates that Corinna's little joke was very explicit."

71. For attempts to fill out the characters of Cithaeron and Helicon, see Page 1953, 21–22; Snyder 1984, 127. Ebert 1978 reconstructs lines 31–34 differently and sees the poem as portraying Cithaeron and Helicon as humans before or at the moment of metamorphosis; Helicon hurls himself from the mountain that was then named after him.

72. Pindar describes the Muses as "golden" in I.8.5, "with golden snood" in P.3.90, I.2.2, and "golden-robed" in fr. 104d.21.

73. See commentaries by Carey 1981; Kirkwood 1982; Instone 1996; also Kohnken 1985; Carson 1982.

74. We may compare the use in line 41 of ἀμφανδόν from ἀναφαίνω: see Instone 1996, 128: "the word occurs nowhere else in Greek literature, and is a conjecture for the unmetrical (but common) ἀμφαδόν."

75. Cf. I.4.70–71, how Melissus of Thebes διπλόαν/ νίκαν ἀνέφατο (brought to light a double victory).

76. Gerber 1997, 291; Vivante 1979, 85, sees similarities in the treatment of the two legends.

77. *PMG* 655.1, line 17, contains Λιβούαν κ[αλάν].

78. See Carey 1981, 79: "some notion of falsehood must be present here, though the precise force of the word must be determined by the context. Apollo's sin is of omission, not commission . . . Chiron's point is that Apollo has come as near to lying as the oracular god may, under the influence of desire."

79. Cf. Rayor 1993, 222: "Her work is neither an imitation and blind acceptance of patriarchal tradition, nor a polemic against it. It is neither simple 'women's folk-poetry' nor the other extreme, a repetition of male misogyny. . . . In none of the fragments does she directly challenge patriarchal tradition. Even so, it would be wrong to read her work, as Skinner does, as being, therefore, blindly patriarchal."

80. Burnett 1985, 47, at the end of her third chapter, "The Epinician Burden" (38–47).

The Power of Memory in Erinna and Sappho

Diane J. Rayor

Erinna's poetry, written in the fourth century BCE, shows a keen awareness of her predecessors Homer (eighth century) and Sappho (seventh century). For example, Erinna's *Distaff*, her lament in epic hexameter over her dead friend Baukis, has a clear Homeric model in Briseis' lament for Patroclus in *Iliad* 19.287–300 (Skinner 1982, 265). In Erinna's poetry, the topic of the absent friend as well as some aeolic forms all reflect Sappho's lyric poetry as Erinna's direct literary influence.[1] In particular, readers (Bowra 1936, 342; Rauk 1989) have long noticed the similarities in Erinna's *Distaff* to Sappho's fragments 94 and 96.[2] These poems by Sappho and Erinna longingly recall absent companions. Both poets focus on women's lives and community, and experiences with beloved female friends. The relationship with the beloved is woman-centered and perhaps could be described as lesbian.[3] Their poetry, however, appears more similar than it actually is on account of untenable assumptions that 94 and 96 are mournful farewells to women who have left to get married. Rather than even mentioning why the women have left, these two poems focus on the continuing bond of the women. In contrast, Erinna's poems focus on Baukis' absence due to her death shortly after marriage.

The use of memory itself, moreover, functions differently in Sappho than in Erinna, primarily as a result of the different performance situations and genre expectations.[4] As did the other early lyric poets, Sappho performed her poetry live to the accompaniment of music for an audience of community members. Erinna, on the other hand, was at the forefront of Hellenistic literacy, at the crux of the transition from performance to readership; her poetry, both epigram and hexameter, was written to be read by whoever had a copy of the text. In the fourth century, as Peter Bing (1988, 17) says, "Poetry . . . became a private act of communication, no longer a public one." For Sappho, memory stimulates ongoing communication and community; for Erinna, memory produces a written record of the past, a memorial.

The contrast in functions of memory is sustained by archaic oral culture and Hellenistic literary culture. As Egbert Bakker (2002, 67) puts it, "'memory' is a function of a culture's dominant medium of communication." In archaic Greece, the performance of poetry makes present the tale sung, whether the story is from myth or current events. Sappho's use of memory aligns with that of Homeric bards, for whom "remembering the song is to enact it, to ensure the presence of its heroic or divine protagonists" (2002, 71). In the literate culture of the fourth century, however, memory functions in a modern way as a retrieval system of stored information (2002, 69). For Erinna and us, remembering is a method of preserving the past.

In Sappho and Erinna, the absent beloved becomes the poet's muse, catalyzing the creation of poetry. In fragment 16 (3–4), Sappho's statement on desire that "whatever one loves" is best (κάλλιστον, ἔγω δὲ κῆν' ὅτ/τω τις ἔραται) derives from the memory of the absent Anaktoria. In explicating this statement, Sappho uses the story of Helen abandoning traditional values (family and husband) for love, followed by her own example of love: "reminding me now of Anaktoria being gone" (]με νῦν 'Ανακτορί[ας ὀ]νέμναισ' οὐ] παρεοίσας, 16.15–16). Fragments 94 and 96 also recall the absent beloveds as their primary subjects. So, too, for Erinna the absence of Baukis, her companion from childhood, provides the impetus for at least three of the six surviving poems and fragments.[5] As told in the hexameter fragment *Distaff* and epigrams 1 and 2, Baukis died soon after getting married.[6] In *Distaff*, Erinna recalls their childhood together, Baukis' marriage and death, and her own grief over the loss of her friend.

While we can recognize the common event in the poems that recall absent female companions, a striking difference appears as well. Sappho's poems mention various women "being gone," although the extant fragments never state the reason for their absence. In contrast, Erinna recalls her sole companion, whose marriage led to her death. Sappho's missing women live elsewhere, continue to remember Sappho, and could perhaps return; Erinna's Baukis is dead.

The critical difference could be lessened if one assumes, with John Rauk and others, that Sappho was an older woman whose circle consisted of young women (*parthenoi*) who departed upon marriage. In this case, marriage could be said to have caused the separations for both Sappho and Erinna. However, as Eva Stehle (1997, 269) notes, "Women who have departed are referred to several times in Sappho's poetry, e.g., 16, 94, 96 V. They may have left because they were getting married (which would mean that they were *parthenoi* while with Sappho), but nothing in the poems indicates as much." I agree with Stehle 1997 (265) and Holt Parker 1996, among others, who find it more plausible that Sappho's circle consisted of other adult female friends (*hetairai*), rather than *parthenoi* ripe for marriage. Women left Mytilene for other reasons, including exile. Sappho does not indicate whether the woman's family, husband, or political situation led to her departure. Instead, she recalls their shared experiences, mutual desire, and continued connection. Just as Eros strikes various women "once again" (δηὖτε, 1.15, 1.16, 1.18, 130.1), the story of the absent beloved repeats itself with different members of the *hetairia*. The community of women continues as they remember the women who have left, and the poems assume the absent women remain connected to Sappho's *hetairia* by their own memories and perhaps even through the gift of the poem itself.[7]

On the other hand, Erinna explicitly states that Baukis' absence was caused by the marriage that led to her death. For Erinna, Baukis' marriage and death is a single life-changing event: Baukis was her only beloved. Erinna preserves Baukis' memory through her poetry—the poet remembers and ensures that the memory of the deceased lives on. Memory is one-sided here, compared to the reciprocal workings of memory in Sappho's poems. Obviously, Baukis cannot carry on the memory of their shared experience, and Erinna gives no hint of any women's community in her poems. While Sappho addresses an intimate audience and specific women who will carry on the memory through song, Erinna addresses only Baukis and the unknown readers of her own poems.

Both poets, in many of Sappho's surviving fragments and perhaps in all of Erinna's surviving six, focus on primary relationships with other women. If we let go of the old unfounded bias toward reading Sappho 94 and 96 as marriage farewells, we can better understand the purpose and function of memory in these poems. Memory transforms the grief of leave-taking or absence into an affirmation and bonding experience between the members of the audience and the one who must leave. In fragment 94, for instance, the recollection of past intimacy "celebrate[s] female erotic desire for the female" (Snyder 1997, 58) and "activate[s] the past and make[s] it come alive in the present" (Greene 1994, 49):

τεθνάκην δ᾽ ἀδόλως θέλω·
<=>ἄ με ψισδομένα κατελίμπανεν
πόλλα καὶ τόδ᾽ ἔειπ·[
ὤιμ᾽ ὡς δεῖνα πεπ[όνθ]αμεν,
=Ψάπφ᾽, ἦ μάν σ᾽ ἀέκοισ᾽ ἀπυλιμπάνω·
τὰν δ᾽ ἔγω τάδ᾽ ἀμειβόμαν·
χαίροισ᾽ ἔρχεο κἄμεθεν
=μέμναισ᾽, οἶσθα γὰρ ὥς σε πεδήπομεν·
αἰ δὲ μή, ἀλλά σ᾽ ἔγω θέλω
ὄμναισαι[··(1·)1]·[··(1·)1]··αι
= ··[   ] καὶ κάλ᾽ ἐπάσχομεν·
πο[οις ἴων
καὶ βρ[όδων   ]κίων τ᾽ ὔμοι
=κα··[   ] πὰρ ἔμοι περεθήκαο
καὶ πό[λλαις ὐπα] θύμιδας
πλέκ[ταις ἀμφ᾽ ἀ]πάλαι δέραι
=ἀνθέων ·[   ] πεποημμέναις
καὶ π·····[   ]· μύρωι
βρενθείωι·[   ]ρυ[··]ν
<=>ἐξαλείψαο κα[ὶ βασ]ιληίωι
καὶ στρώμν[αν ἐ]πὶ μολθάκαν
ἀπάλαν πα·[   ]···ων
=ἐξίης πόθο[   ]·νίδων
κωΰτε τις[   ]··τι
ἰρον οὐδυ[   ]
<=>ἔπλετ᾽ ὄππ[οθεν ἄμ]μες ἀπέσκομεν,
οὐκ ἄλσος ·[   ]·ρος
[   ]ψοφος
<=>[   ]···οιδιαι[8]

"I simply wish to die."
Weeping she left me
and said this too:

"We've suffered terribly
Sappho I leave you against my will."   5
I answered, go happily
and remember me,
you know how we cared for you,
if not, let me remind you
. . . the lovely times we shared.   10

Many crowns of violets,
roses and crocuses
. . . together you set before me
and many scented wreaths
made from blossoms   15
around your soft throat . . .
. . . with pure, sweet oil
. . . you anointed me,
and on a soft, gentle bed . . .
you quenched your desire . . .   20
. . . no holy site . . .
we left uncovered,
no grove . . . dance
. . . sound   (94. 1–24)

We do not know how many stanzas are missing from the beginning of the poem. Our fragment picks up with Sappho recalling
what her lover said to her on leaving.[9] The other woman tries to
make leaving a tragedy, but Sappho corrects her, stops her from
lamenting. She calls on memory to change the leave-taking from
sorrow to joy by remembering their experiences together. Here
memory is a shared activity. The "I" of Sappho, the "you" of the
lover, and the "we" of the two of them with the larger community
of *hetairai* intertwine in the positive recollection of sensuous and
erotic pleasures. Memory sustains them because "the operation of
memory—recalling a past experience in which the speaker's desires
were fulfilled—bridge[s] the gap between . . . the lover and her
beloved" (Greene 1994, 53).

The memories of shared pleasures in fragment 96 includes
singing; the many voices and time frames make the poem more
complex than 94:

[   ]σαρδ·[··]
[=πόλ]λακι τυίδε [ν]ῶν ἔχοισα

ὤσπ·[···]·ώομεν, ·[···]··χ[··]
σε †θεασικελαν ἀρι-
=γνωτασε† δὲ μάλιστ᾽ ἔχαιρε μόλπαι·
νῦν δὲ Λύδαισιν ἐμπρέπεται γυναί-
κεσσιν ὥς ποτ᾽ ἀελίω
=δύντος ἀ βροδοδάκτυλος †μήνα
πάντα περ<ρ>έχοισ᾽ ἄστρα· φάος δ᾽ ἐπί-
σχει θάλασσαν ἐπ᾽ ἀλμύραν
=ἴσως καὶ πολυανθέμοις ἀρούραις·
ἀ δ᾽ <ἐ>έρσα κάλα κέχυται τεθά-
λαισι δὲ βρόδα κἄπαλ᾽ ἄν-
=θρυσκα καὶ μελίλωτος ἀνθεμώδης·
πόλλα δὲ ζαφοίταισ᾽ ἀγάνας ἐπι-
μνάσθεισ᾽ Ἄτθιδος ἰμέρωι
<=>λέπταν ποι φρένα κ[·]ρ··· βόρηται·
κῆθι δ᾽ ἔλθην ἀμμ·[··]··ισα τόδ᾽ οὐ

. . . Sardis . . .
often holding her [thoughts] here   2

*

you, like a goddess undisguised,
but she rejoiced especially in your song.   5

Now she stands out among
Lydian women as after sunset
the rose fingered moon   8

exceeds all stars; light
reaches equally over the brine sea
and thick flowering fields,   11

a beautiful dew has poured down,
roses bloom, tender parsley
and blossoming honey clover.   14

Pacing far away, she remembers
gentle Atthis with desire,
perhaps . . . consumes her delicate soul   (96. 1–17)   17

The singer addresses a woman, perhaps the Atthis named in line 16, recalling how the absent woman, now in Lydia, delighted in her singing in the past when they were together, and that even now, in the present, the absent woman is remembering her "with desire."

In both Lesbos and Lydia, erotic nature is wet and alive. The moon shines equally over both places, the women involved, the sea and fields between them. Just as the light of the moon connects the two women, so does the song of memory. The song recalls other songs in the past, a group of singing women ("us" in line 21), erotic desire among the women, and a present connection through memory. Sappho the singer draws on the memory of the absent woman to keep her present to her audience. Sappho recalls what the woman experienced in the past and is currently feeling while the absent woman herself remembers the individuals and community she left. According to Snyder (1997, 45), "the presence of the beloved's absence is a central feature of lesbian desire as Sappho configures it. . . . The creation of that presence through memory as expressed in song is one of the primary functions of Sappho's lyrics." When women must leave the group, they know that they live on in the song-memories of the others: "the gaps between subjects, figured through time and space, are at the same time constantly bridged by the operations of love and memory" (Williamson 1996, 255). They know that the group remembers them through the reperformance of the song. Songs of farewell focus on the "lovely times [they] shared" (fr. 94.10).

The women of her audience, and later audiences, could recognize themselves in the various situations—friends and lovers leaving and being missed. Stehle (1997, 301) argues that fragment 96 "concentrates on one addressee and allows the audience no way to participate, so I take this poem also as one intended for the addressee to perform for herself." It is possible that Sappho wrote poems down and gave them to individual women, but all of these songs could easily draw in an audience. While each poem may reflect a very specific actual event with a specific woman, the "I" and "us" of the poem can include the whole female audience, all thinking of a particular woman gone or individually of any dear absent friend. Even if we picture a poem written as a parting gift for a specific woman, as Stehle (1997, 324) also says, "Sappho used it [writing] to re-create women's traditions of speaking among themselves in an imaginative, permanently accessible form." The genre of lyric assumes a performance and a persuasive connection between singer and audience. Members of the audience would be connected to each other through the immediacy of the singer's voice and by being among the community of listeners. Or as Margaret Williamson says, "If song itself both arouses and expresses desire, then to sing at all is to enter into an open-ended, unbounded erotic dialogue with the entire group: the erotics of Sappho's poetry implies, therefore, a community of singing, desiring women" (Williamson 1996, 256–57). Sappho invokes memory to express, rejoice in, and continue the life of a community of women.

The performance situation for poetry changed radically in the fourth century BCE. Erinna's poetry, too, focuses on women yet, unlike Sappho's, does not include a community of women, an audience with shared memory. *Distaff*, Erinna's epyllion on Baukis (fr. 401), reads as a heroic lament of women's concerns (Skinner 1982)—childhood games, mothers, daily household tasks such as weaving, fears of and desires for marriage, death (perhaps in childbirth), restrictions in mourning, and fears of old age. The poem expresses essential aspects of women's lives. With early marriage, many women died in childbirth in their teens. According to ancient testimony, Erinna died a virgin at nineteen years old, soon after writing her masterpiece. Although *Distaff* mentions "nineteenth [year?] . . ." (401.35), the poem survives in a fragmentary state.[10] We have no way of knowing whether Erinna actually died at age nineteen, or wrote the poem then but died much later, or perhaps wrote the poem much later, recalling Baukis' death when they were both nineteen. Whenever Erinna wrote *Distaff* and her other poems, they express passion for her close companion (*sunhetairis*, epigram 1.7) and blame marriage for Baukis' death. Erinna's two other surviving hexameter fragments (402, 404) may be part of *Distaff* as well.[11] Even if fragment 404 is not from *Distaff*, it also refers to a female companion (*hetaira*).[12] Epigrams 1 and 2 are about Baukis and epigram 3 about the portrait of a woman named Agatharchis.

Memory in Erinna's poems records the past connection of two friends, not of ongoing community. The individual friend is dead, and the poem has no voice to reach her and no community of singers or listeners to invoke her presence. Erinna's hexameter lacks the traditional bard for epic poetry—both her hexameter and epigram were written for an audience of private readers. We can assume a literate and interested female readership in the fourth century—"women's access to education improved dramatically in the fourth century" (Pomeroy 1978, 19–20)—and it is possible that Erinna passed her poems along to a private group of friends or even gave public readings of *Distaff*. However, unlike Sappho and Korinna before Erinna, and Nossis after, Erinna's work gives no indication of an audience. It is possible to write in the traditional epigram form and still project a sense of intimacy with a community of readers, as Skinner (1991b, 29–30) argues for Nossis. Erinna does not.

Some epigrams traditionally were inscribed on grave monuments, to be read by whoever happens by. Although Erinna's epigrams 1 and 2 explore the traditional form that presupposes permanence, it is unlikely that either of these was actually written on stone at Baukis' grave, especially given that there are two epigrams. Erinna's epigrams were most likely literary, a form that continued with the women poets in the next generation, Anyte and Nossis. As in many sepulchral Hellenistic epigrams, the dead person is given a voice:

Στᾶλαι καὶ Σειρῆνες ἐμαὶ καὶ πένθιμε κρωσσέ,
  ὅστις ἔχεις Ἀίδα τὰν ὀλίγαν σποδιάν,
τοῖς ἐμὸν ἐρχομένοισι παρ᾽ ἠρίον εἴπατε χαίρειν,
  αἴτ᾽ ἀστοὶ τελέθωντ᾽ αἴθ᾽ ἑτεροπτόλιες·
χὤτι με νύμφαν εὖσαν ἔχει τάφος, εἴπατε καὶ τό·
  χὤτι πατήρ μ᾽ ἐκάλει Βαυκίδα, χὤτι γένος
Τηλία, ὡς εἰδῶντι· καὶ ὅττι μοι ἁ συνεταιρὶς
  Ἤρινν᾽ ἐν τύμβῳ γράμμ᾽ ἐχάραξε τόδε.

Stele and my sirens and mournful urn,
which holds the meager ashes belonging to Hades,
tell those passing by my tomb "farewell"
(be they townsmen or from other places)
and that this grave holds me, a bride. Say too,   5
that my father called me Baukis and my family
is from Tenos, so they may know, and that my friend
Erinna on the tombstone engraved this epigram.   (epigram 1)

Erinna, like Sappho in 94.6, uses the verb χαίρω (translated as "go happily" in Sappho and "farewell" in Erinna 1.3), a standard expression on greeting or leave-taking. Both speakers also ask to be remembered. The poems differ radically, however, in direction and tone. Sappho asks the woman to remember their lives together, whereas Erinna's Baukis asks the passing stranger to remember the few details about her life appropriate to epigram form: her name, town, and something about the circumstances of her death. In the last line, though, Erinna makes it clear that it is not really Baukis who speaks: Erinna herself wrote the words. The dead cannot speak, the living cannot hear them, and the poet does not know who will read the written record.

In Erinna's hexameter fragments as well, the lament for the dead may penetrate to Hades, but it is empty, powerless to initiate communication:

τουτόθεν εἰς Ἀίδαν κενεὰ διανήχεται ἀχώ·
σιγὰ δ' ἐν νεκύεσσι, τὸ δὲ σκότος ὄσσε κατέρρει
From here an empty echo penetrates to Hades;
but silence among the dead, and darkness closes their eyes.

(402)

Scholars have thought that the second half of the second line was an anticlimactic redundancy. Bowra (1936, 337) even suggested that the darkness closed Erinna's eyes in a faint. I argue, however, that both parts concern the efficacy of written poetry. Certainly, no communication is possible with the dead—they cannot hear ("silence") and they cannot see ("darkness"). Perhaps Erinna engages the problems or limits of writing: is the "empty" sound that of written hexameter, no longer performed by the bard? The dead cannot hear the silent poem or reply to it—hence the silence. Since the poem is text instead of song, it cannot reach or communicate with the dead. The darkness of death "closes their eyes"—they can no longer even read the written poem. Instead, the text commemorates the dead to whoever happens to read it. The fragment could be part of *Distaff*, since this is the one hexameter poem of Erinna's mentioned in ancient testimony. In *Distaff*, Erinna addresses Baukis, who cannot hear, reply, or read it. Without Baukis, who is there to receive the poem? There is an isolation, a loneliness, not present in Sappho or Korinna, who sing for the community of women who participate in their song.[13]

Even so, Erinna does expect to be read. In the separation of written poem and audience, the anonymous reader provides the only compensation for loss. Her sophisticated poetry is not a naïve diary. Of course, even if the poetry of Sappho and Erinna began from an actual, immediate event of a friend's leaving or dying and was composed at that time for that situation, both Sappho and Erinna were poets who expected their work to be remembered beyond their immediate community and lifetime. According to Sappho herself, "I say someone in another time will remember us" (μνάσασθαί τινά φαιμι †καὶ ἕτερον† ἀμμέων, fr. 147). Both poets "signed" some of their poems by including their names (Sappho 1.20, 94.5; Erinna 401.38 and 1.8), a clear signal that they want to be remembered. Written works travel beyond the physical limitations of the poet. We know Erinna's work was popular, at least by

the next generation: "in antiquity she was second in fame and reputation only to Sappho, to whom the ancients often compared her"
(Arthur 1980, 53). Her poetry influenced the Hellenistic writers,
male and female (Cameron and Cameron 1969, also Gutzwiller
1998). Since Anyte and Nossis come soon after, perhaps there were
other women in Erinna's community with whom she was educated,
who read each other's poems. Does Erinna "speak" for other women
in the community who also experienced separation from friends by
marriage and death?

Broadly put, for Sappho memory in song is a tool for invocation and epiphany, whereas for Erinna memory in writing produces
a historical record or a memorial lament. Erinna suggests that the
written word lacks the potency of the spoken; it cannot come alive.
Epigram 3 calls attention to the contrast between text read and
song performed. The epigrammist may nearly rival the gods in skill,
but her work falls short without voice:

Ἐξ ἀταλᾶν χειρῶν τάδε γράμματα· λῷστε Προμαθεῦ,
    ἔντι καὶ ἄνθρωποι τὶν ὁμαλοὶ σοφίαν·
ταύταν γοῦν ἐτύμως τὰν παρθένον ὅστις ἔγραψεν,
    αἰ καὐδὰν ποτέθηκ᾽, ἧς κ᾽ Ἀγαθαρχὶς ὅλα.

Delicate hands fashioned this portrait: good Prometheus,
there are even humans equal to you in skill.
If whoever painted this girl so true to life
had added a voice too, Agatharchis would be complete.

The portrait (γράμματα) may be "true to life" but still lacks "voice."
The portrait cannot replace or re-create the living girl; the written
text cannot replace song and come alive. In epigram 1.8, Erinna uses
the same word (γράμμ᾽) for epigram: "Erinna on the tombstone
engraved this epigram." The epigram is not able to do what Sappho's song could do within her community because it lacks the voice
to make it complete. Although Erinna's short hexameter fragment
(402) and shortest epigram (3) have been overlooked by scholarship, they provide valuable clues in understanding Erinna's small
surviving body of poems.

Assuming a mid-to-late fourth-century date for Erinna, this is a
transitional time for poetics (Levin 1962, Gutzwiller 1998, 1–7). Performance is on its way out and books are not yet in. The new literary
possibilities of writing, although isolating, reach a different audience of
non–community members. Writing "supposes an intention of deferred

communication, beyond a determined space and time" (Zumthor 1986, 76). The movement from song to text includes the loss of the power of memory to connect the community of women. Yet it also contains the possibility of κλέος (fame), and so memory, beyond continuity of performance or the confines of an individual woman's community to the wider sphere of unknown readers.

For both Sappho and Erinna, the muse of the absent beloved inspires poetry. From this point on, the function of memory differs for the two poets. In Sappho's lyric performance, the shared memory of the beloved provides for a continuing conversation among the women of the community. There is no lament. The circumstance of women leaving, and dying, did not change in the intervening two to three hundred years between Sappho and Erinna. Poised between the oral culture of archaic and classical poetry, and the books of Hellenistic society, Erinna explores textuality, both acknowledging its limits in immediate communication and its power of permanency. Her hexameters are not bardic—they have to do silently what Erinna says she cannot do out loud—mourn Baukis.[14] Epigram's solid inscribed form declares strangers as readers. Erinna's written texts recall the dead without connection to community. In Erinna, the memory of the beloved remains isolated, a memorial.

NOTES

1. In the fourth century, "we see the crossing of genres in . . . Erinna, whose poem transfuses Sapphic material into epic meter and Doric dialect" (Parsons 1993, 154).

2. For *Distaff* see Lloyd-Jones and Parsons 1983: *Distaff* = 401; the other two hexameter fragments are 402 and 404. All Sappho fragments are numbered according to Voigt's edition (1971).

3. Sappho's songs have "a woman-centered framework in which emotional and/or erotic bonds between and among women take center stage" (Snyder 1997, 2). This description fits Erinna's work as well.

4. See Stehle 1997 on the performance of lyric and epic poetry in the archaic period.

5. All six of the Erinna poems should be considered hers. Scholars tend to claim that poems ascribed to women have not really been written by the women; see Rauk 1989, and West 1977. Ancient male poets only mention the "*Distaff*"—perhaps because that is the one that most mattered to them. Gutzwiller 1998 assumes that Erinna's epigrams are indeed hers, that her epigram 3 "stands as a direct model for Nossis' portrait poems" (86) and that Erinna's epigrams influenced Anyte (66) and the male epigrammists (87) as well.

6. The epigrams are numbered according to Page 1975.

7. Stehle (1997, 294) argues that the most famous of Sappho's erotic poems should be read primarily as texts, as parting gifts from Sappho to the specific addressee.

8. Greek texts are from *Thesaurus Linguae Graecae;* all translations of Sappho and Erinna are my own (Rayor 1991).

9. Burnett 1979, 22. Arguments that attribute the first line to the narrator/Sappho call for a much more private and sorrowful poem, without the interesting contrast between voices.

10. Of the surviving first fourteen lines, only the right margin survives; the next twenty lines have both margins, but no middle; out of the last twenty lines, all are the left margin only, except one whole line midway.

11. Rauk 1989 argues that fragment 404 is part of *Distaff,* partly because he believes Erinna only wrote the one poem. While I do not find his argument persuasive for 404 as part of a farewell to Baukis on her marriage, it could be part of *Distaff.*

12. Sappho also uses the term *hetairai* to refer to her audience (160 V) and preferred sleeping companions (126 V).

13. Rayor 1993. Korinna's programmatic poem (*PMG* 655) begins: "Terpsichore [told] me/ lovely old tales to sing/ to the white-robed women of Tanagra" (ἐπί με Τερψιχόρα . . . / καλὰ ϝεροῖ' ἀισομέναν / Ταναγρίδεσσι λευκοπέπλυς).

14. Erinna 401.33: "with my eyes [I may] not see you dead nor lament" (οὐδ' ἐσιδῆν φαε[εσσιν . . . νε]κυν οὐδὲ γοᾶσαι).

4 *dico ergo sum*

Erinna's Voice and Poetic Reality

Elizabeth Manwell

And how Death is that remedy all singers dream
    of, sing,
    remember, prophesy as in the Hebrew
        Anthem, or the
    Buddhist Book of Answers—and my own
        imagination of
    a withering leaf—at dawn—
        —Allen Ginsberg, *Kaddish*

Of all the ancient Greek female poets, perhaps only Sappho intrigues more than Erinna. For like the poetry of her predecessor and model, Erinna's work primarily comprises a tantalizing yet spare set of fragments, from which both ancient and modern scholars attempt to reconstruct her biography, rendering it insecure at best. Most likely a writer of the fourth century BCE, Erinna has bequeathed to us three epigrams, two hexametrical lines quoted in Athenaeus, and a series of fragments from her chef-d'oeuvre, commonly known as the *Distaff*. Those few critics who have considered the body of Erinna's poetry have typically focused on the *Distaff* rather than on the epigrams, yet understandably, despite the comparatively diligent attention that this text has received, because of its fragmentary state there has been no consensus as to its meaning.[1] It has been read variously, as a traditional woman's lament (Skinner 1982), an anti-hymenaeal verse (Arthur 1980), a combination of Sapphic themes and epic meter (Gutzwiller 1997), and most famously a poem of "exceptional ingenium" composed by a man (West 1977).[2] These readings are provocative but tend to exclude epigrams attributed to Erinna, which provide additional clues to her poetic project. By examining the *Distaff* along with the epigrams, one observes an attempt by a female poet to define her identity as a Greek woman. This paper will first examine the techniques Erinna employs to establish a poetic identity in the *Distaff* and then consider similar strategies used in the epigrams. Emphasizing not only the elements and tokens of female life but also the importance of voice as a means of fashioning the self, Erinna both depicts the value of interpersonal ties between women and shapes an identity and poetics of her own.

To argue for Erinna's formulation of a poetic identity presupposes that one can postulate or theorize how identities—poetic or otherwise—are formed. One approach to this issue that provides a framework for considering questions about and problems of identity formation is the application of psychoanalytic theory, which argues that a sense of identity, or individuation, comes into being when the ego separates from, or rather brings into being, an external reality. Various analysts theorize this moment in different ways. For Sigmund Freud (*SE* 19, 25) the ego does not encompass the id but is situated between what we consciously perceive (reality) and the id itself, into which the ego merges. The ego therefore constitutes the part of the id that has "been modified by direct influence of the external world." The differentiation between ego and id grows more pronounced through the process of loss: Freud observed that depression, like mourning, manifests itself in those who, having lost an object, set it up again inside the ego. Subsequent theorists have modified Freud's notions. D. W. Winnicott (1971, 1–6), for example, argues that the lost object is the mother's breast, for which a transitional object must be found. Prior to that moment of separation from the breast, the infant's ego is merged with that of the mother, providing not only a sense of union with another but also rendering the child's nascent ego chaotic, unorganized, and undifferentiated. Only through the process of separation does a child come to understand that she is an individual, that a "not-me" (e.g. the breast) exists. Hans Loewald (1980, 11) takes a slightly different approach, observing that the ego functions as a barrier between an individual's interior world and external reality. Thus, the development of self, of the ego, is what brings about individuation, or as Loewald says, "the ego detaches from itself an outer world" (5). Nevertheless, the ego always desires reunion with that exterior, to become once again a united whole. And Jacques Lacan, whose rewriting of Freud is so distinct and seemingly impenetrable, nevertheless recognizes the ego as an intermediary that produces false judgments or *méconnaissance* in its effort to cover over conflict.[3] The process of ego formation is one of separation, of ordering and reordering, of moving from the more chaotic to the more organized (and back again), of instantiating a moment of loss that one will always strive to bridge but never fully close. Jonathan Lear (1990, 160) notes that Freud recognized that psychic development is dependent upon a "dialectic of love and loss," specifically the tension between desire and the lost object of desire (and human insistence upon obscuring that conflict). Loss, then, represents a fundamental experience of individuation, and the subsequent development of the ego is an attempt to work through that first loss, to further organize and separate while simultaneously attempting to reunite with the other.

If we start from loss, both as a point of departure for the development of an identity (of an individual or of a poet) and as an experience that has the potential to order our lives, then separation from other persons—through death, or physical distance, or emotional rupture—can critically inform identity. In this light Erinna's *Distaff* reads as a prescription for the formulation of the ego, since the losses here are multiple. The poem details the split that has been created between two women, Baucis and "Erinna," first by Baucis' marriage, which leaves "Erinna" without her companion, and finally by her death, which separates them permanently.[4] Adam Phillips (2001, 257) writes that "one of the ironies of the so-called mourning process is that it tends to make people even more self-absorbed than they usually are." In this Phillips alludes to one of the paradoxes inherent not only in the progression of mourning, but more important, also in writing about the process of grief. For lament is inherently personal, and it is the personal that makes the individual turn inward or assert a privileged position ("you can't know what it's like for me"). At the same time, mourning is universal, and the traditional lament, or a poem like Erinna's *Distaff*, only resonates with an audience because there is a common aspect to grief as well, a sense that all feel an investment in or understanding of the process of bereavement, even if they are poorly acquainted with a particular loss. This paradox, the role of lament as both personal and public, compels the author to define herself as both individual and member of her community: a loss that in no way seems personal will not stir an audience; a loss too personal will alienate them.

To bridge the personal and the public requires skill and sensitivity, and although fragmentary, a fairly complete section of the *Distaff* (14–35) demonstrates Erinna's abilities in this arena:[5]

ἐς β]α[θ]ὺ κῦμα[
λε]υκᾶν μαινομέν[οισιν ἐσάλαο π]οσσιν ἀφ᾽ ἵ[π]πω[ν   15

αἰ]αῖ ἐγώ, μέγ' ἄϋσα· φ[   ] χελύννα
] ομένα μεγάλας[   ] χορτίον αὐλᾶς·
τα]ῦτα τύ, Βαῦκι τάλαι[να   ]χεισα γόημ[ι]
τα]ῦτά μοι ἐν κρα[δίᾳ   ] χνια κεῖται
θέρμ' ἔτι· την[   ] υρομες ἄνθρακες ἤδη·   20
δαγύ[δ]ων τεχ[   ]ίδες ἐν θαλάμοισι
νυμ[φ]αι [   ]έες· ἅ τε ποτ' ὄρθον
μάτηρ αε[   ] οισιν ἐρείθοις
τηνασηλθ[   ]να ἀμφ' ἁλίπαστον·
μικραισ [   ]ν φόβον ἄγαγε Μορ[μ]ώ   25
] εν μὲν κ [   ] ατα ποσσὶ δὲ φοιτῆι
]   [ ]σιν· ἐκ δ' [   ] μετεβάλλετ' ὀπωπάν·
ἀνίκα δ' ἐς [λ]έχος [   ]όκα πάντ' ἐλέλασο
ἄσσ' ε [ ] ηπιασ τ [   ] ματρὸς ἄκουσας,
Βαῦκι φίλα· λαθα ε [   ] Ἀφροδίτα·   30
τῶ τυ κατακλα[ί]οισατα[   ] [ ] ε λείπω [·
οὐ [γ]άρ μοι πόδεσ   [ ] [ ] ο δῶμα βέβαλοι·
οὐδ' ἐσιδῆν φαεε[σσιν   ]κυν οὐδὲ γοᾶσαι
γυμναῖσιν χαίταις ν[φο]ινίκεος αἰδὼς
δρύπτει μ' ἀμφὶ πα[ρῆιδας   35

                    Into the deep wave
from white horses [you leapt] with crazed feet.   15
Alas, I shouted loudly . . . tortoise
. . . little enclosure of the great courtyard . . .
these things you, wretched Baucis, . . . I lament . . .
these remnants . . . lie in my heart
still warm . . . already cinders.   20
Of dolls . . . in bedrooms
dolls/brides . . . once near dawn
mother . . . the wool workers
. . . came to you . . . salt-sprinkled
the little girls . . . Mormo brought fear   25
. . . on feet she goes to and fro
. . . and from . . . changes her appearance.
But when into the marriage bed . . . you forgot everything
that . . . having heard from your mother,
dear Baucis. Forgetfulness . . . Aphrodite [brought]   30
therefore loudly bewailing you . . . I leave . . .
for my feet are not permitted/impure . . . the house
nor to look at with eyes . . . nor to bemoan

with uncovered hair . . . blushing shame
tears me about the [cheeks] . . .   35

Much of Erinna's poetry treads a line between personal melancholia
and public pronouncement, through which she constructs herself
specifically, deliberately as a vocal female "I," and nowhere is this
more evident than in the *Distaff*.[6] In part she accomplishes this by
structuring her lament as a *goos*, a traditionally female form of lament.
The *goos*, unlike the professionally sung and male-voiced *threnos*,
articulated a personal loss, and the affinities between Erinna's lament
and this more personal form of mourning have been amply demonstrated by others (Alexiou 1974, Skinner 1982, Gutzwiller 1997).
Yet Erinna's dirge differs from the traditional *goos* in demonstrable
ways; Kathryn Gutzwiller 1997 persuasively argues that Erinna's
hexameters represent a transformation of Homeric lament into a
personal female articulation of grief by incorporating Sapphic themes
of separation from a female beloved.[7] Although the *Distaff* resembles
the laments of Andromache, Hecuba, and Helen found in the *Iliad*
(24.725–45, 748–59, 762–75) in that the narrator publicly articulates her sorrow over the death of one dear to her, it is nevertheless
distinct from such laments because she does not mourn a male hero
but a female friend.[8] Gutzwiller 1997 thus argues that the *goos* is a
song of separation that perhaps corresponds to other women's
songs of separation, such as Sappho's hymns to girls (e.g. Lobel-
Page 94, 96, 131). Yet, the *Distaff* is not a *goos* in the traditional
sense—it is a carefully wrought poem in hexameters addressed neither
to a husband nor to a son, and as a published literary artifact it
remains a very public document, a piece of self-absorption made for
public consumption.

    That Erinna chooses to transform the *goos*, the traditional
woman's oral lament, into a public literary form perhaps alone indicates her interest in establishing herself specifically as a female poet,
a conservator of a traditionally female genre of poetry. Certainly
separation, as seen in the traditional *goos* and in the hymns of Sappho,
is a potent theme that underlies the basis for this poem too, since it
both articulates the division between a married and an unmarried
woman, as well as that between the dead and the living. Furthermore, the separation of "Erinna" and Baucis appears all the more
stark when juxtaposed with the initial affinity between them and the
similarity of their childhood status, which Erinna emphasizes—their
games, their dread of Mormo, and their interest in dolls. The multiple

separations not only denote loss but also serve to highlight the disparity that now exists between the two women, which is enacted on multiple levels but perhaps most notably in the difference in their location, marital status, animation, and occupation. Moreover, similarity and difference are specifically constructed through a gendered experience, namely the transition from girlhood to womanhood and the condition of being female. Thus, Erinna uses traditional symbols of female life to demonstrate the early affinity between "Erinna" and Baucis in an attempt to heighten the sense of their current dissimilarity and simultaneously to effect a reunion. Erinna intimates that the girls were playmates, were engaged in activities together within the household, and feared Mormo. Yet, the poet soon emphasizes the differences between them: "Erinna" is alive not dead, a woman no longer a child, unmarried not a young bride, and mindful instead of forgetful.[9] This mindfulness permits her to recall the times when they were as one, as well as moments of disunity.

The first separation—the differentiation of woman from child or the loss of childhood itself—is actuated on a physical plane, but this motion from one locale to another serves to show connection as well as distance.[10] At every point movement is met with countermovement, as the poet particularly evokes the progression from childhood to adulthood and counterbalances it with the transition of bride to corpse. The passage of a woman's life—from girlhood to womanhood to death—is amply recorded, as Erinna refers to the moon ([σ]ελάννα, 6), the shift from an emphasis on girlish exploits such as the tortoise game (3–15) to life as a married woman (27–28), and the trade of common space in the courtyard and the house (17, 21) to "Erinna's" isolation from Baucis (18, 48). The initial passage as preserved demonstrates a bond between them that is specific both to their status as girls and to their movement within the courtyard space. Within these parameters the girls engage in what Maurice Bowra (1953b) first recognized as the "torty-tortoise" game, a version of tag in which the "tortoise" is surrounded by other girls, who recite a call-and-response poem.[11] The poem, recorded by Pollux (9.122–25), reads as follows:

χελιχελώνη, τί ποίεις ἐν τῷ μέσῳ
μαρύομ' ἔρια καὶ κρόκαν Μιλησίαν.
ὁ δ' ἔκγονός σου τί ποίων ἀπώλετο;
λευκᾶν ἀφ' ἵππων εἰς θάλασσαν ἅλατο.

Torty-tortoise, what are you doing in the middle?
I'm weaving wool and the Milesian woof.
And your child, how did he die?
From white horses he leapt into the sea.

At the end of the final line the tortoise would then jump up and tag the next tortoise.[12]

Marilyn Arthur (1980, 60) has demonstrated how in the first half of the torty-tortoise poem the tortoise acts as a mother, "staying at home and performing traditional tasks, keeping to the interior female space which is construed by the Greeks as a stable and unmoving middle point of a circle." Arthur reads the second half of the children's refrain as the opposite of the first, as nonfemale, perhaps reflecting the actions of warriors as they leap from their chariots. The girl who plays the tortoise does not remain permanently static nor continuously female; by leaping up to tag the next girl she eschews the female state (circumscribed both by boundaries and the activity of weaving) and instead adopts a "male" subject position, like the son who jumps to his death. Although Arthur judiciously distinguishes between the relative positions of the girl in the middle and those who surround her, it is perhaps also possible to read both positions as female.[13] Given the way in which this game involves call and response and the fact that all the girls must participate both as the tortoise and in the group at large, the girls are encouraged to act both as the mother who mourns and the "audience" for the lament. Likewise, each girl must eventually be still (what Arthur would read as symbolic of the married woman), but stasis always returns to motion, allowing the girls to relinquish motherhood (at least for the moment). And so the game continues, ever repeated, the children abandoning their positions in the circle only to return to them. The game then too represents the cyclical nature of women's lives and simultaneously offers respite from mourning, even as it preserves the "son's" memory. The girl who was the tortoise must give up her grief for her son, if only by leaping herself, or forcing another to become the tortoise. The separation of the tortoise from the group—like the separations occasioned both by marriage and by death—are ultimately relieved by the capture of another child (though it is brief and transient), or by the transference of "obligation" and "grief" from one girl to another. Thus, this game employs movement to invoke both commonality and difference; even as a girl is singled out as a tortoise, all are to participate equally in the game.[14] If Bowra is right, that the references to the tortoise refer specifically to a girl's game (which itself reenacts a mother's loss and privileges interior domestic space), then the poet is defining "Erinna's" earliest relationship with Baucis not only as play but as vocal and reciprocal exchange, which is necessitated by the loss of a beloved object, a change of status, and the restoration to the larger group. The bond between the girls is instantiated both through the movement of the proceedings and through the responsion required in the game.

Like the girls playing torty-tortoise, Mormo also moves. An ancient Greek version of a boogey-woman, Mormo, like other evil spirits, was thought to abduct and eat children. Her antipathy toward the young is connected perhaps to the death of her own children (schol. Theoc. 15.40c, Johnston 1999). Tentatively reconstructed as "Mormo [brought] fear" (25), the text suggests that, like the tortoise, Mormo too is a motile entity; accompanied by terror and death she approaches the girls and threatens cannibalistic consumption. Thus, Mormo is analogous to the torty-tortoise who attempts to capture another girl and simultaneously frees herself from her role as mother and assuages her grief through finding a new child. But Mormo's union is darker: she is the all-consuming mother, the one who refuses to let go. Denying the departure of her child and the loss she has suffered, Mormo threatens to ingest small children, symbolically returning them to that state before differentiation and ego formation was possible. Mormo's potency as a symbolic form of the poetic self comes not only from her gender and the associations of motherhood tied to it, but also because she vividly represents the refusal to separate, the denial of loss.[15]

Mormo's "other" or foil might well be the goddess Aphrodite, mentioned later in Erinna's text (30). It is impossible to confirm that "forgetfulness" is the direct object of whatever verb "Aphrodite" governs, yet if we speculate that Mormo brings fear, we might also conjecture that the goddess of love in turn brings forgetfulness.[16] And like that fear that Mormo occasions, the forgetfulness that Aphrodite offers also serves to separate; positioned next to "dear Baucis" (Βαῦκι φίλα, 30) and between her mother (29) and Aphrodite (30), λάθα marks the division between Baucis' previous existence with her family (and with "Erinna") and the new life that marriage brings. Thus, through forgetfulness the connection between "Erinna" and Baucis is effectively severed. The enjambment at the beginning of line 30 serves as a forceful break and offers a pronounced distinction between the girl who used to listen to her mother and the woman whom Aphrodite turns to other concerns. The friendship that existed between Baucis and "Erinna"—represented by a game that joined them through poetic dialogue—has been erased by Baucis' disinterest in its existence, a loss created by the forgetfulness that Aphrodite brings. Though Mormo and Aphrodite represent radically different aspects of feminine experience, they are similar in the threat they pose to Erinna both as companion of Baucis and as poet. For "Erinna" both Mormo and Aphrodite work to remove from view the female companion, and to deny "Erinna" vocal communication with Baucis (Mormo by consuming the other rather than engaging in discourse with her, Aphrodite by rendering her deaf). For Erinna they attempt to erase female agency through the promotion of unions to men and the valuation of children over the production of female-oriented poetry.

Perhaps Erinna means to suggest that her own supposed unfamiliarity with Aphrodite permits her to remember, to assert a poetic voice. If the goddess makes women forget themselves and their pasts (as she asserts Aphrodite does), only those untouched by desire (for husband, children, sexual activity) will remain mindful, will have at the ready the material out of which to construct verses of lament. Thus, Erinna's voice (and "Erinna's" voice as well) is dependent upon the fact that she is unmarried, that the divide between herself and Baucis exists. Just as there can be no lament without the separation, so too can there be no poetry unless there is memory. Erinna as poet and "Erinna" as poetic subject require Baucis' loss and forgetfulness in order to promote their alternative.

The second separation, the distinction between "Erinna" and Baucis based upon their marital status, can be established through references in the extant fragments, in which a distinction is made between the *parthenos* "Erinna" and the *nymphe* Baucis. Though the poet never refers to "Erinna" as a maiden, she does employ a word for bride (22), refers to Baucis' marriage bed (28), and perhaps suggests her own future as a spinster (46). The separation that Baucis' marriage brings and the difference in their status that marriage occasions also permit the poet to structure "Erinna's" experience as distinct from that of her companion. In particular, the designation of Baucis as "bride" also facilitates marking her as a "bride of death." The associations for the Greeks between the experience of a bride and the state of death are voluminous, as can be seen most strikingly in Greek tragedy (Loraux 1987, Rehm 1994). Rush Rehm notes the similarity of the wedding and funeral in that both focus on the activity of the *oikos*:

> Marriage granted a female "outsider" a central place on the inside, opening one family to the influence of another and to contending claims of loyalty and support. A funeral, on the other hand, asked women to consolidate the family in the midst of loss, effecting a transition not only for the deceased but also for the survivors. Both rituals focused on the Greek household, or *oikos*, the private world in which women played their crucial roles—providing heirs, nurturing them as they grew, sustaining the family, and guaranteeing due homage to its dead members. (1994, 8)

Rehm formulates marriage as a motion that brings an "outsider" in and claims that both nuptial and funeral rituals are private rather than public, since they are the purview of women and focus on the interior space of the *oikos*, rather than the exterior world of the polis. The inability then of "Erinna" to attend Baucis' funeral (32–33) further illustrates the extent to which she is separated not only from her former companion, but even from those activities most associated with Greek women.[17] By failing to participate in the funeral rites, "Erinna" fails in her duties as a woman and is denied the opportunity to engage in a new sort of call and response, the *goos* and the keening of female mourners.

The associations of death with marriage appear perhaps nowhere more obviously than in Euripides' *Alcestis*, in which a vocal wife returns from the Underworld a silent bride.[18] While it is not true that death deprives all brides of their voices (in Euripides' *Hippolytus* Phaedra's letter, for example, is read only upon her death), death does literally impose silence. Consequently, perhaps marriage as a bride's symbolic death also silences, at least inasmuch as the separation enacted forecloses the possibility of one's prior existence being restored (and with it the reciprocal vocal exchange between "Erinna" and Baucis). The chasm that marriage creates figuratively compels stillness (a woman's stasis in the interior space) and silence (the loss of voice) upon the bride. Thus, as both bride and bride of death Baucis loses her voice. That is, part of the forgetfulness that Aphrodite brings is a symbolic loss of speech, since only those that remember the past can articulate it.[19]

More critical, however, than Baucis' loss of voice—her removal from the vocal interaction that she and "Erinna" shared as girls—is Erinna's cultivation of her own voice. As a poet Erinna must retain her speech; moreover, the difference that Erinna constructs depends upon these matrices of associated concepts: marriage, death, silence, lament, girlhood, womanhood, fear, desire, forgetfulness, mindfulness. Whereas Baucis represents the silent dead bride, "Erinna" is the vocal living maiden. Thus, Erinna's status as maiden should not be regarded so much as biography (though she may well have been unmarried, as many have argued) as a construct for the purposes of poetic production intended to demarcate a living poet from a dead bride.[20]

The most obvious difference between the two characters, however, lies in the distinction between the living and the dead. Though this opposition can be superimposed upon other dichotomies—vocal/mute, unmarried/married—this distinction between the two women initiates the loss and prompts the production of poetry. If loss brings reality into being through the recognition of the "not-me," then Erinna's *Distaff* creates a space in which to explore the differences between two women in multiple ways. The separation between "Erinna" and Baucis, however, might remain just that were it not for the articulation of that loss, which brings into being two distinct individuals—the mourner and the mourned, the poet and the commemorated. In this sense Baucis' death brings into being Erinna's status as a poet, because she enables "Erinna"/Erinna to make personal claims in a public document. Without Baucis' death there is no poetry.

In fact, the first two verbs extant from the text are in the first person, "I shouted loudly" (μέγ' ἄϋσα, 16) and "I lament" (γόημ[ι], 18), which not only emphasize the role of the narrator ("this poem is about my loss") but denote her voice ("I loudly descry my loss"). In this sense the death of Baucis provides Erinna with an opportunity to articulate loss and separation by means of her voice. The vehicle of the poem becomes a mechanism for Erinna to engage again in dialogue with "Erinna," who becomes the mournful "torty-tortoise" as she explores the tension between all-consuming grief and forgetfulness. The reality of Baucis or Erinna's nineteen years or her homeland becomes of little import when the poem is viewed from the vantage of loss, for this concept and the separation that ensues are what engender the poetry itself. Erinna is permitted this privileged position within her culture—to lament out loud the loss of another.

These various losses—of Baucis' life, of her companionship due to her marriage, of memory—allow Erinna/"Erinna" to separate from Baucis. Yet Baucis is more than just the "other" to Erinna's "self." Rather, it is through these constructs that Erinna is able to distinguish herself as a poet. Here the traditional *goos* is augmented with a series of dichotomies that variously emphasize the reciprocity of the girls' earlier vocality, and Erinna's current status as a sole speaker. Only through this combination of public statement and private emotion can Erinna create a space for herself as a female poet— "I mourn." The space for Erinna as poet is not only physical and emotional but even lexical, as the narrator creates various topographies to demarcate her distinctive status. In her study of Modern Greek lament, Nadia Seremetakis (1991, 117) observes that breathlessness and sobs punctuate a lament, so that they form a "signifying system *autonomous and independent* of any specific verbal content" (original emphasis). Although we can assume that Erinna's original text was not the lacunose fragments we now read, it is perhaps satisfying to take this seemingly postmodern text and read the silences as "breathlessness," as a way of punctuating "Erinna's" emotional outpouring.[21] Thus, out of this loss (including the loss of the text itself) emerges a very vocal, very autonomous, and very female "I."

It is perhaps, one thing to argue for the formulation of a particular poetic identity—one rooted in the vocal femininity of a *parthenos* as opposed to the silence of a bride—in a work about girlhood friends separated by death, but it is something else to argue that such an identity is consciously striven for in every work by a given author. Yet, a similar aesthetic is achieved in the three epigrams attributed to Erinna as well. In each, she emphasizes voice as the medium by which a woman is distinguished as an individual. Perhaps closest in spirit to the *Distaff* are the two epigrams that also concern the death of Baucis, *AP* 7.710 and 712:

Στᾶλαι καὶ Σειρῆνες ἐμαὶ καὶ πένθιμε κρωσσέ,
    ὅστιί ἔχεις Ἀίδα τὰν ὀλίγαν σποδιάν,
τοῖς ἐμὸν ἐρχομένοισι παρ' ἠρίον εἴπατε χαίρειν,
    αἴτ' ἀστοὶ τελέθωντ' αἴθ' ἑτεροπτόλιες·
χὤτι με νύμφαν εὖσαν ἔχει τάφος, εἴπατε καὶ τό·
    χὤτι πατήρ μ' ἐκάλει Βαυκίδα, χὤτι γένος
Τηλία, ὡς εἰδῶντι· καὶ ὅττι μοι ἁ συνεταιρὶς
    Ἤρινν' ἐν τύμβῳ γράμμ' ἐχάραξε τόδε.   (*AP* 7.710)

My stele and Sirens and mournful urn,
    whatever holds this small infernal collection of ashes
tell those who come by my grave to fare well,
    whether they are citizens or of another town;
and tell them that this tomb holds me, a bride, and also
    say this: that my father called me Baucis, that my family

is from Telos, so that they may know; and that my companion
   Erinna inscribed these words upon my tomb.

Νύμφας Βαυκίδος εἰμί· πολυκλαύταν δὲ παρέρπων
   στάλαν τῷ κατὰ γᾶς τοῦτο λέγοις Ἀίδᾳ·
"Βάσκανός ἐσσ', Ἀίδα." τὰ δέ τοι καλὰ σάμαθ' ὁρῶντι
   ὠμοτάταν Βαυκοῦς ἀγγελέοντι τύχαν,
ὡς τὰν παῖδ', Ὑμέναιος ἐφ' αἷς ἀείδετο πεύκαις,
   ταῖσδ' ἐπὶ καδεστὰς ἔφλεγε πυρκαιᾷ·
καὶ σὺ μέν, ὦ Ὑμέναιε, γάμων μολπαῖον ἀοιδὰν
   ἐς θρήνων γοερὸν φθέγμα μεθαρμόσαο.   (AP 7.712)

I am the tomb of the bride Baucis. And you, creeping by this
      much-lamented
   stele, say this to Hades below the earth:
"You are envious, Hades." But to you looking upon them, these
      fair
   monuments will announce Baucis' most cruel fortune.
how with the torches by which Hymenaios was celebrated,
   with the same ones her father-in-law set alight the girl on this
      pyre.
And you, Hymenaios, changed the melodic song of weddings
   into the mournful cry of the *threnos*.

In the first epigram the poem itself is schooled by the poet in what
to say, though only in the final line do we learn that Erinna has provided the tutelage. The convention, of course, of having the deceased,
or a stele or other memorial to the dead, make a pronouncement
about the subject of commemoration is exceptionally common.[22] Yet
of particular interest is one of those addressees named in the first line.
The Sirens are most obviously to be read as architectural elements that
adorned the stele, yet their mention in this epigram is provocative.
Most commonly associated with the voyage of Odysseus, the Sirens
produce a song irresistible to all those who hear it, a song that makes
men forget, so that they may be lured to their death (Hom. *Od.*
12.39–54, 158–200). Their specific appeal to Odysseus is their own
omniscience, with which they attempt to seduce him. As creatures
endowed with a gift for song, they are also often associated with the
Muses (e.g. *Argon.* 4.895f., Alcman *PMG* 30) either as the daughters
of one of the Muses or through a specific equation of the two. Entic-
ing yet baleful, the Homeric Sirens may be categorized with other
dangerous and powerful females in the *Odyssey*, like Circe and Calypso.

Siegfried de Rachewiltz (1987, 16–17) observes that Odysseus' trouble consists in how to approach the Sirens and still maintain his distance. The destructive force of these creatures coupled with their vocal skill places them on the cusp between culture and nature, where they exert a palpable threat to mind, memory, family, social order, and of course, life (de Rachewiltz 1987, 18). Most attempts to analyze the Sirens have essentially stopped here, since the problem they present is in some sense insoluble: they are monsters and temptresses, daughters of the Muse and cannibals, creatures of inherent ambiguity.[23]

Sirens then are seductive not only because of the quality of their voices (musical like those of the Muses) but also because of the content of their speech (that they offer supreme knowledge), and in some sense Baucis becomes a Siren-like figure. The voice that the tomb appropriates is that of Baucis (e.g. my stele, 1; my grave, 3; me, 5). The possessive and personal pronouns serve primarily to emphasize her belongings, such as they are, (my stele, my grave) and her personal relationships (bride, daughter, companion). Baucis, as the Siren of her own tomb, attempts to lure passersby ("come read this inscription") and promises knowledge, though not omniscience. As a Siren, Baucis also occupies a marginal area: the articulation of her fate establishes the very moment where mind, memory, and social order have the potential to break down. But any musicality must be provided by one of the Muses, or one inspired by them, a poet.

In the end we discover that the Sirens, along with the funeral marker and urn, all of which disclose the life and qualities of Baucis, are merely metonyms for Erinna's words, which the poet has caused to be inscribed upon the tomb. As the composer of these verses she creates an odd conflation of monument, commemorated, Siren, and self. These four entities—all ostensibly the first-person narrator of the verses—meld into one, so that not only are Erinna and Baucis virtually indistinguishable one from the other, but they are further given the allure and knowledge of creatures known for their powers of seduction. This charm does not place in peril those who come in contact with the monument; it does, however, strongly articulate Erinna's self-identity within the context of this poem. Naming herself last, the accretion of speakers culminates finally in her own poetic voice, at once inextricable from the others, and yet dominating, since she is the artisan who has imposed the words upon the stone. Her own identity, then, exists not only as an aspect of Baucis (as observed in the *Distaff*), but also as a quasi-historian (or epic poet?

or mythical creature?) who has the final word. Erinna, by giving a Siren's voice to Baucis and in the end appropriating it as her own, deftly positions both herself and her audience in the position of Odysseus. As mourner, Erinna too must negotiate the space between approaching too close and maintaining her distance.

In *AP* 7.712 the stele exhorts passersby to engage in dialogue with Hades, creating a chain of addressees. To those who utter the words that the tomb encourages them to say, the monument responds with the tale of Baucis' funeral: how her bridegroom's father lit her pyre with the wedding torches. The final couplet, addressed to Hymenaios, accuses him of transforming a wedding song into a dirge. In this epigram, whose topic is so similar to that of *AP* 7.710, the voice of "Erinna" as narrator is palpably absent. In her stead there is the responsion of a variety of subjects: a dialogue between the stele and the addressee, an enjoinder by the addressee to Hades, and a direct address to Hymenaios. As in the torty-tortoise refrain, each subject is given the opportunity to articulate his or her loss, and so the tomb recounts the death of Baucis, the "reader" of the inscription scolds Hades for the theft, and Hymenaios alters his song. Although voice is not constructed as it is in the *Distaff* and *AP* 7.710 with Erinna herself as the narrating "I," nevertheless the theme of loss is articulated through the employment of a series of voices, each of which alternately assumes the position of the bereaved, creating an opportunity for identification (among all the subjects, and between the subjects and Baucis), yet simultaneously articulating the failure of reunion.

Erinna's final epigram is unlike the rest of her extant corpus in that the death of Baucis is no longer the subject. Instead she describes a portrait of a woman:

> Ἐξ ἀταλᾶν χειρῶν τάδε γράμματα· λῷστε Προμαθεῦ,
>   ἔντι καὶ ἄνθρωποι τὶν ὁμαλοὶ σοφίαν·
> ταύταν γοῦν ἐτύμως τὰν παρθένον ὅστις ἔγραψεν,
>   αἰ καὐδὰν ποτέθηκ᾿, ἧς κ᾿ Ἀγαθαρχὶς ὅλα.   (*AP* 6.352)

> These figures from tender hands: My good friend Prometheus,
>   there are men even equal to you in wisdom.[24]
> Whoever drew this maiden so true to life
>   if he had also added a voice, it would be the complete
>   Agatharchis.

The poet intimates that the only element that distinguishes the actual Agatharchis from her painted representation is voice. A pictorial representation of a human can approximate reality but cannot quite achieve it. The poem suggests that the animation of the inanimate (or the process by which an object acquires a "life") is achieved by providing it with a voice, by which it is recognized as an individual. It is here that we observe Erinna in the true role of poet (both versifier and "maker"), for as good as craftsmen like Prometheus and his progeny are, they are not equipped to endow a figure with a voice. What these men produce is representation, and no matter its quality, it can never provide verisimilitude. The only way for an artifact to become "real,' it seems, is through the intervention of a poet—who can endow it with the capacity for speech.

Given Erinna's emphasis on the role of voice in fashioning a self—in particular, a poetic female "I"—the emphasis on the endowment to Agatharchis of a voice of her own to make her complete seems more than coincidental. Erinna strongly identifies female animation and perhaps even volition with the capacity to speak, all the while realizing that female speech is in some sense transgressive, that a female who is mindful of her speech is forgetful of something else. It is Baucis' muteness—rendered by both her marriage and her death—that creates the separation and the difference between them. Likewise, Agatharchis is no more than a painting. The distance between the viewer and the viewed exists because this Agatharchis is not a vocal "I." Yet Erinna's poetic foray, her brief description of the painting, her privileging of the aural over the visual (much like the Sirens), makes an attempt to bridge a gap similar to that which exists between the poet and her subject in the *Distaff.*

In each epigram, speech marks the difference between the characters: the painting from the human, the stele from Erinna, the passerby from the tomb. Moreover, the distinction rests on a dichotomy between artifice and reality. For Erinna, vocalization makes something real, actuating it and bringing it to life. The voice provides a tangible means to distinguish self from other, animate from inanimate. Thus, the narrator's voice in the *Distaff* alternately shouts (16), cries out (18), and laments (33, 48). By voicing her anguish the narrator makes real her sorrow and performs it, even though she is forbidden from attending her companion's funeral. The paradox is that, as a poet, Erinna is far from forbidden to mourn. In fact, her vocation as poet allows her to speak on the page (or the tomb, or the painting) through which she fashions memory into a literary form. Through her poetry, and specifically through her emphasis on loss including the loss of voice, Erinna creates a poetic persona, recognizably feminine, yet distinct from her companion. Thus, she transforms the everyday traditions of her companions' lives into a rich tapestry, which both marks the poet as part of a larger female community and yet distinguishes her through her role as poet. In this way she preserves the rituals and interests of women—and the memory of a particular woman—even as she forges beyond them.

NOTES

1. Interpretations of the *Distaff* are all indebted to the pioneering work of Bowra 1953b, whose reading has framed and perhaps colored all subsequent interpretations. The *Suda* tells us that the *Distaff* was a poem of three hundred hexameters, written in an Aeolic-Doric dialect. The portion extant most likely represents the last sixth of the poem (Neri 1997, 62–63; West 1977, 112). For an excellent introduction to the questions surrounding Erinna's poetry and life, see Snyder 1989, 86–97.

2. In addition to the difficulties of interpreting Erinna's poetry, multiple other problems surround her work. On the text of the *Distaff*, see Vitelli 1929, Edmonds 1938, Latte 1953, Levin 1962, West 1977, Lloyd-Jones and Parsons 1983, Pardini 1991, and Neri 1997. On the title of Erinna's major work, see Levin 1962, and Cameron and Cameron 1969. On the controversy surrounding her homeland and biography, see Luck 1954, Levin 1962, Vara 1972 and 1973, and Arthur 1980. Magrini (1975, 225) provides a very comprehensive bibliography on Erinna up to 1973.

3. The discipline of psychoanalysis is populated with practitioners and theorists who espouse diverse and provocative theories on ego formation, though the length and scope of this paper do not allow for their articulation. For further reading on the development of the ego in children, see Tyson and Tyson 1990. For a lucid and illuminating reading of Freud's theory of ego development, see Lear 1990, 156–82. Ego psychology until recently held sway in the United States; one finds some of its more elegant arguments in Hartmann 1964. Lacan 1988 articulates many of his ideas about the ego in *Séminaire* II. For a critical re-reading of Lacanian notions of the ego and their intersections with gender, see Ragland-Sullivan 1989.

4. Because Erinna is both the author of and a narrator in the *Distaff*, it seems necessary to distinguish the poet from the poetic character. Thus, I employ quotation marks when speaking only of the poetic character.

5. My translation of the *Distaff* is based primarily upon the text found in Lloyd-Jones and Parsons 1983. I include some reconstructions suggested by Bowra 1953b, West 1977, and Neri 1997. Though shorter fragments both precede and follow this portion of the papyrus, I have chosen not to translate them here, though I do occasionally refer to them.

6. The poetry of Erinna was well known, as epigrams such as *AP* 7.12, 7.713, 9.190, and 11.322 attest, and the narrator of the *Distaff* is unambiguously female. Yet, Erinna's status as a female poet was, no doubt, circumscribed by the patriarchal society in which she wrote and the tradition of women's writing

available to her. On the "choice" of female Greek poets to write primarily lyric poetry rather than more "public" genres such as epic and elegy, see Gutzwiller 1997, 204. On the transformation of women's traditional poetry into literary formulations, see Skinner 1993b, 131.

7. Gutzwiller's (1997) larger argument contends that the *Distaff* demonstrates a double debt, to both Homer and Sappho. Rauk 1989 also observes Sapphic influence in the *Distaff*, most notably similarities between it and Lobel-Page 1993 (hereafter cited as Lobel-Page), 94. Note also that Alexiou (1974, 13, 103) describes the *goos* as improvisational, and spoken not sung.

8. Gutzwiller 1997 observes that the Homeric *gooi* demonstrate a concern with what will happen to the speaker now that the male warrior has died. Murnaghan 1999 instead investigates women's lament as subversive, contributing an alternate voice and complicating our notions of epic.

9. Arthur (1980, 63–64) observes that maidens and older unmarried women occupy the same "symbolic field." As an unmarried woman of marriageable age, Erinna separates herself out yet again from women who pursue traditional paths. West (1977, 110–11) suggests that Erinna anticipates her fate as a (gray-haired) old woman in lines 45–46.

10. Stehle 2001 has recently argued persuasively that Erinna constructs "herself" as an obedient daughter through the use of motion. That is, motions (e.g. movement outside of the home) are conceived of as transgressive for a female, whereas "Erinna," the "good" daughter, sits in the home working her distaff. An issue that Stehle's article raises but never addresses outright is the extent to which Baucis moves, and how she might have been written as a "bad" daughter, who perhaps committed some violation of Greek mores.

11. The call-and-response structure of the "torty-tortoise" poem is itself suggestive of female lament. Cf. Hom. *Il.* 24.720–22, 746, and Soph. *El.* 823–70 in which women respond to the woman reciting the *goos*. Seremetakis (1991, 99–100) argues that the primary characteristic of female lament in modern-day Greece is its antiphony, which she asserts provides a means for women to establish themselves and exercise influence socially and politically within a male-dominated culture. Cf. Arthur 1980, 61.

12. Magrini (1975, 229–33) reads the χελύννα as a lyre rather than a tortoise. West (1977, 102) effectively counters the argument. Neri 1998 discusses the numphai as dolls that, like the tortoise, both have associations with marriage and allow girls to pretend they are women.

13. Griffith and Griffith (1991, 85) read the girls as actors (*attori*) playing two roles.

14. Arthur (1980, 61–64) reads the movement differently. She sees the tortoise game as manifestation of Erinna's self-conscious employment of commonplace female activities, which then come symbolically to represent both "Erinna" and Baucis. Erinna takes these conventional symbols and invests them with "personal and poetic meaning," reflecting her own situation and her "other self" along her journey of self-knowledge (65).

15. Arthur (1980, 64–65) persuasively argues that Mormo is a site onto which the poet can map both the experiences of Baucis and "Erinna." Johnston 1999 provides detailed analysis of the nature of Mormo and other spirits related to her.

16. Indeed, this is the conjecture of others, including Bowra 1953b, Gutzwiller 1997, and Stehle 2001.

17. Scholars have long debated why "Erinna" was barred from attending Baucis' funeral. See Bowra 1953b, West 1977, Barnard 1978, Arthur 1980.

18. Likewise, unmarried women were referred to as "brides of Hades" (e.g. Eur. *IA* 460–61, Soph. *Ant.* 810–13).

19. Erinna's emphasis on voice and silence is strengthened by lines from the *Distaff* quoted by Stobaeus (4.51.4): "From here to Hades an empty echo penetrates./ There is silence among the dead, and darkness flows down upon their eyes" (τουτόθεν εἰς ᾿Αίδαν κενεὰ διανήχεται ἀχώ./ σιγὰ δ᾽ ἐν νεκύεσσι, τὸ δὲ σκότος ὄσσε καταγρεῖ).

20. For years scholars have asserted and attempted to prove details of Erinna's life: that she originated from Tenos or Telos or elsewhere, that she died at the age of nineteen, that she never married. I think it can be convincingly argued that part of the conceit of the poem requires Erinna to be an unwed girl of nineteen and that this potentially creates interesting echoes throughout her magnum opus, such as the connection between the "old maid" Erinna and others who spin, like the Moirai and Muses, as Arthur notes (1980, 63–64). However, there is no credible evidence that she was nineteen when she wrote the poem, that she died soon thereafter, or that she remained unmarried.

21. Cf. Magrini 1975, 236.

22. Examples from the seventh book of the *Anthologia Palatina* abound, attesting to these tropes as a commonplace, e.g. *AP* 7.15, 17, 26 (the commemorated speaks) and *AP* 7.2, 37, 38 (the monument speaks).

23. Tedesco 1994 investigates the history of the Siren by starting with the difference in the descriptions by Homer and Pindar. Cf. Pollard 1965, 133–34, and de Rachewiltz 1987, 4–5. De Rachewiltz (17–21 observes that the island of the Sirens has numerous qualities that would associate it with death and the Underworld.

24. My translation of τὰ γράμματα as "figures" arises from the ambiguity of the term. Though it surely refers to the portrait of Agatharcis, if translated as "words" it could refer to the poem itself. Note the use of τὸ γράμμα in *AP* 7.710.8 to refer to Erinna's inscription, that is, the poem itself.

5   Homer's Mother

Marilyn B. Skinner

for Daniel

Let me begin at the very end with one of the more curious *testimonia* to the life of a poet surviving from antiquity.[1] Early in the sixth century CE, Christodorus of Coptus in Egypt composed an ecphrastic account of more than eighty bronze statues adorning the baths of Zeuxippus at Constantinople.[2] His descriptions now comprise the entire second book of the *Greek Anthology*.[3] Among those statues stood one of Homer—not the epic poet, Christodorus explains, but a namesake (*Anth. Pal.* 2.407–413):

Ἵστατο δ᾽ ἄλλος Ὅμηρος, ὃν οὐ πρόμον εὐεπιάων
θέσκελον υἷα Μέλητος ἐϋρρείοντος ὀΐω,
ἀλλ᾽ ὃν Θρηϊκίῃσι παρ᾽ ἠόσι γείνατο μήτηρ
Μοιρὼ κυδαλίμη Βυζαντιάς, ἣν ἔτι παιδνὴν
ἔτρεφον εὐεπίης ἡρωΐδος ἴδμονα Μοῦσαι·
κεῖνος γὰρ τραγικῆς πινυτὴν ἠσκήσατο τέχνην,
κοσμήσας ἐπέεσσιν ἐὴν Βυζαντίδα πάτρην.

And there stood another Homer—whom I deem to be not the foremost of epic poets, the god-inspired son of the well-flowing Meles, but him that by Thracian shores his mother Moero bore, the renowned Byzantine, she whom, while still a little girl, the Muses brought up to be skilled in heroic epic. For he himself practiced the learned craft of tragedy, honoring with his verses his native city Byzantium.

Homerus of Byzantium was indeed a noteworthy figure, celebrated not only in his birthplace but also at Alexandria, where he was included as one of the "Pleiad," a group of eight outstanding Hellenistic tragedians.[4] Yet in subsequent literary history his own accomplishments are frequently overshadowed by those of his mother, Moero—as seen here, where she intrudes into the description of her son's honorific statue and claims three of its seven lines for herself. While it is not uncommon for the sons of illustrious Greeks to be identified by their more distinguished fathers, to be designated as the offspring of one's mother is highly unusual and, in classical Athens at least, would have been a terrible insult. This in itself indicates that Moero had a substantial reputation in antiquity, one that persisted, if only at second or third hand, into Christodorus' time and even beyond.[5] In this chapter I propose to review the evidence for her literary activities and reexamine the admittedly scanty remains of her work. There are grounds for revising the date of Moero's literary activity downward, which could in turn explain the close association of mother and son in the biographical tradition. This hypothesis has a further corollary: despite the all but complete loss of what was apparently a large and varied corpus of writings, we may also recover an aspect of Moero's artistic self-fashioning that casts light on that of yet another female poet, the Roman elegist Sulpicia.

Information about Moero's life and career is scattered, and assembling it is made somewhat more difficult by divergent spellings of her name. In a marginal annotation to Parthenius' *Erotica Pathemata* 27, and at Athenaeus'[6] *Deipnosophistae* 11.490e and 491a and several passages in the *Palatine Anthology*, she is called Μοιρώ.[7] Other sources, mostly late, transmit the name as Μυρώ.[8] Baale's attempt (1903, 32–33) to show on the basis of inscriptions and literary parallels that the spelling with upsilon was the correct one runs into trouble because, in the commonly occurring masculine proper name Myron, the first vowel is always short.[9] Likewise, Geffcken's effort (1932, 2512) to explain the alternative form as a simple case of vowel substitution fails to account for the difference in quantity. As the *lectio difficilior*, Μοιρώ must be the right form. The existence of the variant Myro can be traced back to the occurrence of the name in Anyte's epigram Gow and Page (G-P) (*Anth. Pal.* 7.190), which, I argue, is probably a playful *hommage* to the poet from Byzantium.

Moero's date can be roughly established by the *Suda*'s specification of the one hundred and twenty-fourth Olympiad (284–281 BCE) as the *floruit* of her son.[10] She would therefore have been born in the last quarter of the fourth century, at least one generation after Erinna, author of the *Distaff*, and perhaps a little earlier than the epigrammatists Anyte and Nossis, two other canonical female poets.[11] The *Suda* entry on her is brief, identifying her as a Byzantine, a writer of epic, elegiac, and lyric verse (ποιήτρια ἐπῶν καὶ ἐλεγείων καὶ μελῶν), the daughter [*sic*] of Homerus the tragedian, and the wife of Andromachus, nicknamed "the philologist."[12] None of her lyrics survive, but we know of a hymn to Poseidon, mentioned by Eustathius (ad. *IL*. 2.711 van der Valk). We do possess a ten-line hexameter fragment of her epic or epyllion *Mnemosyne*; a prose summary of a tale from an episodic poem, the *Arai* or "Curses," composed in either hexameters or elegiacs; and two elegiac quatrains preserved by Meleager in his *Garland*. Since the majority of the *testimonia* have to do with her longer works, we can begin with those.

EPIC NARRATIVE

In the course of his description of Thebes, Pausanias records that Myro of Byzantium claimed its founder, Amphion, was rewarded with a lyre by Hermes in return for setting up the first altar to the god (9.5.8).[13] The context suggests she was following the lead of an anonymous epic predecessor who had portrayed Amphion as the earliest harpist, taught by Hermes himself. Her poem thus offered a rationale for the divine favor bestowed upon the young musician.[14] In Euripides' *Antiope*, the most influential treatment of this myth, Amphion had defended the contemplative life in the face of objections by his twin brother, Zethos, the man of action.[15] Like Orpheus, he had accordingly become a stock type of the creative artist. If the figure of Amphion played a prominent role in Moero's poem, its theme may have been consciously self-reflexive, in the fashion of much other Hellenistic poetry.

This notion is admittedly speculative, but we can speak more confidently about the hexameter narrative *Mnemosyne*, ten lines of which are quoted by Athenaeus in the *Deipnosophistae* (11.491b = fr. 1 Powell):

Ζεὺσ δ' ἄρ' ἐνὶ Κρήτῃ τρέφετο ηέγας, οὐδ' ἄρα τίς νιν
ηείδει ηακάρων· ὁ δ' ἀέξετο πᾶσι ηέλεσσι.
Τὸν μὲν ἄρα τρήρωνες ὑπὸ ζαδέῳ τράφον ἄντρῳ
ἀμβροσίην φορέουσαι ἀπ' Ὠκεανοῖο ῥοάων·

νέκταρ δ' ἐκ πέτρης μέγας αἰετὸς αἰὲν ἀφύσσων   5
γαμφηλῇς φορέεσκε ποτὸν Διὶ μητιόεντι.
Τῷ καὶ νικήσας πατέρα Κρόνον εὐρύοπα Ζεὺς
ἀθάνατον ποίησε καψι οὐρανῷ ἐγκατένασσεν.
Ὣς δ' αὕτως τρήρωσι πελειάσιν ὤπασε τιμήν,
αἳ δή τοι θέρεος καὶ χείματος ἄγγελοί εἰσιν.   10

Then in Crete Zeus was nursed to maturity, nor did any of the blessed
ones know of him. And he grew great in all his limbs. Timid creatures
nourished him within a sacred cave, bearing ambrosia from the streams of
Ocean. And a great eagle constantly drawing nectar from a rock kept
bringing it in his beak for prudent Zeus to drink. Therefore, after conquering his father Cronus, far-thundering Zeus also made the eagle
immortal and established him in the heavens. In like fashion he bestowed
honor on the timid doves, who are, as you know [*hai dê toi*], the messen-
gers of summer and winter.

The title *Mnemosyne* obviously refers to the mother of the nine Muses,
which would lead us to believe that the poem was concerned with
aspects of poetic creation. At first glance, however, this episode, which
rehearses the sacred tale of Zeus' boyhood on Crete, seems uncon-
nected with such issues. Yet Athenaeus has already informed us (490e)
that matters of Homeric scholarship are being addressed here, because
Moero is proposing a solution to a famous crux.[16] Warning Odysseus
about the Clashing Rocks in book 12 of the *Odyssey*, Circe states that
nothing can fly between them safely: τῇ μέν τ' οὐδὲ ποτητὰ παρέρχε-
ται οὐδὲ πέλειαι/ τρήρωνες, ταί τ' ἀμβροσίην Διὶ πατρὶ φέρουσιν
(by that way no winged things pass through, not even the timid
doves [*peleiai*] that bear ambrosia to father Zeus, 62–63). Alexandrian commentators, preoccupied with epic decorum, had thought it
unseemly (ἄσεμνον γάρ, Ath. 11.490b) that mere birds perform the
office of bringing Zeus ambrosia to drink.

However, use of the expanded form *Peleiades* as a substitute for
Pleiades, the familiar name of the constellation, was a verse convention reaching back through tragic and lyric poetry to the *Astronomia*
attributed to Hesiod. Athenaeus cites three separate phrases from that
poem, all illustrating the same usage (frr. 288–90 Merkelbach and
West 1967, *ap.* Ath. 11.491d). Having reminded readers of the Homeric problem by incorporating the phrase "timid doves" into line 9
(τρήρωσι πελειάσιν), Moero takes the bold step of conflating birds

and star-cluster: when she tells us that they are now the heralds of the
seasons, she unmasks them as the Pleiades. To clinch this identification, she echoes two celebrated episodes in Hesiod, the deception of
Cronus (*Th.* 477–91) and the advice to Perses on the proper seasons
to plough and reap (*Op.* 383–95).[17] Zeus' hidden presence in the
sacred cave (ὑπὸ ζαθέῳ . . . ἄντρῳ) recalls Gaia concealing Zeus "in a
deep cave, below the depths of the sacred earth" (ἄντρῳ ἐν ἠλιβάτῳ,
ζαθέης ὑπὸ κεύθεσι γαίης, *Th.* 483). The revelation that Homer's so-
called doves are in fact the daughters of Atlas is introduced with the
same collocation, *hai dê toi*, with which Hesiod, addressing Perses,
had called attention to their forty-day absence from view after setting
(*Op.* 385). Through these intertextual flourishes, the last line exhibits
due Hellenistic wit and learning as it scores its academic point.

We can pursue this line of investigation further by examining
other poetic passages that bear some resemblance to the *Mnemosyne*
excerpt. Corinna, a Boeotian lyric poet, retells the story of Zeus'
birth from a feminine perspective (*PMG* 654.i.12–18) by playing up
the honor earned by his mother, Rhea, for outwitting Cronus and
saving her son (Rayor 1993, 224–26). Although the question remains
unresolved, scholarly opinion is shifting toward a Hellenistic, rather
than archaic, date for Corinna.[18] In any case, Corinna's focus upon
the role of the mother as rescuer is analogous to Moero's emphasis
upon the kourotrophic role of the eagle and the *Peleiades*. Each
author recasts the Hesiodic creation myth to foreground female
heroism and underscore the infant Zeus' helplessness.

While the parallels between Corinna's use and Moero's use of
Hesiod cannot be pressed too far, comparison of the *Mnemosyne*
passage with Aratus' didactic poem *Phaenomena* sheds further light
on its author's literary strategies. First, we may observe a lexical
similarity: after describing and naming the seven Pleiades, Aratus
states that Zeus "ordered them to indicate that both summer and
winter are beginning" (σφισι καὶ θέρεος καὶ χείματος ἀρχομένοιο/
σημαίνειν ἐκέλευσεν, *Phaen.* 266–67). Moero too employs the
phrase *thereos kai cheimatos*, "summer and winter" (10), although
in speaking of the Pleiades it may well have been formulaic. One
other instance of correspondence is structural, however, and the
resemblance is close enough to preclude coincidence. Embarking
upon his description of the heavens, Aratus begins with the Greater
and Lesser Bears, Helice and Cynosura, whose mythic origins he
narrates. Like Moero's *Peleiades*, these were Zeus' former caretakers

on Crete, rewarded for fostering him by being transformed into major constellations (*Phaen.* 30–35):

> . . . εἰ ἐτεὸν δή,   30
> Κρήτηθεν κεῖναί γε Διὸς μεγάλου ἰότητι
> οὐρανὸν εἰσανέβησαν, ὅ μιν τότε κουρίζοντα
> Δίκτῳ ἐν εὐώδει, ὄρεος σχεδὸν Ἰδαίοιο,
> ἄντρῳ ἐγκατέθεντο καὶ ἔτρεφον εἰς ἐνιαυτόν
> Δικταῖοι Κούρητες ὅτε Κρόνον ἐψεύδοντο.   35

If it is in fact true, they [the Bears] mounted up from Crete to heaven at the desire of great Zeus, because, when he was then a child in fragrant Dicte near Mount Ida, they brought him into a cave and nursed him for a year while the Kouretes of Dicte were deceiving Cronus.

Aratus begins by doubting his source, *ei eteon dê*. Affected uncertainty on the part of the narrator about the credibility of his account points to a local myth treated in an earlier text. That source was probably not Hesiodic, because in a fragment ascribed to the *Pelasgi Progenies* it is not Helice but instead the nymph Callisto who is metamorphosed into the Great Bear (fr. 163 Merkelbach and West 1967 = ps.-Eratosth. *Catast.* 1). Nor could Aratus have taken the tale from Eudoxus' prose *Phaenomena*, which he mined for its astronomical data: surviving fragments indicate that the latter treatise presented a dry and schematic treatment of the various constellations.[19] We should also observe that this episode departs from the well-known account of Zeus' infancy in which he is tended by the Cretan nymphs Adrastia and Ida, daughters of Melisseus, and fed on the milk of the she-goat Amalthea (as in Apollodorus 1.1.6–7). Two of Aratus' contemporaries, Callimachus (*Hymn to Zeus* 45–48) and Apollonius Rhodius (3.133–34), mention the version featuring nymphs and she-goat, so it was doubtless the most popular account in circulation at that time. However, Amalthea does appear later in the *Phaenomena* as the star Aix, "who, as the story goes, gave the breast to Zeus" (τὴν μέν τε λόγος Διὶ μαζὸν ἐπισχεῖν, 163). This substitution at the outset of bears for the more familiar Cretan nymphs must be an intentional deviation from the norm.

Ancient testimony to the location of an Arkesion, or "Bears' Cave," on Mount Ida supports the assumption that the remote antecedent of the story is an indigenous Cretan legend of Zeus being nursed by female bears (Gundel 1924, 40). Imported into the mainstream literary tradition, the myth was then fused by some previous author—or, conceivably, by Aratus himself—with the aetiological component of the bears' transformation into heavenly bodies.[20] Structurally, Moero's tale of the Pleiades offers a striking parallel: Zeus' Cretan nurses, whether doves or bears, are rewarded by becoming important star-clusters and key weather signs. Since the existence of the Arkesion confirms the primacy of the version in which bears are featured, Moero's must be the derivative account, an imitation consciously recalling its source text. The allusion is mischievous, for bears are at home in caves whereas doves, especially timid ones, are not.

In addition to proposing a solution to a Homeric problem, then, Moero is also engaging in intertextual dialogue with a literary predecessor. If Aratus found the motifs of nurture and catasterism combined in a preexisting text, she could be independently emulating the same source. The alternative possibility is that Moero is echoing the *Phaenomena*. Aratus was a close contemporary, born, like her, in the last decades of the fourth century. We have no exact date for the publication of the *Phaenomena*, but if we can trust ancient testimony (e.g., *Vit.* 1.38–43 = Martin 153) that it was undertaken at the suggestion of Antigonus Gonatas, who had invited Aratus to his court, the *terminus post quem* must be Antigonus' assumption of the throne of Macedon in 282 BCE. We do know that Aratus' didactic poem achieved immediate fame upon its appearance.[21] An arch gesture toward a current best-seller would be as much in keeping with Hellenistic literary practice as a bookish reminiscence of an old and perhaps arcane informant.

If that is the case—and, on reflection, it is the more likely option because it bypasses the need to posit an otherwise unknown intermediary—we can draw one further inference. Moero was still poetically active when her son Homerus was a grown man, for, as noted earlier, he himself is attested as writing in the late 280s. This conclusion seems to contradict the biographical information supplied by Christodorus, who states that Moero composed epic verse while only a girl, *eti paidnēn* (*Anth. Pal.* 2.410). Of course, Christodorus or his sources could have got it wrong, perhaps confusing her with Erinna, who represented herself in the *Distaff* as a nineteen-year-old maiden.[22] Or the late antique poet might be aware of verse narratives other than the *Mnemosyne* that Moero produced at the outset of her poetic career. Yet another possibility, however, is that he is referring to a narrative persona affected in her compositions. What modern critics have found jejune about her ten-line fragment—

its paratactic style and stilted archaic diction—could be explained by her writing in the character of a young girl.[23] The artlessness of the actual narration would then be undercut by provocative recollections of other texts and deft interventions in academic controversies.[24] This suggestion, albeit tentative, would further explain the title *Mnemosyne* as a double entendre, referring not only to the mother of the Muses but also to the poetic memory of the author.

CURSE POETRY

Parthenius in his *Erotica Pathêmata* (27) offers a synopsis of the tale of Alcinoe, who was punished by Athena for withholding a servant's wages:

Ἔχει δὲ λόγος καὶ ᾿Αλκινόην, τὴν Πολύβου ἠὲν τοῦ Κορινθίου
θυγατέρα, γυναῖκα δὲ ᾿Αμφιλόχου τοῦ Δρύαντος, κατὰ μῆνιν
᾿Αθηνᾶς ἐπιμανῆναι ξένῳ (Χαμίῳ αὐτῷ ὄνομα). ἐπὶ μισθῷ
γὰρ αὐτὴν ἀγαγομένην χερωῆτιν γυναῖκα Νικάνδρην καὶ
ἐργασαμένην ἐνιαυτόν, ὕστερον ἐκ τῶν οἰκείων ἐλάσαι μὴ ἐντελῆ
τὸν μισθὸν ἀποδοῦσαν· τὴν δὲ ἀράσασθαι πολλὰ ᾿Αθηνᾷ
τείσασθαι αὐτὴν ἀντ᾿ ἀδίκου στερήσεως. (2) ὅθεν εἰς τοσοῦτον
[τε]
ἐλθεῖν, ὥστε ἀπολιπεῖν οἶκόν τε καὶ παῖδας ἤδη γεγονότας
συνεκπλεῦσαί τε τῷ Χάνθῳ. γενομένην δὲ κατὰ μέσον πόρον
ἔννοιαν λαβεῖν τῶν εἰργασμένων, καὶ αὐτίκα πολλά τε δάκρυα
προίεσθαι καὶ ἀνακαλεῖν, ὁτὲ μὲν ἄνδρα κουρίδιον, ὁτὲ δὲ τοὺς
παῖδας, τέλος δέ, πολλὰ τοῦ Χάνθου παρηγοροῦντος καὶ
φαμένου γυναῖκα ἕξειν, μὴ πειθομένην ῥῖψαι ἑαυτὴν εἰς θάλασσαν.

There is likewise a story that Alcinoe, the daughter of Polybius of Corinth, wife of Amphilochus son of Dryas, became madly infatuated with a Samian stranger, whose name was Xanthus, through the wrath of Athena. For Alcinoe had hired for pay a working woman named Nicandra, and later, when the year was up, drove her from the house without paying her full wages. She prayed fervently to Athena to requite Alcinoe for her unjust retention. So it came to such a pass that Alcinoe left her house and the children already born to her and sailed off with Xanthus. But when she was in the midst of the voyage a realization took hold of her of what she had done and immediately she shed many tears and invoked the names, now of her lawful husband, now of her

children, and finally, though Xanthus consoled her mightily and promised
to marry her, unpersuaded, she threw herself into the sea.

The attached manchette, or brief ascription, informs us that Moero
tells the story in her *Curses* ('Aραί).[25] Nothing else is known about
this poem.[26] Comparison with other specimens of Hellenistic curse
poetry, however, can help to locate the story Parthenius sketches
within an ostensible generic context.

The curse poem, whose most notorious exemplar was Callimachus' lost *Ibis*, was an essentially frivolous art form. In the context
of an appeal to the gods for justice and vengeance, a catalogue of
horrific punishments, each illustrated by reference to some historical
or mythic prototype, is called down upon the offender, whose misdeed—stealing a cup, for instance—may be quite disproportionate
to the consequences wished upon him.[27] Such evils can include ill-
fated marriages, shipwreck, incest, cannibalism, death at the hands of
family members, and continued punishment in the afterlife; several
examples of similar fates may be lumped together consecutively, as in
the roll call of murderous brides at Euphorion *Thrax* fr. C col. i.6–17
(*SH* 415). Although curses in real life were a serious business, these
literary imprecations are intentionally over the top; their combination
of pedantic obscurity with extreme brutality is designed to generate
amusement. Even Ovid's *Ibis*, which professes to be motivated by a
genuine injury sustained during the poet's exile, ends with an anticlimactic threat of further invective, patently ridiculous in view of what
has gone before.[28] The ancient reader would therefore approach
Hellenistic curse poetry in a spirit of fun, even though a modern
audience finds it hard to appreciate the humor in narratives of sadism
and violence.

In the *Erotica Pathêmata*, two narratives besides that of Alcinoe
are ascribed to a curse poem. Both the legend of Harpalyce (13),
involving paternal incest, child murder, anthropophagy, and metamorphosis, and that of Apriate (26), which deals with attempted
rape, murder or suicide of the victim, and the later violent death of the
perpetrator, are credited in accompanying manchettes to Euphorion's
Thrax. Since in each case fragments of Euphorion's version luckily
survive, we can observe that what are brief accounts in the *Thrax*,
conforming to the conventions of the genre, are expanded in the
Erotica Pathêmata into detailed anecdotes.[29] This establishes that
Euphorion was not Parthenius' actual source or, at least, not his
only one, which in turn raises suspicions as to how much of the

Alcinoe story was actually taken from Moero. If the *Arai* corresponded to the pattern of other Hellenistic curse poems, the answer would probably be "not very much." This heroine would have been one of several, and readers would have been told only enough of her fate to let them recall the full circumstances, provided they were learned enough to do so. But did the *Arai* in fact resemble the *Thrax?*

Perhaps not. In its tone and incidents, the tale of Alcinoe is not like those found in Euphorion's work. Measured by the standards of Hellenistic sensationalism, the protagonist's original misdeed is a prosaic, bourgeois one, and although her rash infatuation and hasty repentance are melodramatic enough, there is no outlandish horror, and her death is pathetic rather than shocking. There are also a few intriguing elements. Athena is invoked by Nicandra because she is the patroness of weavers (Lightfoot 1999, 522). Although her intervention in that capacity is appropriate, the kind of punishment she inflicts upon Alcinoe is not in keeping with the character of a virgin goddess and is a vengeance regularly associated with Aphrodite. Again, both the heroine and her paramour have provocative names. Lightfoot (1999, 520–21) observes the similarity between Alcinoe and Alcyone, a name bestowed upon other heroines who perish by drowning, including the wife of Ceyx famously metamorphosed into a seabird (Ovid *Met.* 11.410–748). The name Xanthus suits a handsome philanderer; yet, in a context otherwise so reminiscent of Helen and Paris' elopement, one cannot help but recall that in both the *Iliad* and the *Odyssey* it is, ironically, the formulaic epithet of Helen's wronged husband.[30] Finally, the title *Arai* could equally well derive from one prominent incident in a longer narrative, even though it is obviously appropriate for an episodic catalogue of curses.[31] Hence it is possible that the account in Parthenius supplied the frame for a curse speech uttered by the disgruntled woolworker, which because of its dramatic centrality would have given the poem its title. Moero's inventiveness would then be displayed in the conflation of two previously distinct genres, epyllion (or idyll) and curse poem; one, in a focus on the subjectivity of the woolworker, reflecting Hellenistic preoccupation with daily life; and two, in retelling a high epic theme, the abduction of Helen, from a middle-class perspective. While this notion is advanced only as a conjecture, the points enumerated above appear to support the premise that Moero's composition was a bird of a different color from Callimachus' *Ibis.*

EPIGRAMS

Finally, let us turn to Moero's two elegiac quatrains. Each is an ecphrastic epigram featuring bold and imaginative portrayal of vegetation. The first (G-P 1 = *Anth. Pal.* 6.119) addresses a grape cluster dedicated to Aphrodite:

κεῖσαι δὴ χρυσέαν ὑπὸ παστάδα τὰν Ἀφροδίτας,
    βότρυ, Διωνύσου πληθόμενος σταγόνι,
οὐδ᾽ ἔτι τοι μάτηρ ἐρατὸν περὶ κλῆμα βαλοῦσα
    φύσει ὑπὲρ κρατὸς νεκτάρεον πέταλον.

You rest within the golden chamber of Aphrodite, cluster filled with the liquid of Dionysus. No longer will your mother, casting around you her lovely tendril, put forth a nectarous leaf over your head.

The epigram may have memorialized a dedication of real grapes, though that seems a somewhat trivial gift; alternatively, it might describe a still life painting of fruit, as in frescoes preserved at Pompeii. Whatever its presumed occasion, the poem's ostensible stylistic excesses displease modern readers. Luck (1954, 182) observed that the image of tender maternity in line 3 is actually a sepulchral formula and pronounced it a somewhat "false" and "insensitive" attempt at sentimentality. Snyder (1989, 85) concurs; in her opinion, the metaphors of the grapes as containers of wine and the vine as their mother are exaggerated and artificial.

Although this is a dedicatory epigram, its language is funereal throughout. While *keimai* (lie) is a colorless verb suitable for an object consecrated in a temple, it is often applied to fallen or buried corpses (LSJ 1:4–5), and the latter implications are clearly brought to the surface by the accompanying particle *dê.* "The emphasis conveyed by δή with verbs is for the most part pathetic in tone, and it is peculiarly at home in the great crises of drama, above all at moments when death or ruin is present or imminent" (Denniston 1950, 214).[32] These paratragic overtones are reinforced by *oud' eti,* for the complaint that an accustomed action will no longer be performed by or for the deceased is a topos of sepulchral epigram.[33] Although an isolated phrase might well aim at pathos, this pileup of threnodic expressions suggests parody—of what, we will consider shortly. Here I will simply remark that casting the vine as a bereaved mother is amusing, not maudlin, if taken as tongue in cheek.

Moero's other preserved epigram (G-P 2 = *Anth. Pal.* 6.189) assumes the form of a prayer on behalf of a dedicant:

Νύμφαι Ἁμαδρυάδες, ποταμοῦ κόραι, αἳ τάδε βένθη
    ἀμβρόσιαι ῥοδέοις στείβετε ποσσὶν ἀεί,
χαίρετε καὶ σῴζοιτε Κλεώνυμον, ὃς τάδε καλά
    εἵσαθ᾽ ὑπαὶ πιτύων ὔμμι, θεαί, ξόανα.

Hamadryad nymphs, daughters of the river, divinities who forever tread these depths with rosy feet, hail, and may you safeguard Cleonymus, who set up for you beneath the pines these lovely carvings.

The quatrain is reminiscent of Anyte's evocations of rural life in Arcadia, especially G-P 3 (*Anth. Pal.* 16.291), also involving a dedication to nymphs. Here the speaker requests a particular group of woodland spirits, the Hamadryads, to watch over the worshiper, presumably a shepherd, who has erected wooden statues in their honor. Much scholarly ink has been spilled over the identity of these divine beings: technically, Hamadryads are tree spirits, a species distinct from the water nymphs connoted by "daughters of the river."[34] Yet the metaphor might easily be applied to trees standing on the bank of a river and watered from that source (Waltz vol. 3 [1960] p. 101 n. 1), especially if the image of them treading the river bottom with their feet is understood as a whimsical description of roots extending out of the bank beneath the surface of the water.

The evocative features of these two poems are very much in keeping with the thematic interests of other female epigrammatists. Ecphrasis of nature and art was, as I have argued elsewhere (Skinner 2001), a preoccupation of Hellenistic women poets, recognized as gender specific by male contemporaries. What is striking about Moero's quatrains, however, is the visualization of natural entities in human terms and the imposition of anthropomorphic qualities upon them. Nothing similar is found in Erinna and Nossis, who instead concentrate upon describing the effect of the perceived object upon the viewer. The only epigrams comparable to Moero's in this respect are those of Anyte, particularly G-P 12 (*Anth. Pal.* 7.215), in which a stranded dolphin poignantly recalls his pleasure at leaping in the waves, and G-P 14 (*Anth. Pal.* 9.745), describing a mountain goat in a relief or a painting as being inordinately vain of his appearance.

Moero's indebtedness to Anyte is regularly assumed.[35] The poets are in fact mentioned together three times in the ancient *testimonia*, although two instances may be fortuitous. Antipater of Thessalonica leads off his canon of women writers with "Praxilla, Moero, [and] Anyte, the female Homer" (*Anth. Pal.* 9.26.3). This juxtaposition of names could be accidental, as there is no evident principle of organization, chronological or generic, in Antipater's list. Tatian's report (*ad Graec.* 33) that Cephisodotus, the son of Praxiteles, made statues of both Anyte and Moero also means little, since it occurs in a catalogue of portraits of female poets in which the names of several sculptors are repeated. However, Meleager's testimony carries considerably more weight. In the proem to the *Garland*, he couples Anyte and Moero as two varieties of the same species of flower (Baale 1903, 35): πολλὰ μὲν ἐμπλέξας Ἀνύτης κρίνα, πολλὰ δὲ Μοιροῦς/ λείρια (having entwined many white lilies of Anyte and many Madonna lilies of Moero, G-P 1.5–6). *Krinon* and *leirion* may be used as synonyms (Philinus *ap.* Ath. 15.681b, cf. Nicander *ap.* Ath. 15.683d, Dsc. 3.106 Sprengel).[36] Yet in the poetic tradition, the two names have distinct semiotic implications: the latter was associated with the delicate voice (ὄψ λειριόεσσα) of cicadas (*Il.* 3.152) and Muses (Hes. *Th.* 41); the former was an emblem of death.[37] Meleager's flower symbolism seems pointed, *krina* perhaps recalling Anyte's sepulchral epigrams on people and animals and *leiria* distinguishing Moero's verse for its musical features. It is evident that the anthologist perceived a close literary connection between the two women writers.[38]

Reciprocal intertextual echoes may lie behind this association. I have suggested above that Moero 1 is parodic. Linguistically and thematically, we find its closest echoes in Anyte's trademark epitaphs for animals, whose sentimentalism, though measured, might well tempt a lampoonist. For example, δή appears as the introductory particle of a funerary epigram three times in Anyte. In G-P 7.1 (*Anth. Pal.* 7.646), λοίσθια δὴ τάδε, it emphasizes that these were the *very last* words the dying girl Erato spoke to her father, a justifiably pathetic use (Geoghegan 1979, 82). However, Ὤλεο δή ποτε καὶ σύ (you too perished at length) at G-P 10.1 (Pollux 5.48) is an epic reminiscence addressed to a young hound[39] and οὐκέτι δή (no longer) is placed in the mouth of the dying dolphin (G-P 12.1 = *Anth. Pal.* 7.215). As an opening phrase, the collocation *ouketi dê* became formulaic for imitators of Anyte's animal epigrams, indicating that it must have struck her readers as idiosyncratic in that context.[40] I submit that Moero's introductory κεῖσαι δὴ and subsequent οὐδ' ἔτι replicate Anyte's linguistic mannerisms in memorializing dead animals; the joke consists in taking the humanizing process one degree further, into the realm of plant life. It is arguable, too, that the image of the vine as bereaved mother recalls funerary epigrams such as Anyte 5 (*Anth. Pal.* 7.486) and 7 (*Anth. Pal.* 7.646), in which the separation of child from grieving parent is fore-grounded.[41] Ancient parody frequently hinges upon incongruity (Herrlinger 1930, 72); on my reading, this would certainly be the case here.

We may now turn to Anyte's poetry. An ostensible funerary epigram (G-P 20 = *Anth. Pal.* 7.190) commemorates the tomb made by a little girl, Myro, for her two insect pets:[42]

ἀκρίδι τᾷ κατ᾽ ἄρουραν ἀηδόνι καὶ δρυοκοίτᾳ
    τέττιγι ξυνὸν τύμβον ἔτευξε Μυρώ,
παρθένιον στάξασα κόρα δάκρυ· δισσὰ γὰρ αὐτᾶς
    παίγνι᾽ ὁ δυσπειθὴς ᾤχετ᾽ ἔχων Ἀΐδας.

> For her grasshopper, the nightingale of ploughed land, and her oak-dwelling cicada Myro built a common mound, a maiden who shed a virginal tear, for Hades, hard to persuade, had carried off both her playthings.

This quatrain was well known to readers of the *Garland* in the first century CE.[43] Thus a garbled reference to it in the elder Pliny has justifiably puzzled commentators. At *Natural History* 34.57 Erinna's verse is cited as authority for the claim that the fifth-century BCE sculptor Myron constructed a memorial (*fecisse . . . monumentum*) for a cicada and a locust. Clearly Myro has been mistaken for the artist known, among other achievements, for his realistic image of a cow; but the confusion of two female poets is less explicable. Gutzwiller (1998, 66) infers that Anyte is imitating a lost epigram by Erinna. It is possible, however, that the faulty recollection of the compiler was triggered by an adaptation of Erinna's own language in the last line. The phrase βάσκανος ἔσσ᾽, Ἀΐδα (Hades, you are malicious) occurs in a sepulchral epigram ascribed to Erinna (G-P 2.3 = *Anth. Pal.* 7.712.3). Leonidas of Tarentum (or, alternatively, Meleager) quotes it as her most memorable phrase, with the implication that it was also found in the *Distaff* (Leon. 98.4 G-P = *Anth. Pal.* 7.13.4).[44] Anyte's epithet *duspeithês* (hard to persuade), characterizing the god as intractable, seems to echo Erinna's reproach of cruelty: in each case death is naively viewed from the perspective of a child's or of a young woman.

The picture of the little girl crying as she inters her pets is taken at face value in recent feminist readings of this quatrain, which speak of Anyte's insight into children's behavior (Barnard 1991, 167) and her delicate combination of compassion and mock solemnity (Snyder 1989, 72, Gutzwiller 1998, 65–67). However, the number of metapoetic tropes contained in these lines would suggest that their import is literary, rather than funereal. Apart from the allusion to Erinna, invoked as a female predecessor in the genre of *epicedeion*, cicadas and grasshoppers are, for Greek poets, quintessential songsters and emblems of their craft. If Myro is grieving for the loss of her pets' music, she is a girl of creative leanings (Gutzwiller 1998, 66–67).[45] The very word *paignia* (playthings) has an artistic pedigree, being the title of a book of epigrams by Anyte and Moero's older contemporary Philetas (frr. 10 and 11 Powell). Anyte, then, may be alluding to poems on insects composed by Moero.[46] When one ancient author speaks of another, it is conventional to represent the latter in a setting reminiscent of his or her verses; thus the Byzantine writer is depicted as herself burying the creatures she immortalized. The hypothesis that "Myro" was a sobriquet invented to suit this fiction—but not understood as such by later readers—would explain why the variant spelling of the poet's name entered the biographical tradition. If my interpretation is accepted, it provides corroboration that Moero had adopted the persona of a child in her writings, since she is again characterized as a small girl when her poetry is discussed.

CONCLUSION

Why would Moero have chosen to represent herself as a child? The first-person speaker of Erinna's *Distaff* was a young woman of marriageable age—a persona demanded by the dramatic scenario of the poem (Stehle 2001, 186). But that figure of a maiden poet putatively silenced by death touched a sentimental nerve in later Hellenistic authors, and its popularity might have given rise to a stereotype of precocious feminine creativity. Resorting to such self-characterization may also have been a defensive strategy to avoid possible stigma attached to the woman who assumes a male public role. Sappho had originally legitimated the function of poet for women, but her name had meantime been linked in Middle Comedy with sexual license, and claiming her as a precedent, as Nossis did, was to risk being tarred with the same brush—as happened to Nossis (Bowman 1998, 52–53). Self-portrayal as a preadolescent girl would deflect whatever sinister suspicion could threaten a respectable woman's claim to a public voice. Later, in a somewhat different literary environment, the Roman poet Sulpicia, while herself posing as a young girl, could interrogate the notion that female appropriation of a literary posture constitutes sexual exhibitionism (Flaschenreim 1999, 37–45). In his verse epistle to his supposed protégée Perilla (*Trista* 3.7), Ovid finally deconstructs the stereotype of virginal feminine creativity as an internalized mechanism of self-censorship.[47]

The icon of the gifted maiden silenced by untimely death—or timely marriage, for the two are symbolically equivalent—was gratifying to male readers because it reinforced a general belief that adult female nature was essentially oriented toward body rather than mind. In the case of Moero, though, it may be quite removed from historical reality. Even if the argument presented above for revising the date of her poetic activity downward is not accepted, she is still unlikely to have laid down her stylus upon marriage. Had this occurred, her name would not have been coupled so persistently with that of her son to a degree that casts even the achievements of his father into shadow. It is a more plausible hypothesis, instead, that she continued to be poetically active and maintained a high literary profile even after Homerus began his own writing career. Is it possible they gave readings together? Several inscriptions of the Hellenistic period commemorate visits by professional female poets who performed at civic festivals; would Moero have toured with her son, like Aristodamia, daughter of Amyntas of Smyrna, who traveled from city to city in the company of her brother?[48] We will never know, but it should be evident from the preceding observations that Homerus of Byzantium had a formidable maternal role model to live up to—or live down.

Let us hope he did not compose a tragedy on Orestes.

NOTES

1. My thanks to Ellen Greene and the helpful comments of the anonymous Press reader. The subject of this essay is referred to throughout as "Moero," the Latinized version of Greek *Moirô*. All translations are my own.

2. On Christodorus see *PLRE* 2:293.

3. After first circulating independently, Christodorus' poem may have been bound into a single Byzantine codex with the anthology of ancient epigrams, compiled about 900 CE by Constantine Cephalas that later became the basis of the Palatine and the Planudean Anthologies (Cameron 1993, 147–48).

4. On this group of tragedians, see Frazer 1972, 1:619–20.

5. Byzantine scholia to the metrical handbook (*Enchiridion*) of Hephaestion identify Homerus as ὁ Μυροῦς τῆς ποιητρίας υἱὸς τῆς Βυζαντίας (the son of the Byzantine poetess Moero), with no mention of his father, Andromachus (Consbruch 1906, 236, cf. p. 279), as does the tenth-century *Suda*, s.v. Σωσίθεος.

6. Athenaeus, from Egypt (circa 200 ACE), was a Greek author of a fifteen-book work called the *Deipnosophistae*, the *Learned Banquet*, in which he cited some 1,250 authors, including many early Greek lyric poets.

7. Apart from Christodorus' epigram, these passages include Meleager's preface to his *Garland* (*Anth. Pal.* 4.1.5), Antipater of Thessalonica's versified list of nine canonical woman poets (9.26.3), and the lemmata of the two epigrams ascribed to the poet herself (6.119 and 189). However, in the Palatine codex the scribe's reading Μοιροῦς Βυζαντίας (of Moero the Byzantine) in the lemma to 6.119 is corrected to Μυροῦς (of Myro) see Baale 1903, 31.

8. Pausanius 9.5.8, Tat. *ad Graec.* 33, two scholia to Hephaestion (Consbruch 1906, 236, 279), the *Suda* thrice (s.v.v. Μυρώ, Ὅμερος, Σωσίθεος), and finally Eustatheus ad *Il.* 2.711.

9. At *Anth. Pal.* 2.410, 4.1.5, and 9.26.3 the meter requires a long first syllable. Baale (1903, 34–35) ascribes the change from upsilon to the diphthong at those points to poetic license and further suggests that Christodorus, Meleager, and Antipater may have believed the poet's name was derived not from μύρον (perfume), with a short vowel, but from μύρομαι (flow, melt into tears). Gow and Page (1965, 2:413–14) are duly skeptical of the latter hypothesis.

10. As Gow and Page (1965, 2:414) note, the dating is approximate. This Olympiad was merely the first to fall completely within the reign of Ptolemy Philadelphus, during whose time in power the tragic Pleiad was active. It is doubtless too early for Homerus' *acmê* or prime of life, conventionally understood to be a man's fortieth year.

11. Eusebius places Erinna's *floruit* in the mid-fourth century (Ol. 106.4 or 107.1). Nossis is dated to the early part of the third century by her epitaph for Rhinthon, a writer of mythological burlesques (*Anth. Pal.* 7.414 = G-P 10); according to the *Suda*, Rhinthon was active during the reign of Ptolemy I, who died in 282 BCE We have no firm evidence for Anyte's period of activity. Conventional assignment of a date around 300 BCE is based upon stylistic considerations and belief that her work was imitated by Nicias and Mnasalces, two epigrammatists writing in the first half of the third century (G-P 2:90). Baale's arguments (1903, 7–9) for the existence of a widely circulating ancient canon of women poets are fundamental to the understanding of the Greek female poetic tradition.

12. While admitting we have no evidence that Moero lived or wrote anywhere else than at Byzantium, Wilamowitz (1924, 1:45 n. 2) doubts that the intellectual resources of the city at that time would have permitted her husband to pursue his occupation there. West (1996a, 27) intimates that Andromachus' professional visibility may have helped his wife gain recognition as a poet among a learned readership.

13. The scholiast to Apollonius Rhodius 1.740–41 (Wendel 1958) gives two additional sources for Amphion's lyre: according to Dioscorides, he received it from Apollo, whereas Pherecydes, among others, makes it a present from the Muses.

14. Both writers are naturally looking back to Hermes' invention of the lyre in the archaic Homeric Hymn (*h.Merc.* 24–61).

15. Numerous excerpts from the celebrated *agôn* survive, but their exact placement is disputed. See frr. 184–202 Nauck²/Snell; Pl. *Grg.* 484e3–486d1; Hor. *Ep.* 1.18.41–44; cf. Snell 1967, 70–98, Webster 1967, 205–11.

16. Athenaeus insists that Moero was the first to understand the Homeric passage correctly, although, he adds, her explanation was subsequently plagiarized: the Homeric scholar Crates of Mallus (a contemporary of Aristarchus of Samothrace [*c.* 216–144 BCE] and a vigorous proponent of the Stoic method of allegorical interpretation), appropriated it (σφετερισάμενος) and published it as his own. This snatch of academic gossip raises an intriguing though unanswerable question. Allegations of plagiarism are not uncommon in ancient scholarly circles (e.g., the grammarian Ser. Clodius was accused of purloining his father-in-law's unpublished book, Suet. *Rhet.* 3), but how did this incident become so notorious that Athenaeus would have heard of it more than three centuries later? Does it imply that, by Crates' time, Moero's epic was no longer widely read or that, on the contrary, it was well enough known that alert readers quickly spotted the theft?

17. The familiarity of this passage is evident from the fact that in the *Contest of Homer and Hesiod* from the Antonine period Hesiod is made to recite it as illustrative of his finest work and is then awarded the tripod (*Certamen* 321).

18. Snyder (1989, 41–44) gives a lucid summary of the arguments on both sides. Later (86) she observes the similarity between Corinna's and Moero's treatments of the infancy of Zeus.

19. In citations preserved by Hipparchus (1.2.3, 8, 11 Manitius), Eudoxus simply gives the positions of the constellations, without mythic or other elaboration.

20. Boll and Gundel (1937, 871) credit Aratus himself with combining the two motifs.

21. Most scholars date publication of the *Phaenomena* in the late 270s BCE; Wilamowitz (1924 2:276) put it in the 260s. The poem was celebrated in epigrams by two contemporaneous poets, Callimachus (G-P 56 = *Anth. Pal.* 9.507) and Leonidas of Tarentum (G-P 101 = *Anth. Pal.* 9.25).

22. Attested in the laudatory epigrams *Anth. Pal.* 7.11. 2 (Asclepiades) and 9.190.4 and apparently confirmed in the papyrus of the *Distaff* (*SH* 401 col. iii.37). The author's self-portrayal cannot, of course, be taken as biographical fact; like Manwell in this volume, I regard it as "a construct for the purposes of poetic production" (82).

23. Corinna offers an instructive parallel. Taking her direct, unelaborated style at face value, Page (1953, 76) remarked condescendingly: "We may judge her narratives rather dull and childish, and herself lacking in the force of intellect and character necessary to inspire them with life and interest: but at the same time we shall not fail to acknowledge her talents for clarity, conciseness, and perfect control of such language as is requisite to express her simple meaning." Page's verdict has lately been reversed by scholars who find allusiveness, sly

humor, and artistic sophistication in Corinna's fragments and define her osten-sible simplicity as a deliberate archaizing stance. See Segal 1975; Skinner 1983a; Snyder 1989, 53; Rayor 1993; Clayman 1993.

24. Tension between a speaker's naive perceptions and an ironic density of poetic reference in the statements she or he makes is a common phenomenon in ancient poetry. In Theocritus' *Idyll* 2, for example, echoes of Sappho and of the *Odyssey* in Simaetha's report of her seduction "add the dimension of literary his-tory to a poem which purports to be an account of a transient contemporary event of everyday life" (Segal 1984, 204).

25. I borrow the term "manchette" from Lightfoot. These short notices, which derive from later scholarly activity, do not necessarily indicate Parthenius' source but may simply refer to places where the same story is told, possibly in a very different form (Lightfoot 1999, 248–49).

26. On the assumption that the *Arai* was composed around the turn of the third century BCE, Moero is often credited with being the first to write a curse poem, but this distinction probably belongs to another writer. Two recently joined papyrus fragments, *P. Brux.* 8934 and *P. Sorbonn.* 2254, together supply almost fifty lines of an elegiac text whose authorship is disputed, but which, on metrical and stylistic grounds, appears to be pre-Callimachean (see Huys 1991, 77–98, who assigns it to Hermesianax of Colophon). The speaker repeatedly threatens to tattoo (στίξω, *P. Brux.* i.5, *P. Sorbonn.* i.4, ii.18) various parts of the addressee's body with depictions of assorted mythic punishments. The elegy already displays many of the characteristic features of subsequent curse poetry, such as an explicit invocation of the goddess Dike (*P. Sorbonn.* i.1–3, see Watson 1991, 92) and a tendency to employ obscure and uncanonical mythic variants (Watson 1991, 261–62). If the generic paradigm was so well established by the first quarter of the third century BCE, precursor texts must have been in exis-tence much earlier. As we have seen, there appear to be grounds for shifting at least some part of Moero's creative activity downward to the reign of Ptolemy Philadelphus. It is likely, then, that in the *Arai* she is following an already estab-lished trend rather than inventing one, and possibly even turning it in a new direction. Cameron (1995, 386) proposes Moero herself as a candidate for the author of the "Tattoo Elegy." Greek female poetic production, however, is grounded in female public speech genres such as hymns, laments, and wedding songs (Lardinois 1994; Skinner 2001, 201), and speaking in a masculine per-sona to curse a male transgressor seems to fall outside the thematic range of ancient women's writing.

27. Watson (1991, 79–149) presents an extensive survey of the conven-tions of Hellenistic curse poems, which, as he shows, "conform to a very elabo-rate, not to say artificial pattern" (81). He argues persuasively that their subject matter is tongue in cheek and that they are meant to be appreciated as a comic jeu d'esprit (135–39).

28. "If Ovid sets any store by his curses, 'Ibis' ought by rights to have been dead a hundred times over by the end of the poem" (Watson 1991, 138).

29. Harpalyce's story occurs in *SH* 413.12–16. The fragmentary lines touch upon the cannibalistic meal she served to her father, Clymenus; her own metamorphosis into a bird, described as "Athena's servant"; and Clymenus' suicide. *SH* 415.i.12–21 contain Apriate's pursuit by Trambelus, her leap into the sea and attempted rescue by dolphins, and Trambelus' death at the hands of

Achilles. Parthenius departs from Euphorion in significant ways—for example, in giving two separate versions of Apriate's death. For discussion, see Lightfoot 1999, 516–18.

30. Μενέλαος at *Il.* 3.284, 4.183, etc., and *Od.* 3.168, 4.30, etc. There are variants in the dative (*Il.* 3.434, etc.) and the accusative (*Od.* 1.285).

31. Cf. another poem of this kind by Euphorion, the Ἀραὶ ἢ Ποτηριοκ-λέπτης (*Curses* or *Cup-Thief*), a title preserved in Steph. Byz. s.v. Ἀλύβη; see fr. 8 Powell 1925.

32. Euripides' *Andromache* offers a close parallel. The heroine is speaking to her son Molossos (510–12): κείσῃ δή, τέκνον, ὦ φίλος,/μαστοῖς ματέρος ἀμφὶ σᾶς/νεκρὸς ὑπὸ χθονὶ σὺν νεκρῷ (you will lie, child, o dear one, / beside the breast of your mother, / corpse with corpse beneath the earth).

33. Geoghegan (1979, 116; *ap.* Anyte G-P 11.1) observes that it is frequently used to open funereal epigrams, citing numerous examples. See also Herrlinger 1930, 59; Luck 1954, 180.

34. White 1980 attempts to remove the difficulty by arguing that the phrase "daughters of the river" refers to Oceanus, from whom in certain sources all nymphs, including the Hamadryads, are said to descend. This seems strained. One proposed correction is Ἀνιγριάδες, a reference to nymphs presiding over a cave and healing cult that specialized in curing skin diseases beside the river Anigros in the eastern Peloponnese (Paus. 5.5.11, cf. Strabo 8.3.19). The emendation has been widely accepted, most recently by Larson 2001, 159. However, both Pausanias and Strabo mention the peculiarly disgusting smell of the river water and note that writers cite aetiological myths to account for it. Allusion to this cult, then, might well have summoned up associations that were out of keeping with the evocation of a bucolic *locus amoenus*.

35. So Geffcken 1932, 2512, and Luck 1954, 181. Reitzenstein (1970, 135 n. 1) observes a close resemblance between the two poets but believes the question of priority cannot be decided.

36. In Theophrastus *History of Plants* 6.6.8–9, however, *krinon* is the generic name for *Lilium candidum*, while *leirion* is another designation for the narcissus, whether *Narcissus serotinus* or *Pancratium maritimum* (Amigues 1993, 190–92).

37. It is proverbially contrasted with the colocynth or bitter-apple (*Citrullus colocynthis*), a symbol of health: ἢ κολοκύντην ἢ κρίνον (living or dead, Diph. fr. 98 Kock).

38. Baale (1903, 38–39) postulates an actual friendship between Anyte and Moero, but this biographical inference is unjustified.

39. Gow and Page translate *pote* as *olim* (once, formerly) and believe it means that the quatrain was composed some time after the actual event. On metrical grounds it seems better to take *dê pote* together (cf. Denniston 1950, 212–13) as an adverbial expression modifying the verb *ôleo*. The epic solemnity of this apostrophe (Geoghegan 1979, 105–107) contrasts movingly with the information, provided in the next line, that its addressee was a puppy who had loved to run and bark (φιλοφθόγγων ὠκυτάτα σκυλάκων). Observing the echo of Andromache's lament for Hector at *Il.* 24.725–26, Greene (2000, 25) notes that it "serves to elevate the ordinary activities of everyday life to heroic stature and, at the same time, to deflate the solemnity and grandeur associated with heroic lament."

40. See *Anth. Pal.* 7.189 (Aristodicus), 192 (Mnasalcas), 200 (Nicias), 201 (Pamphilus), all on locusts or cicadas; for the nicht mehr formula as especially characteristic of funerary poems for animals, see Herrlinger 1930, 2.

41. Barnard 1991 labeled Anyte a "poet of children and animals." Gutzwiller (1998, 55–56 and 74) adds that such interests distinguish a unique feminine persona, reflected in what was originally a representative sample of her poetry. If we posit that the verses preserved by Meleager were indeed typical of Anyte's larger corpus, we can observe that Moero 1 condenses two of her characteristic thematic concerns.

42. Although the epigram is ascribed to both Anyte and Leonidas of Tarentum in the *Anthology*, for stylistic reasons it is usually assigned to Anyte (G-P 2:101; Geoghegan 1979, 171).

43. Marcus Argentarius, probably a younger contemporary of Ovid, carefully imitated it, retaining the figure of Myro and the joint burial of the two insects but attributing the death of the cicada to Hades and that of the grasshopper to Persephone. The effectiveness of his adaptation requires a reader's close familiarity with the original.

44. Gow and Page (1965, 2:394) see "no compelling reason" to assign the epigram to Meleager, but authorship of the poem does not affect my argument.

45. For this reason alone, readers might surmise that Anyte is paying tribute to her fellow poet from Byzantium. Baale (1903, 35–39) was the first to suggest that Anyte is referring to Moero; Geoghagen (1979, 173) also entertains the possibility that the poetess could be meant.

46. The expression "common tomb" might even refer to a published collection.

47. "Ovid stresses Perilla's virginal modesty as part of a persistent endeavor to desexualize Perilla, to de-emphasize her female sexuality and even her acquisition and literary display of sexual knowledge" (Hallett 1990, 192). In his exile poetry Ovid frequently casts himself as Perillus, the legendary sculptor destroyed by his talent (Skinner 1993a); Perilla may certainly be read, then, as a trope for Ovid's own art. Her desexualization would comment ironically upon Augustus' effort to censor it.

48. Aristodama was granted proxeny by two cities of mainland Greece, Lamia (SIG 532 = *IG* 9.2.62, 218/17 BCE) and Chalaion (SEG II.263). Alcinoë of Thronion was honored by Tenos in similar fashion (*IG* 12.5.812, third century BCE). Each poet celebrated the special traditions of her host city: Aristodama versified the founding legends of Lamia and Chalaion, and Alcinoë composed hymns to the chief divinities of Tenos, Zeus, Poseidon, and Amphitrite (Pomeroy 1977, 54–55).

6 Nossis *Thêlyglôssos*

The Private Text and the Public Book

Marilyn B. Skinner

Eleven quatrains accidentally preserved in the *Greek Anthology* comprise the literary remains of the woman epigrammatist Nossis, a native of the Greek colony of Locri Epizephyrii in southern Italy active around the beginning of the third century BCE.[1] Together with her predecessors Sappho and Erinna, both of whom situated their poetry within the sphere of women's religious and domestic lives and created poetic speakers who proclaimed their deep emotional attachments to other women, Nossis may be one of the earliest Western European exemplars of the recognizably female literary voice.[2] Certainly her slight body of texts gives the impression of a forthright personality with an idiosyncratic point of view that upon close reading emerges as strongly woman-identified.[3]

For anyone planning to demonstrate the peculiarly female timbre of Nossis' poetic voice, however, the fact that she chose to work within the epigrammatic tradition presents an initial interpretative difficulty.[4] The majority of her surviving quatrains are dedicatory, honoring gifts made by women to goddesses. There is nothing particularly unusual in her subject matter, for male poets also wrote about women's offerings to female divinities. Moreover, the dedicatory epigram is by its very nature a public and impersonal mode of poetic discourse.[5] Destined to commemorate a votive offering, usually by being affixed to a temple wall alongside the donor's present, such testimonial verses necessarily addressed the world at large, and their preoccupation with the votive object itself left scant room for authorial subjectivity. Then too, most dedicatory epigrams were probably commissioned from professional writers. Although dedicants might have hoped for some share of literary immortality in having their individual offerings memorialized by a Callimachus or a Leonidas of Tarentum, what they surely expected from any poet, no matter how talented, was no more than a new and clever way of dealing with mandatory formulaic elements—the donor's piety, the gift's value, the god's consequent obligation. The work of Anyte, another woman epigrammatist who often treats novel subjects—women, children, animals, and the Arcadian landscape—but employs traditional epigrammatic strategies in doing so, indicates that even innovative dedications may still conform to a conventional pattern.[6]

Contrasted with Anyte's verse, and with similar verse produced by male epigrammatists, Nossis' dedicatory epigrams display some exceptional features. First, the speaker is not a detached observer: she invariably expresses warm personal feeling for the dedicant conveyed in familiar, in fact intimate, tones. Again, she speaks explicitly to an audience of women companions who are themselves presumed to know the donors in question. Finally, in the course of describing the dedicated object, she sometimes articulates sentiments decidedly at variance with the values inscribed in the mainstream poetic tradition. Thus, despite the overtly "public" character of Nossis' chosen subgenre, we receive the distinct impression of writing directed exclusively toward a relatively small, self-contained female community.[7] The paradox can be explained if we postulate that these quatrains operate as literary texts abstracted from their original commemorative function. Though they record actual donations, they would have been written primarily for private circulation among the members of a tightly knit circle rather than for public display in a temple; and they must accordingly have served a poetic purpose far more complex than merely preserving a dedicant's name. We shall see that the author herself ultimately issued these pieces in book form accompanied by prologue and epilogue poems: to that extent, at least, she did treat her dedicatory epigrams as purely literary documents.

The use of a quasi-public verse form for poetic statements really designed for a private female readership would draw attention to the culturally meaningful distinction between the sheltered domestic interior and the much more accessible temple precinct.[8] This tension would then be augmented by book publication, with its corresponding change in readership from a coterie of women friends to a bigger, predominantly male audience dwelling beyond the confines of Locri. Consequently Nossis may be important not only as an ancient embodiment of the "private" female voice but as an illustration of how that voice might subsequently have been heard by the larger "public" world. I shall return to the latter question after we have had the opportunity to examine Nossis' poetry.

One of the few references to her in later Greek literature furnishes evidence that ancient readers regarded her as an intensely woman-centered poet. By the beginning of the Christian era, Alexandrian literary scholarship had already constructed a roster of major women writers.[9] These figures, nine in number by a predictable analogy with the nine Muses, are listed by Antipater of Thessalonica in his declamatory epigram *Anth. Pal.* 9.26. There Nossis is characterized by the lone adjective *thêlyglôssos*. Because the word does not occur elsewhere, its exact meaning is uncertain, but it is generally thought to denote "one who spoke like a woman"—a curiously redundant epithet for a canonical woman poet.[10] Alternatively, *thêlyglôssos* may be translated as "one who spoke specifically to women." So construed, it would imply that ancient readers perceived Nossis' poetry as oriented toward her own sex to a degree unusual even for female writers. This interpretation of *thêlyglôssos* can be supported by a detailed examination of her most typical productions, the dedicatory epigrams 3 through 9, where analysis quickly reveals the extent of her interest not only in women's religious activities but also in women as subjects of representative art.

In form a commemoration of a gift to Hera Lacinia, poem 3 (*Anth. Pal.* 6.265) is in reality an autobiographical *sphragis* or "signature-poem":

Ἥρα τιμάεσσα, Λακίνιον ἃ τὸ θυῶδες
    πολλάκις οὐρανόθεν νισομένα καθορῇς,
δέξαι βύσσινον εἶμα τό τοι μετὰ παιδὸς ἀγαυᾶς
    Νοσσίδος ὕφανεν Θευφιλὶς ἁ Κλεόχας.

Most reverend Hera, you who often descending from heaven
    behold your Lacinian shrine fragrant with incense,
receive the linen wrap that with her noble child Nossis
    Theophilis daughter of Cleocha wove for you.

The first distich tactfully reminds the goddess of the constant honors paid her at her temple on the Lacinian promontory near Croton—

the most celebrated shrine in southern Italy, known for its wealth no less than its sanctity (Livy 24.3.6). Hera is then requested to accept a textile produced by the author's mother, Theophilis, with the help of her daughter. This robe is no ordinary piece of home-spun: its imported material, linen, singles it out as a costly garment.[11] The central ritual event of the Panathenaic festival at Athens, immortalized in the processional frieze from the Parthenon, was the presentation to Athena of a peplos woven by the leading women of the polis; and fifth-century votive tablets indicate that at Locri itself a similar practice obtained for the cults of the great goddesses Persephone and Aphrodite.[12] Nossis' epigram may memo-rialize just such a solemn public offering to Hera. If so, the dedicants would certainly have been of prominent social rank. The adjective *agaua* (noble), with which the poet modifies her own name, validates this inference: infused with Homeric associations of antique eminence, it testifies to her membership in one of the old aristocratic families of the geographical region served by Hera's temple.[13]

At the conclusion of the epigram Nossis identifies her mother as *Theuphilis ha Kleochas* (daughter of Cleocha) tracing her elite ancestry back two generations through the female line. The phrase cannot be used as evidence for an exceptional public custom of matrilineal descent–reckoning at Locri, as W. A. Oldfather argued, for it was common practice for Greek women in general to desig-nate each other by metronymics, rather than patronymics, when speaking privately among themselves.[14] Accordingly, the poet called her mother "daughter of Cleocha" to show that she is addressing an audience composed of female companions. By stressing her grandmother's name, she directs attention to Cleocha's dis-tinguished position within that Locrian community. The ceremo-nial gift of a choice piece of women's handiwork to Hera, queen of the gods, has already established her mother's consequence and her own. Furthermore, the conventional metonymic association between weaving and poetry also allows Nossis, in casting herself as apprentice to Theophilis the dominant artisan, to pay loving tribute to her mother as her earliest creative mentor.[15] This epigram is therefore a comprehensive statement of personal identity in which a woman writer "thinks back through her mother" both biologically and artistically. At the same time, it provides a glimpse of an alternative cultural environment set apart, to some degree, from the male-dominated public order, a milieu in which religious observance, social position, and creative self-consciousness all find expression in activities and language derived from women's domestic experience.

Poems 4 and 5, describing two dedications to Aphrodite, touch upon those aspects of her divine personality that were apparently the particular concerns of her cult at Locri: sexuality as a cosmic principle, and the realm of sexual activities not institutionalized within marriage, "its illicit and 'aberrant' forms which do not serve society."[16] In the first epigram (*Anth. Pal.* 9.332), Nossis summons her companions to go and view a statue of Aphrodite set up by the courtesan Polyarchis:

ἐλθοῖσαι ποτὶ ναὸν ἰδώμεθα τᾶς Ἀφροδίτας
    τὸ βρέτας ὡς χρυσῷ δαιδαλόεν τελέθει.
εἵσατό μιν Πολυαρχὶς ἐπαυρομένα μάλα πολλάν
    κτῆσιν ἀπ᾽ οἰκείου σώματος ἀγλαΐας.

Let us go to Aphrodite's temple to see her statue,
    how finely it is embellished with gold.
Polyarchis dedicated it, having made a great fortune
    out of the splendor of her own body.

Placed for emphasis as the opening word, *elthoisai*, the participle denoting the act of departure, is grammatically feminine. Once again the sex of the addressees is specified as exclusively female; meanwhile the hortatory *idômetha* (let us see) imposes a shared viewpoint upon the entire group of observers. We readers are welcomed into the circle of women surrounding the speaker and invited to discover in Polyarchis' statue what that speaker herself beholds: we are to confront it, that is, from a woman-oriented perspective. Elaborately crafted and gilded, obviously very expensive, the figure testifies not only to the dedicant's wealth but also to its source in her physical perfections. The overtones of metallic brightness in the word *aglaïas* (splendor) combine with the prior description of the statue as *chrysôi daidaloen* (embellished with gold) to create an impression of exact correspondence between gift and donor: like her offering, the lovely Polyarchis was herself an exquisitely wrought artifact. Mention of her great fortune recalls the literary stereotype of the mercenary courtesan.[17] Yet the speaker's undeniable admiration for Polyarchis finally counteracts any censorious implications. We are left with the conviction that her riches, themselves no more than her elegance deserved, were put to good use in the creation of a votive image as elegant as herself. This is not the only epigram in which we find Nossis pointedly correcting misogynistic or androcentric tenets embedded in the patriarchal literary tradition.

Whereas poem 4 conveys a female observer's response to a dedicated object, poem 5 (*Anth. Pal.* 6.275) attempts to voice the reaction of its divine recipient:

χαίροισάν τοι ἔοικε κομᾶν ἄπο τὰν Ἀφροδίταν
    ἄνθεμα κεκρύφαλον τόνδε λαβεῖν Σαμύθας·
δαιδάλεός τε γάρ ἐστι καὶ ἁδύ τι νέκταρος ὄσδει·
    τούτῳ καὶ τήνα καλὸν Ἄδωνα χρίει.

Joyfully indeed, I think, Aphrodite receives this gift,
    a headdress from Samytha's own hair.
For it is elaborate, and smells sweetly in some way of nectar.
    With this she too anoints the beautiful Adonis.

Like Polyarchis' statue, Samytha's headdress is sumptuously worked (*daidaleos*), but it is also redolent of the pomade with which its former owner scented her hair. Use of rich balms and incenses was intrinsic to the cult of the dying god, Aphrodite's consort, and we may therefore assume that Samytha has recently participated in the yearly Adonia.[18] Nossis calls attention to the similarity of interests between goddess and mortal woman by dwelling upon their mutual pleasure in Samytha's perfume, by investing that perfume with associations of divine nectar, and by concluding the poem with a subtle ambiguity: the antecedent of the rhetorically and metrically accentuated "she too" (*kai têna*) could be either Aphrodite or Samytha herself.[19] Although we are given no explicit indication of Samytha's social position, passages in Middle and New Comedy show *hetairai* observing the Adonia in a particularly lavish manner, and later authors depict them playfully using "Adonis" as a nickname for their lovers.[20] Perfumed oils, too, have an erotic as well as a ritual significance. Nossis thus sets up a sly correlation between Aphrodite and Samytha: both derive sensual enjoyment from unguents—and from the company of a young male friend. This flattering analogy finds a parallel in poem 4, where we must understand Polyarchis to have served as the actual model for the statue ostensibly dedicated as an effigy of the divinity. Aphrodite accordingly looks with favor upon the two dedicants Polyarchis and Samytha because their physical allure and sexual expertise bear compelling witness to her own divine power. Though herself of aristocratic birth, Nossis does not patronize or condemn either woman; on the contrary, her poetic statements reflect a positive attitude toward sexuality and a keen awareness of the pleasures to be gained from the skilled gratification of sight, smell, and touch.

Poems 6 through 9 belong to the venerable tradition of *ekphrasis*, the verbal reproduction of a work of plastic art.[21] All four deal with paintings in encaustic, the regular medium of ancient portraiture.[22] Descriptions of art objects recur with unusual frequency in the small number of extant epigrams written by ancient Greek women. Erinna 3 (*Anth. Pal.* 6.352), which insists upon the lifelikeness of a girl's painted countenance, seems to have furnished a prototype for the next generation of women poets: Moero 1 (*Anth. Pal.* 6.119) must have accompanied a picture of a grape cluster, and of Anyte's twenty-one genuine epigrams, two are obviously ecphrastic.[23] In one respect, though, Nossis' quatrains differ strikingly from those of most other female and male poets working within the same tradition: she is pre-occupied not so much with the painter's success in effecting a physical likeness as with his ability to capture distinctive traits of the sitter's personality. Her ecphrastic poems thus become brief character sketches of members of the Locrian community—perhaps her own relatives and acquaintances. Like the very portraits she affects to describe, these quatrains were apparently designed to put her original audience in the imagined presence of a known individual.

The only one of these *pinakes* (wooden panels) clearly designated as a temple offering is that of Callo, who in poem 6 (*Anth. Pal.* 9.605) dedicates her picture to Aphrodite:

τὸν πίνακα ξανθᾶς Καλλὼ δόμον εἰς Ἀφροδίτας
  εἰκόνα γραψαμένα πάντ᾽ ἀνέθηκεν ἴσαν.
ὡς ἀγανῶς ἕστακεν· ἴδ᾽ ἁ χάρις ἁλίκον ἀνθεῖ.
  χαιρέτω, οὔ τινα γὰρ μέμψιν ἔχει βιοτᾶς.

> This tablet Callo set up in the house of blonde Aphrodite,
>   a portrait she had painted, like her in every way.
> How tenderly she stands! See how her charm blooms!
>   May she fare well: her way of life is blameless.

Here, as in poems 4 and 5, the text insists upon a mysterious affinity between goddess and worshiper. The proper name Callo at once recalls *kallos* (beauty), the distinguishing hallmark of Aphrodite's darlings (*Il.* 3.54–55). Though common in inscriptions, as Gow and Page observe, the name still gives the impression of being carefully chosen. At any rate, it is very appropriate for a young woman whose tender, blooming appearance elicits the speaker's warm approval. Furthermore, we are told that the painted image is *pant'* . . . *isan* (wholly like), with no object specified; this portrait, then, could be either like the sitter or like the divinity who receives it. Remembering the provenance of those other dedications to Aphrodite mentioned in poems 4 and 5, we may conclude that the subject of the present epigram is quite probably another *hetaira*. If so, its last line must be construed as a bold defense of her way of life, the forthright proclamation of a judgment already implicit in the two quatrains previously examined. In addition, the express identification of Polyarchis, Samytha, and now Callo with the Locrian Aphrodite transforms all three women into avatars of a goddess honored as the demiurgic principle of sexuality operating outside the sphere of marriage.

Nossis' eulogies of courtesans and their profession are remarkable. It is tempting to speculate that poems 4, 5, and 6 were commissioned and that such sentiments were intended to gratify a paying clientele.[24] Yet similar views are not expressed in epigrams written by male poets, where verses commemorating actual dedications by *hetairai* limit themselves, discreetly, to a bare inventory of votive objects. Although fictive dedications by notorious courtesans do provide the occasion for gnomic pronouncements, the speaker always elects to moralize upon the ephemerality of physical beauty rather than the might of *erôs*. In Nossis' quatrains, however, the female audience constructed by the text does not object to frank praise of *hetairai*. The hypothesis of commissioned verses thus casts an intriguing light upon respectable women's attitudes toward nonrespectable women and also suggests the possibility of some degree of acquaintance between the two groups. Apart from their literary merits, these texts are therefore of considerable importance as cultural documents, for they raise provocative questions about the possible relaxation of rigid caste distinctions between respectable and nonrespectable women in third-century BCE Locri.

In two other ecphrastic epigrams Nossis addressed the problem of how female selfhood is achieved and manifested. Poem 7 (*Anth. Pal.* 9.604) conveys a vivid impression of an adolescent girl's personality through sharp verbal dissonances combined with subtle humor:

Θαυμαρέτας μορφὰν ὁ πίναξ ἔχει· εὖ γε τὸ γαῦρον
τεῦξε τό θ᾽ ὡραῖον τᾶς ἀγανοβλεφάρου.

σαίνοι κέν σ᾽ ἐσιδοῖσα καὶ οἰκοφύλαξ σκυλάκαινα,
  δέσποιναν μελάθρων οἰομένα ποθορῆν.

This tablet shows Thaumareta. Well indeed it portrayed
  the pride and the ripeness of the tender-eyed girl.
Even your house-guarding puppy would wag her tail on seeing
    you,
  thinking she gazed on the mistress of the mansion.

Although young (we should recall that Greek girls frequently married in their early teens), Thaumareta is already installed as manager of a great household. Her portrait reveals a piquant combination of character traits: endowed with the ripe physical charm of youth, she is also arrogant, doubtless because of her recent accession to this position of responsibility.[25] The young woman's underlying vulnerability—intimated by the descriptive adjective *aganoblepharos*, (tender-eyed)—betrays itself in her attachment to her pet dog, an emotion somewhat unsuited to a haughty *despoina melathrôn*. With arch magniloquence, Nossis calls this animal an *oikophylax skylakaina* (house-guarding female puppy) that would wag its tail in greeting were it to see its mistress's picture.[26] The oxymoron draws a parallel between dog and owner, insinuating that the latter ought to refrain from giving herself airs inappropriate to her age; and the final hyperbole, a neat reminiscence of Odysseus' encounter with the aged dog Argos (*Od.* 17.301–304), lightly mocks Thaumareta's pretensions to authority and so completes the genial process of deflation.

In a more serious vein, poem 8 (*Anth. Pal.* 6.353) addresses the biological and psychological complexities of the mother-daughter relationship:

Αὐτομέλιννα τέτυκται· ἴδ᾽ ὡς ἀγανὸν τὸ πρόσωπον.
  ἀμὲ ποτοπτάζειν μειλιχίως δοκέει.
ὡς ἐτύμως θυγάτηρ τᾷ ματέρι πάντα ποτῴκει·
  ἦ καλὸν ὅκκα πέλῃ τέκνα γονεῦσιν ἴσα.

Melinna herself is fully wrought. See how tender her face is.
  She seems to gaze upon us benignly.
How truly the daughter resembles her mother in all things!
  Indeed it is good when children are like their parents.

Into the verb *tetuktai* (fully wrought), ostensibly predicated of Melinna's painted representation, Nossis retrospectively inscribes a startling biological analogy: like the painter, the girl's mother has created a likeness by reproducing her own self in her daughter's flesh. While the speaker marvels at the wonderful physical similarity of mother and daughter, the text meanwhile underscores the fundamental tension between Melinna herself (*automelinna*) and Melinna as the genetic reincarnation of her parent: by juxtaposing those two contradictory notions without reconciling them, it hints at the struggle over the daughter's autonomy latent in the mother-daughter dyad. At the same time, the epigram ingeniously appropriates the patriarchal tenet that sons should resemble fathers as proof of their legitimacy and converts it into a confirmation of the hereditary bond between female parent and female child.[27]

In contrast to Thaumareta and Melinna, Sabaethis, the subject of poem 9 (*Anth. Pal.* 6.354), is definitely a mature woman:

γνωτὰ καὶ τηλῶθε Σαβαιθίδος εἴδεται ἔμμεν
ἄδ᾽ εἰκὼν μορφᾷ καὶ μεγαλειοσύνᾳ.
θάεο· τὰν πινυτὰν τό τε μείλιχον αὐτόθι τήνας
ἔλπομ᾽ ὁρῆν. χαίροις πολλά, μάκαιρα γύναι.

Even from far off this image is known as Sabaethis'
    because of its beauty and stature.
Look! From this spot I observe, I think, her wisdom and kindness.
    Fare you very well, blessed lady.

The language of this quatrain is charged with religious nuances, for Sabaethis' external and internal qualities are elsewhere associated either with female deities or with heroines singularly favored by the gods.[28] Conspicuous in her picture and making recognition possible even at a distance, her shapely form and stature (*morpha kai megaleiosyna*) are distinctive attributes of the goddess who reveals herself to human eyes. Her prudence, observable at close quarters, is a gift bestowed upon divine protégées, most notably the virtuous Penelope, and the benevolence that accompanies it informs the relationship of gracious divinity to pious mortal. The transition from external appearance to internal character is marked by adverbs of place that seem to designate two separate planes of existence, the transcendent as in *têlôthe* (from afar off) and the mundane as in *autothi* (on this spot).[29] Nossis' parting salute to Sabaethis, *chairois polla, makaira gynai*, is therefore a studied equivocation: although the use of such heightened language is not unusual in encomiastic contexts, the epithet *makaira* (blessed) here eradicates the boundary between mortal and immortal already blurred by the preceding description. Surrounding this older woman, clearly a person of some standing, with an awesome numinosity, the *ekphrasis* of her portrait approximates a divine epiphany.

In this cursory examination of poems 3 through 9 I have attempted to show that Nossis was in actual fact *thêlyglôssos*, a woman who speaks in her epigrams specifically to members of her own sex. Her identification with women extends far beyond the mere celebration of their dedications to female divinities. It manifests itself most conclusively in the assumption of a female audience to whom the speaker can identify herself both as artist and as artist's daughter, employing a private, gender-linked form of speech common to the women's quarters. The ecphrastic epigrams then attempt to re-create the experience of living within a closely affiliated female community by evoking the essential personality of each sitter insofar as it was known to her companions and has now received enduring visual expression. Nossis' value system also differs in noteworthy ways from that reflected in the androcentric public culture. Her candid tributes to the physical charms of *hetairai*, which betray no consciousness of her own social or moral superiority, may be contrasted with the presumed hostility of respectable Athenian women toward the former courtesan Neaera, as alleged by the male speaker of [Demosthenes] 59.110–11.[30] Similarly, her personal interest in the transmission of skills and attributes from mother to daughter, glanced at in the quasi-autobiographical poem 3, surfaces again in poem 8, which implicitly repudiates the very structures of patriarchy by transforming the evidential basis for claims of paternity into a proof of the mother's vital role in the reproductive process.

While those seven poems dealing with women constitute the majority of Nossis' surviving pieces, two other quatrains indicate that she also devoted some attention to traditional epigrammatic themes. Despite their surface preoccupation with male pursuits and ostensible adoption of a conventional masculine stance, these texts can also be read as the expression of a markedly idiosyncratic point of view. Poem 2 (*Anth. Pal.* 6.132) is a patriotic commemoration of a Locrian victory over the Bruttians, an indigenous tribe that had long posed a threat to Greek settlements in southern Italy:

ἔντεα Βρέττιοι ἄνδρες ἀπ᾽ αἰνομόρων βάλον ὤμων
θεινόμενοι Λοκρῶν χερσ῾ν ῾πὺ ῾κυμ῾χων,

ʼν ῾ρετʼʼν ῾μνεʼʼντα θεʼʼν ῾πῦ ʼʼνʼʼκτορα κεʼʼνται,
οʼʼδʼʼ ποθεʼʼντι κακʼʼν πʼʼχεας οʼʼς ῾λιπον.

These shields the Bruttians cast from doomed shoulders
as they fell by the hands of the battle-swift Locrians.
Hung beneath temple roofs, the shields praise the Locrians' valor
and do not long for the arms of the cowards they deserted.

Anyte's epigrams prove that it was not unthinkable for a woman to celebrate martial prowess, but the austere solemnity of her dedication poem for Echecratidas' spear and of her epitaphs for fallen combatants, human and equine, finds no echo in Nossis.[31] The Locrian poet instead applies her energies to reviling the defeated enemy. Initially she alleges that the Bruttians had thrown away their shields in flight—for a soldier, the ultimate act of cowardice. In the last line, however, she reverses herself, claiming that the shields themselves chose to desert their unworthy masters and do not, even now, miss them. This statement negates the sentimental conceit whereby a warrior's horses or personified weapons grieve for him, a topos already present in Homer and popular with composers of dedicatory epigrams.[32] Meanwhile the reiterated motif of defection invokes the supposed etymological derivation of the tribal name Brettioi from an Italian dialect word for "runaway slave" or "rebel."[33] This allusion to their unsavory origins defames the Bruttians, but it also undercuts the ethical posture of the shields, whose condemnation of their former masters' pusillanimity is itself tainted by implications of having abandoned a comrade in the heat of battle. In contrast to Anyte's idealization of the warrior and his deeds of valor, Nossis tenders an undeniably patriotic, but still wry, comment upon the equivocal operations of the heroic code.

On the other hand, poem 10 (*Anth. Pal.* 7.414) does convey strong partisan admiration, but for a literary product—the work of Rhinthon, composer of *phlyakes*, or parodies of classic tragedy:[34]

καὶ καπυρὸν γελάσας παραμείβεο καὶ φίλον εἰπών
ῥῆμ᾽ ἐπ᾽ ἐμοί. Ῥίνθων εἴμ᾽ ὁ Συρακόσιος,
Μουσάων ὀλίγα τις ἀηδονίς, ἀλλὰ φλυάκων
ἐκ τραγικῶν ἴδιον κισσὸν ἐδρεψάμεθα.

Laugh, and loudly. Then pass by, saying a kind word
over me. I am Rhinthon of Syracuse,

a small nightingale of the Muses, but from my tragic burlesques
    I plucked for myself a personal ivy crown.

In this quatrain Nossis assumes a masculine persona as she makes
use of the poetic convention that permits the dead man's grave-
stone to speak for him in his own voice. By attaching the super-
fluous feminine suffix *-onis* to *aêdon* (nightingale), however, she
emphasizes the grammatical gender of that noun and so appears to
call attention to the female poetic presence behind the male mask.[35]
Metaphorically, the epigram pleads the necessity of evaluating any
literary composition on its own proper merits, independent of
genre—for the sacred ivy garland earned by the successful dramatic
poet is owed to the parodist Rhinthon no less than to his illustrious
tragic forebears Aeschylus, Sophocles, and Euripides. In true
Hellenistic fashion Nossis affirms the possibility of extraordinary
accomplishment within an "inferior" poetic form and so challenges
the time-honored Greek conception of an objective literary hierarchy with the sober genres of tragedy and epic poised at its apex.[36]
This defense of Rhinthon has obvious relevance for Nossis' own
painstaking efforts in the slighter genre of epigram; but it would
have been inherently applicable to all literary production by women,
who, because of the exigencies of their private lives, were less likely
to attempt the *mega biblion* (weighty masterpiece) that Callimachus,
a generation later, would magisterially condemn. Nossis 10 is
therefore a literary manifesto in which the figure of Rhinthon, the
hyperfeminine *aêdonis*, fronts for the author, who tacitly professes
her own allegiance to that emerging principle of Hellenistic taste
that renounces magnitude and high seriousness in favor of a deft
and playful textual finesse.

In reviewing Nossis' surviving epigrams I have reserved poems
1 and 11 (*Anth. Pal.* 5.170 and 7.718) for last, as both quatrains
pose special textual and interpretative problems.[37] Their unique
literary purpose also sets them apart, for they are Nossis' only two
demonstrably public poems—"public" insofar as they patently
speak to an audience larger than her coterie of women friends. It
was a standard Hellenistic poetic convention to preface and end a
book-length verse collection with programmatic pieces identifying
the author and commenting directly or indirectly upon the contents
of the volume.[38] Nossis 1 and 11 exhibit many of the formal
generic elements that characterize such studied manifestos: each
mentions the author's name, and Nossis 11 also informs us of her

birthplace; each invokes a primary literary model—in this case, Sappho—either forthrightly or through carefully deployed reminiscences; and each claims the patronage of a presiding deity, Aphrodite or the Muses. Scholars have reasonably concluded that 1 and 11 were designed to perform the respective functions of preface and epilogue for Nossis' epigram collection.[39] The poet herself, then, would have prepared her quatrains for broader circulation. Consequently her introductory and concluding statements may be examined as a twofold attempt to communicate her artistic intentions to a new, overwhelmingly male reading audience that would have known little, if anything, about her.

Poem 1 begins with a blunt pronouncement that the joys of *erôs* are supreme:

ἄδιον οὐδὲν ἔρωτος· ἃ δ᾽ ὄλβια, δεύτερα πάντα
    ἐστίν· ἀπὸ στόματος δ᾽ ἔπτυσα καὶ τὸ μέλι.
τοῦτο λέγει Νοσσίς· τίνα δ᾽ ἁ Κύπρις οὐκ ἐφίλασεν,
    οὐκ οἶδεν τήνας τἄνθεα, ποῖα ῥόδα.

Nothing is sweeter than desire. All other delights are second.
    From my mouth I spit even honey.
Nossis says this. Whom Aphrodite does not love,
    knows not her flowers, what roses they are.

This gnomic utterance is arrestingly programmatic in two quite different ways. First, it proclaims that *erôs* is the controlling theme of the book and the crucial ingredient of the poems to follow. Second, and more audaciously, it contradicts Sappho's archetypal personification of desire as paradoxically both sweet and bitter (*glukypikros*) and intimates the possibility of an alternative construction of human sexual experience in which love can offer absolute pleasure untempered by any concomitant suffering.[40] From that initial urgent pitch, the rhetoric becomes still more impassioned, rising through a sweeping dismissal of "all other goods" to culminate in a bold conflation of metaphorical and literal "sweetness": by comparison with the lusciousness of *erôs*, honey itself is spat out. Yet this paratragic expression, *apo stomatos d' eptusa*, with its intertextual echoes of violent and horrified repudiation, interjects an unexpected note of bathos, allowing the speaker to mock her own rhetorical ardor.[41] Just as we have begun to relate to this engaging authorial voice, however, it switches abruptly to the impersonal mode: in the next line the poet formally identifies herself with *touto*

legei Nossis, a third-person *sphragis* that distances her psycho-
logically from her earlier proclamation even as it endows that
proclamation with objective authority. She then concludes with the
almost apologetic assertion that those not in Aphrodite's favor
cannot know her *anthea*—in programmatic terms, her poems—for
the Sapphic roses they are.[42] It appears that Nossis has confronted
the possibility that the erotic element in her art might well be
misunderstood and is therefore attempting to forestall the censure
of a hostile reading public.

Poem 11, however, assumes a much more trusting posture
toward the general reader, for it adapts a motif common in funerary
epigram, the request to a passerby to bear a farewell message to the
dead person's homeland.[43]

ὦ ξεῖν᾽, εἰ τύ γε πλεῖς ποτὶ καλλίχορον Μιτυλήναν
    τᾶν Σαπφοῦς χαρίτων ἄνθος ἐναυσόμενος,
εἰπεῖν ὡς Μούσαισι φίλαν τήνᾳ τε Λοκρὶς γᾶ
    τίκτε μ᾽· ἴσαις δ᾽ ὅτι μοι τοὔνομα Νοσσίς, ἴθι.

Stranger, if you sail to Mytilene of the lovely dances
    to be inspired with the flower of Sappho's graces,
say that the Locrian land bore me, one dear to the Muses
    and to her. Having learned that my name is Nossis, go.

In all other instances of the motif, the subject feels nostalgia for his
or her own native land; this speaker, though, directs her thoughts
across time and space to Sappho's city-state, Mytilene. Sappho plainly
served as Nossis' sovereign literary model: poem 1 is a tissue of
Sapphic allusions, and several other epigrams contain unmistakable
echoes of her language.[44] In the epilogue to her collection Nossis
accordingly represents herself as a lost companion of Sappho
yearning hopelessly for her mistress, like Atthis' beloved (in L-P 96),
homesick in far-off Lydia. By asking a *xenos* bound for Mytilene to
inform its citizens of her literary ties with their great countrywoman,
Nossis admits to a sense of creative isolation caused by her temporal
and spatial distance from her predecessor: in death she will have to
rely on a male stranger or friend, her one last addressee, to effect a
tenuous affiliation between Sappho and herself. Thus the *envoi*
sounds a final chord of lingering uncertainty, for the dead speaker
will never know whether her message was received, her connection
with her model fully understood. It is not an auspicious note on
which to end a book and send it forth into the world.

These two authorial statements are self-conscious attempts to gain the goodwill of an anticipated reader and explain those features of Nossis' poetry that he, the *xenos*, might find exceptional or even shocking. The prologue singles out her eroticism as problematic, and rightly so: it would have been unusual, to say the least, for a woman of Nossis' elite background to have written openly about sexual passion. Sappho, herself an aristocrat, is therefore brought forward in poems 1 and 11 as an enabling precedent.[45] Elsewhere (1989, 14) I have suggested that this appeal to Sappho, taken together with certain homoerotic nuances in the surviving epigrams, must indicate that Nossis' texts would have looked to women, rather than men, as objects of desire. At any rate succeeding generations certainly did categorize her as a love poet. Meleager, the first-century BCE anthologist who excerpted some of her pieces for his epigram collection, the *Garland*, states that he "wove in at random the myrrh-breathing, well-blooming iris of Nossis, for whose tablets Eros melted the wax" (G-P 1 = *Anth. Pal.* 4.1.9–10). His selection of the iris as her flowery token surrounds her with a heady and exotic, yet refined, sensuality; and the conceit of Eros melting wax, a reference to the encaustic process and therefore to her ecphrastic quatrains, hints at an undercurrent of physical desire permeating those poems that claim to transmit the speaker's spontaneous reaction to a compelling visual image.[46]

Meleager furnishes an example of the male reader well disposed toward Nossis: an expert connoisseur of epigram, he savors the delicate sensuality of those pieces he has chosen to anthologize. The only other recorded references to her are trivializing and prurient. Herodas, for example, a writer about whom little is known but who was probably her much younger contemporary, composed *mimiambi*, sketches based on a popular dramatic form, for the amusement of the bookish intelligentsia of Alexandria.[47] In his sixth and seventh mimes, he portrays middle-class housewives first discussing the merits of and then shopping for leather dildoes. The first of these two works gratuitously designates a "Nossis daughter of Erinna" as the illegitimate possessor of such an implement (6.20–36); the second, in which the running joke involves an analogy between dildoes and women's shoes, puns on Nossis' name and that of Baucis, Erinna's dead girlhood companion, as specific kinds of footwear (7.57–58). Nossis and Erinna have been singled out, then, as emblems of perverted female sexuality, given to practices either solitary or indulged in with another woman but in either case devoted to ends other than the gratification of a male partner. As the reference to Baucis indicates, it was Erinna's passionate attachment to her friend—expressed in both her epigrams and her greatly admired epyllion, the *Distaff*—that invited this insulting appropriation of her name.[48]

Nossis must figure in Herodas' mimes for a very similar reason. The extended use made of her in mime 6 implies not only that her own name was known to an educated audience as Erinna's certainly was, but that it could be relied upon to arouse salacious laughter. Since the initial mention of Nossis straightaway prompts a misogynistic attack upon women's disloyalty to one another, an attack tellingly placed in the mouth of a woman speaker, the Locrian poet's glorification of female community and absorption in female culture appear to have been targeted for coarse parody. These two mimes by Herodas, featuring matrons outwardly priggish but grossly amoral in private, operate as a harsh male corrective to Nossis' woman-centered, erotically charged world.

Vastly different in their appreciation of Nossis, Meleager and Herodas display reactions that are nevertheless alike in one instructive way: both foreground and isolate her eroticism at the expense of all other components of her work. By the Hellenistic period, sensational literary portrayals of Sappho had already conditioned the general reading public to imagine a woman who had written about love as herself experienced in such matters, if not actually promiscuous.[49] Furthermore, and despite the evidence of Sappho's own lyrics, the Sappho figure of fourth-century comedy and sentimental legend is not attracted to women; rather, she is the beloved of a whole company of archaic male poets or, alternatively, the aggressive pursuer of the handsome youth Phaon. We see much the same tendencies present in subsequent representations of Nossis. Herodas' unsubtle devaluation looks back to that lurid popular notion of an "amorous Sappho" for its image of another woman poet given to artificial penile stimulation. Meleager takes a vicarious delight in the sexual undercurrents pervading her ostensibly descriptive impressions of painted portraits. These reductionist readings detach the author from her female community— the milieu in which her texts were originally conceived and her woman-identified sensibility fostered. In a new and fundamentally inhospitable literary environment, Nossis thus became a stereotype of aberrant female sexuality, to be romanticized or denigrated as the reader saw fit, and at length to be as good as forgotten.

Ancient male readers' inability to comprehend Nossis' special woman-oriented poetic discourse seems to be shared by contemporary classical scholars, which would account for her continued neglect by historians as well as literary critics. Absurdities of interpretation occur when commentators fail to perceive that a woman writer like Sappho, in speaking privately to members of her own sex, is making use of a semiotic code of emotional and sensual imagery—an evocative strategy better adapted to communication among women than to rational academic exchange.[50] Nevertheless, despite the hardships she poses for some readers, Sappho is still recognized as both a major poet and a key source for uncovering the realities of Greek women's lives. Nossis, however, has been utterly ignored until recently: it is only in the last decade that scholars have begun to cite her texts as evidence for a female perspective upon religious cult, visual art, sexuality, or personal relationships. Yet if my assumption of an original female audience for her poetry is correct, the sentiments expressed in her verses must largely mirror attitudes common to her circle of friends, for she would not have been moved to publish her works in book form had they not met with approval from her first readers. I submit, then, that the values she affirms—values, as we have seen, quite distinct from those found in mainstream Greek literature—furnish evidence for the existence of a relatively autonomous women's subculture at Locri, one in which such an alternative perspective could be generated, nurtured, and transmitted, notwithstanding the pressures toward androcentric conformity exerted by the dominant culture.[51] We cannot, of course, term this perspective "feminist" in any modern sense, but it does concur with modern feminist thought in advocating the transcendent importance of women's experience–of intimate bonding, especially the bonding of mother and daughter; of physical desire and sensual enjoyment; of affectionate contact with divinity; and not least, of the immediate aesthetic pleasure imparted by the woven, sculpted, painted, or written artifact.

At this point some caveats should be issued. We have hardly any reliable data about the sociohistorical circumstances of Sappho's life, and none about Nossis'; nor do we know how closely the cultural systems of their respective city-states conformed to prevailing models of Greek social organization.[52] It would be rash, then, to draw general conclusions about the overall "status" and "emancipation" of Lesbian or Locrian women from their texts. Again, though it is obvious that the two authors share many poetic concerns, their statements should not be used to prove a historical continuity of thought among all Greek women (or even among all elite women) extending from sixth-century BCE Lesbos in the eastern Mediterranean to southern Italy three hundred years later. We cannot project a characteristically female point of view onto Greek womanhood as a whole.

What we can extrapolate from Nossis' epigrams is, instead, the impact of Sappho's poetry upon later women readers. Nossis assumes a learned audience capable of apprehending deft allusions and pointed modifications of standard poetic tropes. If I am correct in assuming that her original readership was female, the fact that she made such demands upon it tells us something about literacy among women of her class at this period.[53] Her efforts to imitate Sappho in the epigrammatic genre must reflect an admiration for the archaic poet within her own community, and her appeal to that figure as ideal reader in the epilogue to her book implies that she speaks not only as an individual woman, Nossis daughter of Theophilis, but also as emissary for a group of friends who have discovered a literary prototype of themselves in the Sapphic circle of companions. Her objective in appropriating the age-old formulas of the dedicatory epigram and infusing them with an unwonted subjectivity then becomes more intelligible: like Sappho, she attempted to transpose the public literary discourse of her time into forms more palatable to women, here blending the cool monumentality of the traditional graven inscription with the emotive urgency of the lyric moment. The misreadings of her critics, ancient and modern, are partial proof that she succeeded in this project. In turn, my cursory overview of her poetry now attempts to restore to Nossis her own proper female audience, an audience more distant in time and space than the Sappho she envisioned as an ideal reader, but one no less attentive to her woman-identified art.[54]

NOTES

1. This essay, originally a paper presented at the Seventh Berkshire Conference on the History of Women on June 21, 1987, and later published as a chapter in Pomeroy 1991, has received considerable revisions including updated endnotes and bibliography. I regret that limitations of space do not permit me to take account of all the important scholarship appearing in the interim. The standard commentary on all epigrams of Hellenistic date, which also established the present convention of numeration, is Gow and Page 1965. All page references are to vol. 2, *Commentary and Indexes*. To facilitate

references to texts, I provide the number of the poem first in Gow and Page and then in the Loeb Classical Library edition of the Palatine and the Planudean anthologies (Paton 1918). Other epigrams are cited by *Greek Anthology* number only; pertinent commentary references are provided in endnotes. Unless otherwise indicated, abbreviations are the standard ones from *L'Année philologique* and the third edition of the *Oxford Classical Dictionary*. For the text of Nossis I follow Page's Oxford Classical Texts edition of Greek epigrams (1975). All translations are my own. Although Nossis 12 (*Anth. Pal.* 6.273), a prayer to Artemis for a woman in labor, would furnish one additional example of the poet's interest in the female sphere, I prefer to exclude it from consideration here, as the attribution to Nossis may be erroneous (on the evidence against its authenticity, consult Gow and Page 1965, 443). For Nossis' generally accepted date see Maas 1936, col. 1053.

2. My underlying postulate of a culturally constructed female consciousness and a corresponding female literary voice, extant in antiquity no less than in modern times, was largely shaped by late twentieth-century feminist literary criticism, especially Diehl 1978, Gilbert and Gubar 1979, and Showalter 1979 and 1981. Since the original publication of this essay, other scholars have analyzed Nossis' characterization of her speaker as a woman addressing women: see, for example, Snyder 1989, 77–86 (unfortunately published too late to be taken into account in the preceding version of this essay); Furiani 1991; Williamson 1995, 18–20; Gutzwiller 1997, 211–22, and 1998, 74–88; and my further thoughts in Skinner 2002. Recent examinations of Sappho's female poetic voice are too numerous to list in full; representative works include Winkler 1990, 162–87; Skinner 1993b; Greene 1994, 1996c, 2002; Lardinois 2001; Snyder 1997; Stehle 1997, 262–318; Williamson 1995, esp. ch. 3; Wilson 1996. Much of this work is collected in Greene 1996a. For Erinna as a strongly woman-identified poet see Arthur 1980 and recent studies by Gutzwiller 1997; Stehle 2001; Manwell, this volume. West 1977 hypothesizes that Erinna's masterpiece, the *Distaff*, was an elaborate literary forgery and denies the historical existence of the poet; but his arguments have been answered by Pomeroy 1978.

3. Gutzwiller (1998, 83–84) suggests that the employment of a consistently characterized dramatic narrator as the first-person speaker of a collection of epigrams is Nossis' own invention. In Herodas' *Mimiamb* 4, the conversation of the protagonists Kynno and Kokkale, two local women who tour the votive objects housed in a temple of Asclepius, may satirize the interaction of Nossis' poetic speaker and her internal addressee (Skinner 2001, 217).

4. Important early studies of Nossis as an epigrammatist include Luck 1954 and Barnard 1978. Gigante 1974 examines her as a learned Hellenistic poet who draws upon the cultural and religious traditions of south Italian Locri. My own readings of Nossis owe much to his exposition of her indebtedness to Sappho.

5. The development of the dedicatory epigram as a genre is analyzed by Raubitschek 1968.

6. Wilamowitz's notorious observation (1924, 1:136) that there is "nothing at all personal, not even anything feminine" in Anyte's work has been challenged by several recent studies that establish her particular interest in the domestic and rural world: see Barnard 1991; Gutzwiller 1992 and 1998,

54–74; Greene 2000. For Anyte's use of language and topoi from the mainstream literary tradition, consult the remarks of Gow and Page 1965, 89–104, together with Geoghagen's 1979 commentary.

7. Bowman (1998, 46–48) draws sharp distinctions among the audiences addressed by Nossis. The internal audience constructed by the text is a group of Locrian women, most likely respectable citizen wives. But we cannot presume that these were really the poet's original readers; instead, she might have been writing all along for an actual audience that was predominately male. I agree with Bowman that Nossis ultimately sought recognition from the larger public and consequently invoked Sappho as an enabling predecessor. Yet her epigrams, like Sappho's songs, take for granted a personal familiarity with their female subjects that strangers would not possess. Granted, intimate dealings among women are also depicted in Theocritus and Herodas, but I have pointed out elsewhere (Skinner 2001) that those male writers consciously imitate Nossis. Bowman (1998, 49) concedes that Nossis' quatrains commemorate real dedications by women. It seems reasonable, then, that in practice they were not merely inscribed alongside the votive offering but also shared with members of the dedicant's circle. The alternative is to assume that the epigrams are simply literary exercises about fictitious dedications composed to give a male reader the vicarious experience of immersion in a woman's world. Both hypotheses are arguable, and neither, I am afraid, can be securely established; I adopt what seems to me the more plausible one.

8. The contrast of domestic and public space, with the particular significance of each for women, is also a central concern in Theocritus 15, where the transition from suburban household to royal palace is marked by a vivid dramatic realization of the physical dangers of ancient city streets (Griffiths 1981).

9. On the evidence for such a canon see Baale 1903, 7–9. Barnard (1978, 204) believes the selection of names originated with Antipater himself; but it was much more in keeping with epigrammatic practice to versify lists already in circulation. Gow and Page (1968, 2:36) supply several parallels for this epigram, which they designate as Antipater 19.

10. Gow and Page (1968, 2:37) observe that the adjective is "not very descriptive." For a parallel to the standard interpretation one could point to *theoglôssous*, "god-voiced," in line 1 of the same poem, where the meaning is obviously "who spoke *like* divinities [i.e., Muses]." But Hellenistic conventions of poetic wit would have not only sanctioned but in fact encouraged the proximate use of morphologically similar compounds with a different syntactical relationship of parts.

11. The word *byssos* can be used of other fabrics besides linen but retains its connotations of oriental luxury and expense. See Olck 1897.

12. On the evidence for such ritual dedications at Locri see Prückner 1968, 42–43, with Abbildung 5. Barnard (1978, 213) cites the literary parallel at *Il.* 6.286–311, where the women of Troy, led by Queen Hecuba, offer a robe to Athena. For the well-known offerings of women's clothing to Artemis of Brauron see Linders 1972 (this reference was provided by one of the anonymous referees for the University of North Carolina Press). Sarah B. Pomeroy reminds me that at Elis a group of elite women termed "the Sixteen" wove a robe for Hera every fourth year (Pausanias 5.16.2, 5.16.6, 6.24.10). Many

other instances of private and public dedications of textiles by wealthy or prominent Greek women could be cited.

13. In the *Iliad*, *agauos* is a regular epithet for the Trojans and for heroes
(for example, Tydeus at 5.277, Laomedon at 5.649 and 6.23, Achilles at
17.557, Nestor at 18.16). In the *Odyssey* it becomes the characteristic epithet
for the suitors; it is also applied thrice to the goddess Persephone (11.213, 226,
635; cf. *Hymn. Hom. Cer.* 348 and *Orphei Hymni*³ [Quandt] 41.5–6; my
thanks to J. Henderson for his help with the latter reference). Thereafter it is
rarely found, even in poetry. The noun-epithet combination *pais agauos* (noble
child) occurs just once, interestingly enough at *Od.* 11.492, where Achilles in
the underworld desires to learn of his son and is informed that by his deeds of
valor Neoptolemus has proved himself his father's successor. If Nossis has this
famous passage in mind, she is neatly reversing gender roles.

14. Against the contentions of Oldfather 1927, cols. 1345–46, I argue in
Skinner 1987 that identification by mother and mother's mother is a gender-specific
speech trait. For other arguments against Oldfather's thesis see Pembroke 1970.

15. For more extensive discussion of this point see Skinner 1989.

16. Sourvinou-Inwood 1978, 120. On the joint worship of Persephone
and Aphrodite and its implications for female participants, cf. MacLachlan 1995.
I regret that Redfield 2004, a much broader investigation of the distinctive religious cults and institutions of Locri, appeared just too late to be dealt with in
revisions to my essay. Considerations of space do not allow me to examine the
problematic evidence for ritual prostitution associated with the cult of Locrian
Aphrodite (see especially Justin 21.3), though such a practice, if its actual existence could be demonstrated, might have important ramifications for our understanding of poems 4, 5, and 6. For very different evaluations of this evidence see
Prückner 1968, 4–14; Sourvinou-Inwood 1974; and Woodbury 1978.

17. Rapaciousness of both fictive and living courtesans had become a staple
complaint of Middle Comedy, for example in Anaxilas' *Neottis* (ap. Athenaeus
13.558a–e). On the courtesan as a dramatic character in Middle and New
Comedy, see Fantham 1975 and Henry 1985; McClure 2003 studies the later
cultural meanings of the courtesan figure.

18. For Samytha's likely association with the Adonis rites, see Gow and
Page 1965, 438. Detienne 1977 [1972] regards the use of exotic perfumes and
spices as one of the primary and essential ingredients of this cult. Theocritus
15.114 furnishes one well-known example of the practice.

19. On the divine and magical powers of nectar, imagined as a quintessen-
tially sweet fragrance, see Lilja 1972, 19–30. I am grateful to R. Ridinger for
calling my attention to this study.

20. For courtesans celebrating this feast see Menander *Sam.* 38–48; cf.
Diphilus as given in Athenaeus 7.292d, 10.451b (Meineke, FCG⁴, pp. 394–95,
399). At Alciphron *Epist. Meret.* 14.8, a woman invited to just such a celebration is asked to bring along *ton son Adônin* (your own Adonis) and at Lucian
Dial. Meret. 7.297 an older courtesan scornfully refers to her daughter's boy-
friend in virtually the same words. For discussion of these passages see Detienne
1977 [1972], 64–66.

21. Downey 1959 provides a basic overview of *ekphrasis* as an ancient literary convention. On the theory and practice of pictorial description in Hellenistic
literature, see Zanker 1987, 39–112.

22. On the encaustic technique see Pliny *HN* 35.149 and Vitruvius 7.9.3; Cagiano de Azevedo 1958–1966; Swindler 1929, 319–24; Pfuhl 1955, 124–25.

23. For Erinna 3 (*Anth. Pal.* 6.352) as our oldest ecphrastic epigram see Luck 1954, 171, and Scholz 1973, 21, with earlier bibliography. On Anyte 13 and 14 (*Anth. Pal.* 6.312, 9.745) as descriptions of artworks see Geoghegan 1979, 131, 137. I treat this subject at greater length in Skinner 2001.

24. I am indebted to Sarah B. Pomeroy for the idea that these three epigrams were written to order for paying customers. Examples of poems by male authors apparently testifying to real offerings by *hetairai*, and so presumably also commissioned, include Leonidas 2 (*Anth. Pal.* 6.211) and Callimachus 20 (*Anth. Pal.* 13.24), both scarcely more than lists. Contrast the purely literary epigram, allegedly by Plato, that converts the courtesan Lais' presentation of her mirror to Aphrodite into an object lesson in mutability (*Anth. Pal.* 6.1); the topos is later taken up by Philetas 1 (*Anth. Pal.* 6.210) and Julianus (*Anth. Pal.* 6.18, 19, 20). In fragment 122 (Snell-Maehler), Pindar exempts from blame an entire troop of slave women sent to serve Aphrodite of Corinth as temple prostitutes, but his remarks are meant to dignify the male donor's generosity. For the primary patriarchal class distinction between "respectable women" living under a man's protection and "disreputable women" whose sexuality is public and commercial, see Lerner 1986, 123–40.

25. Gow and Page (1965, 439) propose that *to gauron* here means "sprightliness" rather than "insolence." But the latent notion of overweening pride in *gauron* would be brought to the surface by the bombastic expression *despoina melathrôn*. This phrase is a variant of the positive term *oikodespoina*, found at Babrius 10.5 and Plutarch *Quaest. conv.* 612f and etymologically analyzed by Fraenkel 1952–1953, 32 (I owe this reference to H. Lloyd-Jones). Gow and Page themselves note that *melathrôn* seems "a curiously stilted word to use of a house in such a context." Moreover, *despoina* can easily take on negative overtones; cf. Menander fragment 333.7, where the word is applied to the tyrannical wife Crobule.

26. Gow and Page (1965, 440) observe that the form *skylakaina* does not occur elsewhere and that the feminine ending *–aina* furnishes the authors of Old Comedy with humorous material. At Aristophanes *Nub.* 658–67, the locus classicus, the joke springs from Socrates' pedantic insistence upon constructing a distinct feminine form for the names of female domestic animals normally subsumed under the generic masculine. It is conceivable that Nossis is intentionally alluding to this passage, thereby giving the description of Thaumareta's puppy additional comic flavor. My reading of this line has benefited from the incisive comments of H. Lloyd-Jones and J. Russo.

27. For conventional expressions of the sentiment see the parallel passages cited by Gow 1952, 2:334, on Theocritus 17.44 and by Fordyce 1961, 253, on Catullus 61.214–18.

28. For the stature of a divinity manifest note especially *Hymn. Hom. Cer.* 275 and *Hymn. Hom. Ven.* 173–74; cf. the political trick played by Pisistratus at Herodotus 1.60. Agamemnon identifies Penelope's wisdom (*pinutê*) as her characteristic feminine trait at *Od.* 11.445–46; compare the remarks of Telemachus at 20.131 and 21.103 and of Odysseus at 23.361. We may also adduce Hera's gift to the daughters of Pandareus at 20.70–71.

29. If the original manuscript reading *tênôthe* (thence) is retained, the suggestion of an alternative plane of reality becomes even more pronounced: note the significance of the plausible conjecture *toutothen* at Erinna fragment 402.1 *Supp. Hell.* and cf. the phrase *ho ekeithen angelos* at Plato *Resp.* 619b.

30. Lacey (1968, 172–74) cites this statement as a factual illustration of Athenian women's domestic influence upon the public actions of male family members; but we should take into account the tendentious character of the oratorical passage.

31. On the epic tone and diction of Anyte 1, 4, 9, and 21 and their close thematic parallels with other epigrams see the discussions of Geoghegan 1979, which show that in idealizing warfare she faithfully follows the dominant literary tradition. Luck (1954, 172–81) makes the same point.

32. The key Homeric passage is *Il.* 17.426–40, where the horses of Achilles weep for Patroclus; cf. 11.159–61, where runaway horses miss their fallen charioteers. Leonidas 35 (*Anth. Pal.* 6.131), Mnasalces 4 (*Anth. Pal.* 6.125) and Hegesippus 1 (*Anth. Pal.* 6.124) extend Homer's conceit by making dedicated weapons express devotion to their former owners.

33. This etymology is given in Diodorus 16.15.1–2 and Strabo 6.255.

34. For Rhinthon as a self-conscious and sophisticated parodist, see Taplin 1993, 48–52.

35. Gow and Page (1965, 441) find the use of this form unusual; but it may have been in vogue among Hellenistic poets. Cf. Callimachus *Lav. Pall.* 94 and Theocritus 8.38.

36. Aristotle's *Poetics* epitomizes the classical notion of an inherent superiority of genres: see especially 1462b15, where the highest place is finally awarded to tragedy over epic. In contrast, Callimachus 57 (*Anth. Pal.* 9.565) counterposes the poetic immortality of Theaetetus, possibly an epigrammatist, to the brief moment of glory accorded victors in dramatic competitions. On Aristotle and Callimachus as representative spokesmen for antithetical critical positions on measure and scale, see further Onians 1979, 121–34. For the Hellenistic admiration of the "perfect small work" applied to poetry by women, note the praise of Erinna's *Distaff* by the anonymous author of *Anth. Pal.* 9.190, who pronounces her three hundred lines "equal to Homer," and the even more effusive celebration of her lasting fame in Antipater of Sidon 58 (*Anth. Pal.* 7.713).

37. Gow and Page (1965, 435–36) provide an excellent summary of critical opinion on the crux involving the demonstrative pronoun *tênas* in the final line of poem 1. Their suggestion that the pronoun may refer to Nossis herself, rather than to Aphrodite or to the implied antecedent of *tina*, seems the most economical and acceptable solution. On the textual difficulties in the last distich of poem 11 see the survey of scholarship by Cazzaniga 1970, along with the remarks of Gow and Page 1965, 442; Luck 1954, 186–87; and Gigante 1974, 38–39. A rationale for following the corrected text of Page is provided in Skinner 1989, 12.

38. For this convention see Clayman 1976 and Van Sickle 1981. The pioneering treatment of the poetic *sphragis* is Kranz 1961. That the convention was already in force in Nossis' lifetime is evident from a signature poem by her contemporary Posidippus (Lloyd-Jones 1963). Its function in the Hellenistic

epigram collection is discussed by Gutzwiller 1998 s.v. *sphragis*.

39. The possibility that Nossis 1 was conceived as an introduction to a book-length epigram collection was first advanced by Luck 1954, 183. Long before, Reitzenstein (1893, 139) had proposed that Nossis 11 had once served to round off a book of poems, a suggestion that won the approval of Wilamowitz (1924, 1:135). For the programmatic character of poem 1 see especially Gigante 1981. Riedweg (1994, 141–50) attempts to dismiss a "poetological" reading of the quatrain by objecting to individual pieces of evidence; he does not take their cumulative weight into account.

40. Sappho *LP* 130.2, the famous description of the god as a "bittersweet irresistible crawling thing." Posidippus 1 (*Anth. Pal.* 5.134) and Meleager 61 (*Anth. Pal.* 12.109) employ Sappho's phrase in epigrams; Plutarch (*Quaest. conv.* 681b) indicates that by his time it had become proverbial. Carson has now traced out the complex psychological and literary resonances of the expression in a long meditative essay (1986). My deep thanks to D. Boedeker for observing this direct allusion to Sappho and remarking upon its significance.

41. Figurative use of the verb *apoptuein* is frequent in tragedy, always with the suggestion of something abominable. Note Clytemnestra's horrified reaction to the news of Agamemnon's impending sacrifice of their daughter, *apeptus', ô geraie, mython* (Euripides *IA* 874), and cf. these other instances: Aeschylus *Ag.* 1192, *Ch.* 197, *Eu.* 303; Euripides *Hec.* 1276, *Hel.* 664, *Hipp.* 614, *IT* 1161.

42. Degani (1981, 51–52) follows Gow and Page 1965 *ad loc.* in assuming that the poet's own name, emphatically stated one line above, is the immediate antecedent of *tênas*; he then interprets *anthea* as a figurative expression for her poetic compositions. The metaphor of poems as flowers is as old as Pindar *Ol.* 6.105 and common in programmatic literary statements: we need look no further than the proem to Meleager's *Garland* (Gow and Page 1 = *Anth. Pal.* 4.1). For the direct reminiscence of Sappho *LP* 55 in the last line see Gigante 1981, 244–45.

43. On the funerary motif of "conveying the message" see Tarán 1979, 132–49; Nossis 11 is examined on pp. 146–48. Tarán observes that the epigram utilizes expressions and conceits regularly associated with this motif but differs from other fictitious epitaphs, even those composed by poets for themselves, in its general tone and intention.

44. Gigante (1974, 25–26) lists a number of these reminiscences, claiming that Nossis' epigrams repeatedly attempt the imitation of Sappho in a Hellenistic key ("l'emulazione di Saffo in chiave ellenistica," 25).

45. Bowman (1998, 42–46) examines Nossis' recourse to Sappho as predecessor at much greater length. On the similarities in class outlook between Nossis and Sappho, especially in their joint construction of an elite female internal audience, see Gigante 1974, 25–26. The unconscious conviction that a woman who frankly affirmed the joys of love would not have been respectable may have induced Reitzenstein (1893, 142) to postulate that Nossis was herself a *hetaira*. Wilamowitz (1924, 1:135) objected to Reitzenstein's notion, which has since been decisively refuted by Cazzaniga 1972.

46. Meleager's epithet *myropnoun* almost certainly points to the white iris (*Iris florentina*), which yields orris root, the principal ingredient of the unguent *myron irinon*: see Theophrastus *Hist. Pl.* 1.7.2, 9.7.3–4, and Athenaeus 15.689e. Pliny (*HN* 21.19) states that this flower is not used in garlands; but see the refer-

ences in Lilja 1972, 185. On the exotic origins of myrrh see Herodotus 3.107 and Theophrastus *Hist. Pl.* 9.4, along with the remarks of Detienne 1977 [1972], 5–8; for its erotic aspects cf. Detienne 60–66 and Lilja 60–76. Because the process of encaustic painting involved laying pigmented wax onto a panel with a heated implement to fuse the colors, Greek epigrammatists hit upon the topos of the enamored painter whose heart is softened by desire for his sitter: for example, in *Anth. Plan.* 16.80.5–6, *isa gar autôi/ kêrôi têkomenôi têketai hê kradiê* (for his heart is melted like the melted wax itself). Meleager's capsule description of Nossis is unquestionably a clever variant of that conceit. *Deltos*, the standard Greek noun for the wooden writing tablet with a waxen interior surface, may also be applied, at least metaphorically, to the wooden panel that served as support for the image depicted in encaustic: see Aristophanes *Thesm.* 778.

47. On the spelling of Herodas' name, his likely *floruit* (the late 70s and early 60s of the third century BCE), and the nature of his compositions, see the introductory comments of Cunningham 1971, 1–17. Mastromarco 1984 establishes that Herodas wrote for an educated audience.

48. Crusius (1892, 118) was the first to claim that 6.20–21 is a malicious slur upon both women poets, a suggestion that has won general acceptance. H. Lloyd-Jones is credited by Cunningham (1964, 32 n. 3) with observing the sinister significance of Herodas' insertion of *Baukides* along with *Nossides* in the ostensible catalogue of footwear at 7.57–58. Taking a hint from Crusius, who supposed that Herodas was attacking these poets for their artistic failings, Stern (1979, 254) theorizes that Erinna and Nossis are denounced for "taking the art of poetry in wrong directions." In the previous version of this paper I dismissed this idea, attributing Herodas' barbs to "ordinary misogyny," but I have since concluded (Skinner 2001, 216 n. 61) that Stern is correct, and that Herodas' attacks upon Hellenistic women writers in general and Nossis in particular were provoked by their growing influence upon the mainstream literary tradition.

49. Seneca *Ep.* 88.37 provides evidence that Sappho's alleged unchastity was a topic of scholarly debate; cf. the slanders mentioned by the biographer of *P. Oxy.* 1800 fr. 1, col. 1.16–19. For the tradition of portraying Sappho as the beloved of numerous male poets see Dover 1978, 174. Menander fragment 258 alludes to the most famous Sapphic legend, that of her suicidal leap from the white rock at Cape Leukas in pursuit of the boatman Phaon. By the first century ACE the tale had been incorporated into her biography; see Ovid *Her.* 15. For its likely mythic origins see Nagy 1973 and Lefkowitz 1981, 36–37. On this later "heterosexualization" of Sappho's erotic life see Hallett 1979, 448–49.

50. Using examples of the critical reception of texts by Charlotte Perkins Gilman and Susan Keating Glaspell, Kolodny 1980 demonstrates that readers accustomed to an exclusively male-oriented conceptual system are often inadequate interpreters of literary products dealing with women's conceptual and symbolic worlds. Snyder 1991 shows that this is true for earlier work on Sappho. For a hypothetical (and decidedly controversial) model of a "woman's poetics" see Lipking 1983.

51. On female subcultures and their role in shaping the outlook of the woman writers who participate in them, see Showalter 1977, 11. For the possibility that the domestic sphere of Greek women constituted a likely matrix for such a subculture see Skinner 1987, 41–42.

52. Lefkowitz (1981, 36–37) notes that Sappho's ancient biography simply portrays her as conforming (or not conforming) to expected patterns of female behavior. Against those who conclude from her poetry that Lesbian women enjoyed high status and esteem Arthur (1973, 38–43) contends that Sappho's lyrics, like those of male poets of the same era, create an idealized, aristocratic fantasy world of refinement and romantic passion having little to do with reality. Even in antiquity there was some spirited argument about the foundation and customs of Italian Locri, as evidenced by the historian Timaeus' attack on Aristotle's account of its origins and Polybius' later polemic against Timaeus' assertions (Polybius 12.5–11). While Timaeus had apparently insisted that Locri was a normal Greek city, Polybius explicitly states that some of its usages were borrowed from the native Sicels (12.5.10); for an attempt to determine what Timaeus actually wrote see Pearson 1987, 98–104. The supposed evidence for *Mutterrecht* at Locri as a remnant of indigenous Italian customs is laid out in Oldfather 1927, cols. 1345–49; cf., however, the skeptical comments of Dunbabin 1948, 183–86. Redfield (2004, 385) attempts to show that Epizephyrian Locri constituted a third type of city-state, differing from the antithetical models of Sparta and Athens; at Locri, he concludes, sexual complementarity and the celebration of the honorable state of the married woman provided validation, within an "Orphic" context, for the entire social order.

53. On this topic see Pomeroy 1977 and Cole 1981.

54. Those who have contributed to the final version of this essay include Ellen Greene, Judith Hallett, Hugh Lloyd-Jones, Amy Richlin, Joseph Russo, Jane McIntosh Snyder, and Eva Stehle. I owe particular thanks to Deborah Boedeker for her excellent literary insights and her friendly encouragement. I also appreciate the suggestions of the two anonymous referees for the University of North Carolina Press who reviewed the Pomeroy volume and the referee for the University of Oklahoma Press who reconsidered it for this collection. None of these people is responsible in any way for whatever faults remain.

7   Playing with Tradition

Gender and Innovation in the Epigrams of Anyte

Ellen Greene

As Sylvia Barnard has observed, Anyte's poetry has received scant critical attention.[1] Indeed, the work of Anyte's Hellenistic contemporaries Erinna and Nossis has provoked feminist scholars to investigate their peculiarly feminine forms of discourse and to see in their poems evidence of an alternate female poetic tradition reaching back to Sappho.[2] Anyte's epigrams, on the other hand, have often been viewed as reflecting the concerns and sensibilities of patriarchal culture.[3] Some recent scholars, however, have sought to define the feminine qualities in her poetry and to establish Anyte as a distinctly feminine writer whose work merits significant attention.[4] Kathryn Gutzwiller (1998) argues persuasively that Anyte's focus on feminine concerns and her deviation from masculine themes and values found in traditional epigram identify Anyte's literary voice as particularly feminine. My own analysis is an attempt to map out a middle ground between earlier views of Anyte as a writer who merely apes prevailing patriarchal values and more recent discussions of Anyte that emphasize the feminine sensibilities and values in her work.[5] I argue that Anyte's art lies in her innovative use of conventional literary genres, her ability to blend the personal and domestic with the "high" art of the heroic. The set of concerns and points of view expressed in Anyte's poems may be identified as feminine, yet much of Anyte's work can be linked to traditionally masculine forms of expression.

I will focus primarily on Anyte's laments and pet epitaphs, and more specifically on how Anyte's transposition of Homeric vocabulary to the personal and domestic sphere deflates heroic conventions and, at the same time, elevates the domestic to the heroic. While Anyte wrote her poems in the form of traditional epigram and largely confined herself to its dedicatory and funereal genres, she nonetheless introduced important innovations into the epigram that appear to have had a significant impact on later writers—particularly her pet epitaphs and pastoral poems.[6] As D. Geoghegan (1979) has shown in his commentary on Anyte's epigrams, we find numerous references to and borrowings from Greek literary culture in Anyte— particularly an abundant use of Homeric vocabulary. Indeed, Geoghegan points out that in antiquity the phrase θῆλυν Ὅμηρον (female Homer) may have been applied to Anyte.[7] Her use of Homeric imagery and her laments for slain warriors and their horses have contributed to the view of Anyte as a poet who merely imitates the dominant literary tradition. Yet Anyte transforms traditional epigram through her application of the heroic language of Homeric verse to a context that is often personal and idiosyncratic. Unlike Sappho and Erinna, whose work may reflect a parallel women's literary tradition, Anyte, at least in some of her poems, maintains the tensions of "high" and "low" art and thus creates a unique interplay between established male literary culture and the domesticity typically associated with women.

My investigation begins with a discussion of three of Anyte's four epitaphs for young unmarried women—whose deaths are lamented either through the voice of the speaker or through the voice of the deceased girl's mother.[8] Anyte's focus on female concerns appears to figure most prominently in this group of epigrams, and thus it is reasonable to assume that in these poems we would most likely be able to discern a distinctly feminine voice and poetic identity. Indeed, four out of five of Anyte's human epitaphs represent a mother's grief for a deceased unmarried daughter. These epigrams, as Gutzwiller 1998 has shown, clearly express an affirmation of the worth of women's lives and particularly attest to the value of the mother-daughter relationship. In the process, Anyte's poems often invoke the Homeric tradition and thus overturn masculine genres of epic and epigram and the celebration of masculine heroic endeavor so integral to those genres.

In 5 G-P (*AP* 7.486) the dramatic figure of a mother, named Cleina, laments for the death of her daughter who died before her marriage—before the point that marked the apex of a woman's life. In the context of a society that often valued women chiefly for their use as vehicles of procreation, the pathos expressed by Cleina at the death of her daughter emphasizes the importance of the mother-daughter relationship and celebrates the worth of the young woman's life for its own sake.

Πολλάξυ τῷδ' ὀλοφυδνὰ κόρας ἐπὶ σήματι Κλείνα
    μάτηρ ὠκύμορον παῖδ' ἐβόασε φίλαν,
ψυχὰν ἀγκαλέουσα Φιλαινίδος, ἅ πρὸ γάμοιο
    χλωρὸν ὑπὲρ ποταμοῦ χεῦμ' Ἀχέροντος ἔβα.   (5 G-P=*AP* 7.486)

Often in lamentation at this tomb of her daughter, Cleina,
    the mother, cried out for her dear child who died
too soon. Calling on the soul of Philaenis, who before
    marriage crossed over the pale stream of the river Acheron.

Surviving literary epigrams before Anyte typically celebrate the heroism of men slain in battle. Commemorating the life of a woman whose only worth is authenticated through the love of her mother, and not through the *kleos* (glory) achieved by the deceased, emphasizes the power of the mother-daughter bond, but more important, it validates the public expression of female grief. As Nicole Loraux (1987, 1–3) points out, in classical Athens no public comment on a woman's death was considered acceptable, and it was the husband's duty to ensure that his wife not be the subject of either praise or blame among men. In the case of the death of an unmarried woman, the standard for public silence would be even higher. The lamentation of a mother for her daughter was expected to occur in the private sphere—where women conducted their personal relationships in general. However, the image of Cleina lamenting at the tomb, that is, in a public space, evokes a tradition of lament in which women's prominent roles in lamenting the dead both reflect and reinforce realms of experience exclusive to women.[9] Indeed, the narrator's emphasis on Cleina's loss of her daughter's potential marriage attests to the value Cleina attaches to marriage itself as a defining feature of a woman's worth and identity. As scholars have argued, however, the celebration of women's traditional roles in women's laments for one another constituted a female history, a "female line of transmission" that may be considered an alternative to masculine models of heroic lament.[10]

In addition, the image of Cleina lamenting for her daughter, whose soul is described as "crossing the river Acheron," may evoke the myth of Demeter and Persephone—a myth that is emblematic of mothers lamenting their daughters' premature deaths. As Helene Foley (1994, 123) argues, the Demeter/Persephone myth stresses the "intergenerational chain of relations from mother to daughter" and "concentrates on the experience of female protagonists in a female world." As in the myth, Anyte's poem clearly celebrates the centrality of the mother-daughter relation and seems to authorize the mother's public expression of grief. However, Anyte's evocation of the Persephone myth here seems ironic. Unlike Demeter, Cleina cannot revive her daughter from the dead, cannot recall her from the depths of Hades. The finality of Cleina's separation from her daughter heightens her sense of irremediable loss, and it serves as a reminder that human mothers have no power to reverse the course of natural events.

The Homeric allusions in the poem also serve to accentuate Cleina's unmitigated loss. Geoghegan (1979, 65–68) points out that Cleina's lament echoes both Achilles' mourning of Patroklos in *Iliad* 23 and Thetis' mourning for Achilles. Although Achilles' lament for Patroklos clearly celebrates homosocial bonds between men, in *Iliad* 16 (7f.) Homer implicitly compares Achilles to a mother where Patroklos is likened to a child crying after his hurrying, anxious mother. Thus Anyte's Homeric allusions here point to mothers lamenting their "sons'" tragically premature deaths on the battlefield. Cleina and Achilles "cry out for the souls" of their loved ones, and both Cleina and Thetis lament their children who died too soon (ὠκύμορον). As Sheila Murnaghan (1999, 204) points out, lamentation in the *Iliad* threatens to imperil the "*kleos*-conferring function of epic because it stresses the suffering caused by heroic death rather than the glory won by it." Achilles' lamentation for Patroklos, coupled with his withdrawal from battle, emphasizes his alienation from warrior culture and also links him with a mode of speech most closely associated with women—whose plight as survivors, captives, and victims of war is often expressed through verbal expressions of grief.

The laments of both Achilles and Thetis clearly differ in a profound way from that of Cleina. Although both Achilles and Thetis may be considered mothers, their laments do not express merely

personal loss. While Homer emphasizes the tremendous pathos in
their expressions of grief, those laments are, nonetheless, cast within
a framework in which the memory of the glorious deeds of the
deceased offers compensation for personal loss.[11] Both Patroklos
and Achilles die in the service either of their armies or of personal
glory. Their deaths, while presented as tragic, will be mitigated by
the *kleos* they will receive, a *kleos* to which Homer's poem constantly
attests (particularly in Achilles' case). Although Achilles' lamentation for Patroklos is among the most extravagant laments in the
poem, Achilles' grief ultimately turns into action—a passionate
desire for revenge that will lead to his death and ensure his *kleos*.[12]
Achilles himself acknowledges this at *Iliad* 18.120–24 when he
announces to Thetis that he now embraces his death and the glory
attendant upon it: "So I likewise, if such is the fate which has been
wrought for me, shall lie still, when I am dead. Now I must win
excellent glory, and drive some one of the women of Troy, or some
deep-girdled Dardanian woman, lifting up to her soft cheeks both
hands to wipe away the close bursts of tears in her lamentation."[13]
Even Thetis, who laments Achilles' death as a human mother, orders
armor from Hephaistos to help ensure Achilles' *kleos*. While both
Thetis and Achilles are never fully assuaged by the knowledge of the
glory their beloved ones will receive, the audience is, nonetheless,
constantly aware of the larger context within which death and
mourning are presented. In the end, even Achilles champions the
suppression of lamentation as he becomes reidentified with his warrior identity. Thus he tells Priam in book 24 to stop mourning, since
"there is not any advantage to be won from grim lamentation"
(*Iliad* 24.524). Moreover, Patroklos and Achilles are both made
worthy—as subjects of lament—through their tremendous, larger-
than-life deeds on the battlefield. Cleina's daughter Philaenis, on the
other hand, is lamented by her mother because she died too soon,
before she was able to fulfill her roles as a wife and mother. Achilles'
initial expression of grief over Patroklos occurs after Homer elabo-
rates at length the heroic deeds of Patroklos on the battlefield. The
arête (valor) of the hero is inextricably tied to the hero's death. And
in the *Iliad* it is only through a glorious death that a hero will be
remembered and his heroic stature guaranteed.

Anyte's allusions to Homer in her laments also evoke the role
of women in the *Iliad* in their lamentations over the dead male warriors (husbands, sons, brothers, etc.). As Holst-Warhaft has pointed
out, the most elaborate treatment of lament in Homer is the funeral

of Hector.[14] Not only do women lead the laments as professional mourners and as kinswomen, but they also offer a perspective on death that emphasizes the particular qualities of the deceased and a sense of personal loss without the compensations of *kleos*. In her lament Andromache addresses Hector directly, and rather than praising him for his heroic deeds, she emphasizes her sense of loss and abandonment. Similarly, the narrator in Anyte's epigrams 6 and 8 speaks in the first person, and in 6 the poetic voice addresses the deceased Thersis directly, specifically acknowledging in both poems that death destroys both beauty and wisdom.

> παρθένον Ἀντιβίαν κατοδύρομαι, ἇς ἐπὶ πολλοὶ
>   νυμφίοι ἱέμενοι πατρὸς ἵκοντο δόμον
> κάλλευς καὶ πινυτᾶτος ἀνὰ κλέος· ἀλλ' ἐπιπάντων
>   ἐλπίδας οὐλομένα Μοῖρ' ἐκύλισε πρόσω   (6 G-P = AP 7.490)

I mourn the maiden Antibia, for whom many desiring young men
    came to her father's house,
drawn by her reputation for beauty and wisdom.
    But destructive Fate rolled away out of reach
the hopes of all of them.

> ἀντί τοι εὐλεχέος θαλάμου σεμνῶν θ' ὑμεναίων
>   μάτηρ στᾶσε τάφῳ τῷδ' ἔπι μαρμαρίνῳ
> παρθενικὰν μέτρον τε τεὸν καὶ κάλλος ἔχοισαν,
>   Θερσί, ποτιφθεγκτὰ δ' ἔπλεο καὶ φθίμενα.   (8 G-P = AP 7.649)

Instead of a bedchamber and the holy rites of marriage
    your mother has placed upon this marble tomb
a maiden's statue having your shape and beauty,
    and you, Thersis, though dead, can be saluted.

In epigram 6, the mourner speaks in the first person, and thus in Gutzwiller's view (1998, 60) "merges of course with Anyte herself, whose sorrow for Antibia seems emblematic of the grief she feels for all the maidens lost to a premature death." This apparent merging of poet and persona leads Gutzwiller to assert that this group of epigrams offers a "feminine perspective on death expressed through a chorus of female voices—grieving mothers, dying daughters, and the epigrammatist herself." In epigrams 5 and 8 it is clear that the narrator describes a mother's expression of grief for her daughter, and in 6 the speaker both expresses grief over Antibia in a first-person utterance and at the same time ruminates in a general way on the pointlessness of her death. While I agree with Gutzwiller that the speaker of the poem expresses a feminine perspective through (her) evocation of women's lament, I think the last two lines of the epigram introduce an impersonality of tone that draws not only on the tradition of epigram itself but also on genres of epic and public lament.[15]

Geoghegan (1979, 73) points out that repeated echoes of Homer occur in epigram 6, especially in line 3. The phrase κάλλευς καὶ πινυτᾶτος ἀνὰ κλέος (referring to Antibia's reputation for beauty and wisdom) alludes both to *Iliad* 13 (364ff) and to *Odyssey* 20 (70–71). With regard to the Iliadic reference, Anyte substitutes πολέμοιο μετὰ κλέος (after the rumor of war) with her phrase πινυτᾶτος ἀνὰ κλέος. In the *Iliad* a soldier is drawn to the κλέος of battle, while in Anyte's poem Antibia's potential bridegrooms are attracted by the κλέος of the maiden's beauty and wisdom. In the Homeric context, the use of κλέος has the implication of both the rumor (of battle) and the glory the soldier will potentially receive as a result of his participation and eventual death in battle. In Anyte's poem κλέος is usually translated as "word," "fame," "report," or "reputation."[16] Not only does Anyte equate the κλέος of beauty and wisdom with the κλέος of battle, she implicitly elevates Antibia's virtues to heroic status by linking her death to the Homeric tradition. Moreover, the allusion to Homer suggests an expansion of the sense of κλέος here. Antibia's suitors are drawn by her reputation, but in Antibia's death the "I" of the poem grants her immortality by proclaiming her beauty and wisdom. Despite the senselessness of her death, the κλέος conferred on Antibia by the speaker does, to some degree, have a mitigating force. The same can be said of epigram 8, where the apostrophizing voice of the speaker "saluting Thersis though she is dead" has an even stronger mitigating effect. In this way, Anyte's poems go beyond traditionally feminine perspectives on death in the way they bring the ordinary lived experiences of women into dialogue with male heroic tradition.

In addition, in line 3 of epigram 6, the first three words in the phrase κάλλευς καὶ πινῦτατος ἀνὰ κλέος recalls in the *Odyssey* the story of Pandarus told by Penelope in her prayer to Artemis.[17] Like Antibia, the daughters of Pandarus died before marriage. In her prayer, Penelope asks Artemis to take the life from her just as Zeus once carried away the orphaned maidens to the "hateful Furies." Comparing her situation to that of Pandarus' daughters emphasizes Penelope's sense of abandonment and loss, but more important, it accentuates the notion that beauty and wisdom (πινυτή) can do nothing to prevent an often unjust Fate from running its course.[18] Penelope's unfortunate situation causes her not only to express her personal grief but to contemplate more generally the μοῖρα and ἀμμορίη (the "luck" and "lucklessness") that afflicts mortals.[19] Likewise, the last line of epigram 6 emphasizes the bitterness of Antibia's death and also suggests the tragedy of the human condition in general. The pathos that comes through in Penelope's prayer to Artemis depends as much on her personal loss as on her awareness of the unpredictability of an often destructive Fate that can snatch away all hope from even the most innocent and judicious of mortals. Indeed, scholars have argued that, since antiquity, women's laments often express grievances that sometimes amount to a form of protest against various forms of injustice.[20] Protest against death itself is frequently one of the complaints expressed in women's laments.

In epigram 6 the speaker shifts from the declaration of Antibia's beauty and wisdom to the more general statement about the capricious, destructive nature of Fate in taking away what is most dear in life. The bitterness implicit in this statement recalls, in Andromache's lament, her sense of outrage at the host of injustices to which she will be subject as a result of Hector's abandonment of her. As Anna Caraveli (1986, 182) argues, the element of protest in women's laments sometimes takes the form of "an attack against a vast, all-encompassing category of evils." But Caraveli also points out that no matter how general the grievance being lamented may be, the focus is almost always on the particular suffering it brings to the female mourner. And in many cases the grievances expressed by women relate to the particular injustices women experience as a result of their vulnerable positions in a social order largely controlled by men. Penelope and Andromache lament not only the (potential) deaths of their husbands, but also their own loss of identity and social status as a result of losing the men through whom they are defined.

While in some ways Penelope epitomizes femininity in the *Odyssey* through her association with female chastity and devotion to the *oikos* (household), she is also the only figure in the poem (male or female) who rivals Odysseus for cleverness and prudence. Homer emphasizes her heroic stature (that may be said to outshine Odysseus') in book 24 by accentuating her valiant achievement in remaining faithful—despite women's more typical behavior, which is presented throughout the poem as disruptive of the stability of the *oikos*. Thus, the allusion to Penelope in the poem, in my view, reflects a "double consciousness," a consciousness that incorporates female helplessness (as in the case of Pandarus' daughters) and, at the same time, a rational awareness about the capricious workings of Fate.[21] While the last line in epigram 6 has a generalizing force that recalls the element of protest in women's laments, the speaker's statement does not evoke the suffering of any particular (female) mourner. Caraveli points out that one of the most important criteria for defining a "true" lament is the expression of emotional engagement and intensity on the part of the mourner. In the *Iliad*, both Achilles and Andromache express such emotional intensity; their laments not only communicate their intense feelings of loss, but also their powerful personal bonds with the deceased (Caraveli 1986). While the speaker in Anyte's poem expresses personal grief (κατοδύρομαι), she also takes on the impersonal voice of the (male) epic poet whose ability to confer κλέος assures the heroic stature of the deceased.

In addition, epigrams 6 and 8 both have qualities that may be associated with funeral orations in classical Athens. As scholars have shown, changes in attitudes toward mourning began to occur in the sixth century BCE in Athens, and then in a number of places in the Greek world through the third century.[22] In particular, women's formerly prominent role in mourning rituals became severely restricted, and in the later classical period mourning was explicitly characterized as both unmanly and un-Greek.[23] Plutarch, for example, described mourning as "something feminine, weak and ignoble; women are more inclined to it than men, barbarians more than Hellenes."[24] It is difficult to know to what degree Anyte may have been influenced by Athenian attitudes toward mourning. But it is not unlikely that some of those attitudes affected her epigrams. As Holst-Warhaft (1992, 5) points out, classical funeral orations for those who die in battle make a "virtue of death, provided it is death in the service of the state." What is relevant for our purposes here is that in all surviving classical orations the dead are praised rather than lamented.[25] Although the speaker in epigrams 6 and 8 does not lament a fallen soldier, she (or he), nonetheless, focuses on the remarkable traits that will bring κλέος to the deceased rather than on the plight of the survivors. Further, unlike in traditional women's laments, the speaker in these poems never expresses the strong personal bond with the deceased that would precipitate intense grief. Like the praise accorded to those who die in the service of the state, the praise bestowed on Antibia and Thersis places them "in a realm of glory beyond the reach of death" (Holst-Warhaft 1992, 120). The mourner's emphasis on the virtues of the dead, on salutation rather than on pathos, imparts to these epigrams a quality of public praise that borrows from the male genre of classical funeral oration. The epigram as a whole thus offers a unique blend of masculine and feminine perspectives on death, a complex intertwining of personal and impersonal modes of expression.

A number of scholars have suggested that Anyte's pet epitaphs represent the most innovative examples of her work which were also copied by later authors.[26] What is particularly striking about these poems is their extensive application of the heroic language of Homeric verse to the sphere of ordinary and everyday life—a sphere with which women and children were typically associated. Gutzwiller (1998, 62) argues that, unlike male authors who treat similar themes, Anyte's expressions of sympathy for and commiseration with dead animals is "entirely consistent with the nurturing and care-giving function that women performed in Greek society." Gutzwiller's analysis of Anyte's animal epitaphs offers a convincing argument that Anyte's identification with animals helps to identify her voice as distinctly feminine. In addition, Gutzwiller (1998, 64) argues that Anyte shows us a way of perceiving animals differently—not as "servants of men" or as "objects of utility"—but as creatures in whom we may find a profound sense of commonality and kinship. Anyte's abundant use of Homeric references and witty wordplay suggest an ironic stance toward male heroic tradition and also reflect the "double consciousness" that we have seen in her human laments. Anyte's epigram 10, her lament for a puppy killed by a snake, offers a striking illustration of this.

The epigram opens with an echo of Andromache's lament for Hector in the *Iliad* (24.725).

Ὤλεο δή ποτε καὶ σὺ πολύρριζον παρὰ θάμνον,
    Λόκρι, φιλοφθόγγων ὠκυτάτη σκυλάκων,
τοῖον ἐλαφρίζοντι τεῷ ἐγκάτθετο κώλῳ
    ἰὸν ἀμείλικτον ποικιλόδειρος ἔχις. (10 G=P)

You perished, even you, once beside a many-rooted bush,
    Locris, swiftest of noise-loving puppies,

Into your nimble limb a speckle-necked snake
    put such harsh poison.

Like Andromache to Hector, the speaker here uses the word ὤλεο
(you perished) to address the dead puppy (Gutzwiller 1998, 63).
This direct reminiscence of Andromache's lament playfully characterizes the perished puppy as a great hero who has given his life to
protect his homeland. This serves on the one hand to elevate the
ordinary activities of everyday life to heroic stature and, at the same
time, to deflate the solemnity and grandeur associated with heroic
lament. Andromache's lament, however, is pervaded by recrimination
and blame. Not once in her lament does Andromache praise Hector
for his heroic qualities. She focuses exclusively on how he is to blame
for all the suffering and hardship she and her son will endure as a
result of being abandoned. And Andromache ends her lament by
reproaching Hector for not even giving her the satisfaction of sharing
some final words with him on his deathbed. While ὤλεο may have
been common in women's laments, the self-conscious and pervasive
use of Homeric references in Anyte's epigrams suggests that this
Homeric allusion may have a more specific purpose here. Unlike
Andromache, the speaker in the poem praises the deceased puppy for
his particular traits of swiftness and noise-loving and does not, as
Andromache, focus on her anger at the deceased for leaving.

  Moreover, the phrase καὶ σύ (and you) in line 1 is puzzling.[27]
The specificity of the dog's identity is emphasized by the speaker's
naming of the animal as well as by her direct address to him. Thus
the phrase "you too perished" does not seem to fit within the context of lamenting the death of a particular pet. Surely the speaker
cannot mean that Locris is one of many pets who have perished.
Accordingly, I take the phrase to mean something like "even you,
Locris, perished," implying that the speaker is not merely mourning
the death of this particular animal but, as in the human laments,
reflecting in a more general way on the capricious and inevitable
nature of mortality. The death of this puppy makes the speaker
aware of the mortality of all living things; even an energetic puppy
can meet death suddenly and unexpectedly. But the way this is
expressed is strikingly devoid of the bitterness in Andromache's
lament. Indeed, the tone of the speaker's lament is neither
anguished nor resigned, instead it expresses calm reflection and
rational awareness. Although its poison is harsh, the snake itself is
described as beautiful, as ποικιλόδειρπς—a word that is used by

Hesiod of a nightingale and by Alcaeus of ducks.[28] This description of the snake suggests that the speaker has no bitterness toward death but sees it as part of the natural world.

Although the speaker clearly expresses compassion for the puppy, she does not express any emotion, any sense of personal pathos over the death of this animal.[29] The use of epic diction throughout the poem, as well as the words ποτε (once) and καὶ σύ, give the lament a quality of narrative that imparts a distance to the speaker's presentation of the puppy's death. This distance is characteristic of the objective style of epigram; indeed, the phrase καὶ σύ is fairly common in epitaphs in the *Anthology* and often suggests the commonality and inevitability of death.[30] The phrase καὶ σύ is also formulaic in funerary contexts and would thus link the speaker's expression of grief to masculine funeral oration as well.[31]

While the poem's reminiscence of Andromache's lament may suggest that the speaker in the poem is female, it does not necessarily imply that the narrator's voice reflects traditional feminine perspectives and values. The speaker at the end seems to praise predator and prey alike; indeed, they are both presented as having qualities worthy of admiration. The poem appears to take an ironic stance not only toward heroic tradition but toward the tradition of women's lament as well. The speaker's calm acceptance and dispassionate tone show a departure from the intense emotional engagement characteristic of women's laments. At the same time, the manner of the speaker's lament for the puppy, marked in the poem by praise rather than pathos, suggests a close affinity with public forms of encomia designed to affirm the glorification of death as compensation for personal loss. Clearly, Anyte's poem does not fit neatly into generic categories but draws on elements of traditional epigram, women's lament, and on the male-centered discourses of public funeral oration. What is perhaps most innovative is that it crosses traditional boundaries between public and private, between male and female modes of expression. In its concern for the death of a noisy little puppy, the poem evokes the personal sphere more associated with women than with men. Yet the speaker's calm philosophical attitude presents the death of Locris the puppy as neither heroic nor trivial but simply as part of a natural process to which all life is subject.

Epigram 4, one of two of Anyte's surviving epitaphs for a soldier slain in battle, appears to follow the traditional pattern for human

epitaphs through its ostensible celebration of masculine achievements and values. While, in the poems discussed above, Anyte elevates the lives and experiences of women by linking them to male
heroic tradition, in epigram 4 Anyte reverses this process. Here the
speaker commemorates the death of a warrior in battle, yet by
means of a simile Anyte performs a kind of gender inversion that
significantly transforms male-centered discourses of public praise for
the dead.[32]

Ἥβα μέν σε, πρόαρχε, ἔσαν· παίδων ἅτε ματρός,
   φειδία, ἐν δνοφερῷ πένθει ἔθου φθίμενος,
ἀλλὰ καλίν τοι ὕπερθεν ἔπος τόδε πέτρος ἀείδει
   ὡς ἔθανες πρὸ φίλας μαρνάμενος πατρίδος.

(4 G-P = *AP* 7.724)

The youth buried you, captain. Dying, Pheidias,
   you cast them into dark grief, just as
children for their mother. But the stone
   above you sings this beautiful song,
that you died fighting for your beloved country.[33]

The opening of the epigram departs dramatically from Anyte's
other surviving laments, which typically begin with personal expressions of grief. Here the mourner is Ἥβα (a body of youth) rather than
an individual. This initial emphasis on collective grief suggests a reminiscence of classical funeral oration. In Athens, the war dead were
publicly praised and commemorated not as individuals but as citizens
of the state. Although it is the captain who is remembered here, those
who are "cast into dark grief" are an unnamed, undifferentiated body
of soldiers whose relationship to the deceased is defined by a public,
official, perhaps even political affiliation. Holst-Warhaft (1992, 124)
argues that in the new democracy of Athens the old forms of lament
in Homer and in the folk tradition were abandoned in favor of new
forms of praise for the dead: "The *polis*'s substitution of public praise
for private mourning, at least as it presents itself in the context of the
funeral oration, involves a rejection of tears and laments for the dead
as feminine, barbaric, trivial." Indeed, Anyte's poem, on the surface,
seems to substitute public praise for private mourning and to celebrate the (masculine) ideal of death in service to one's country and
the glory attendant on such a death.

Anyte's simile in the first line, however, significantly alters the
masculine perception of death and the discourse of public praise

apparently endorsed by the poem.[34] First, by comparing the captain to a mother who is mourned by her children, Anyte reverses the usual position of mothers as passive mourners.[35] Not only is the mother herself mourned, but she is implicitly presented as active and as someone whose deeds in life merit commemoration perhaps equal to those of a soldier on the battlefield. Second, and more important, through the simile Anyte takes the more abstract "love" of a body of youth for its captain (and a captain's love for his country) and makes it more personal. By linking that love to the sphere of the family—in particular to the intense bonds between mothers and their children—Anyte imparts an element of individuality and specificity to the abstract, public quality of praise and lament for those who have died in battle. The impersonal relationship between a soldier and his captain and between soldiers and the abstract aims of the state are linked in Anyte's poem with the more personal values of care and nurturance associated with women in general and mothers in particular. I am not arguing, however, that Anyte is simply trying to elevate women's experiences and values over those of men. By adding this simile to what would be a traditional celebration of masculine κλέος on the battlefield, Anyte shows that public praise and private mourning need not be in opposition to one another. Rather, Anyte presents private and public grief here as parts within the totality of human experience. Anyte challenges traditional oppositions between private and public spheres, familial and political bonds, and between what may be considered strictly "masculine" and "feminine" sensibilities.

In the last two lines of the epigram, the deaths of the captain Pheidias and (implicitly) of the unnamed mother appear to be mitigated by what Geoghegan (1979, 62) calls the "bold metaphor of the singing stone." Gutzwiller (1998, 60) discusses these last two lines as a departure from Anyte's usual (feminine) perspective on death—a perspective that "offers no comforting excuses . . . but sees in death only the senseless destruction of the goodness and beauty in life." But as I argue here, Anyte's epigrams present a complex picture of death and mourning that often emphasizes links between public and private spheres and forms of lament. Consolation is thus almost always an integral part of lamentation.

In contrast to Anyte's allusions throughout the poem, the metaphor of the singing stone is, according to Geoghegan, an innovation of Anyte's. Scholars typically read the last two lines of the poem as offering a conventional celebration of heroic death in battle, but it seems to me rather that Anyte's poem takes an ironic twist. The qualifying force of ἀλλὰ (but) in the emphatic first position at line 3 introduces an adversative element into the mood of praise and lamentation that characterizes the first two lines of the poem. The image of a singing stone is, if taken literally, paradoxical. The living grief of the youths and the children gets no voice on the stone. Rather, the stone, itself cold and dead, merely extols the abstract glory of death in battle. While the first two lines vividly evoke the pathos of personal and communal grief, the ἔπος (word, speech) on the stone, although καλόν (beautiful), only expresses an impersonal notion of duty to country. Moreover, the assonance in πέτρος (rock) in line 3 and πατρίδος (πατρίς, fatherland) in line 4 links the image of the "cold" stone with an impersonal fatherland.

The "dark grief" of the youths for their captain is, ironically, a more personal memorial to the life of Pheidias than is a stone that "sings" only of an impersonal death in the service of the abstract goals of the πατρίς. This emphasis on the impersonality of death in battle is reinforced by the speaker's shift from direct address in the first two lines to third-person narrative in the last two. Moreover, the last line includes the Homeric formula φίλην ἐς πάριδ' and recalls other epigrams commemorating the deaths of warriors. Indeed, the stone's message seems hollow in comparison with the speaker's expression of personal commiseration for mourners and mourned alike; the threefold use of the vocative in lines 1–2 (σε, πρόαρχε, Φειδία) heightens this effect. In addition, the contrast between ματρός (mother) in line 1 and πατρίς (πατρίδος) in line 4 reinforces the opposition in the poem between the more personal, feminine form of lament in the first two lines and the more abstract, masculine mode of commemoration in the last two. The consolation in this poem arises not out of the "comforting excuses" for death that come through glory in battle, but rather out of the sense of a commonality between the often irreconcilable worlds of male and female grief—a commonality evoked in the poem's opening simile.[36] As Geoghegan has said, the metaphor of the singing stone is a bold one. But the boldness of the image lies in the way it brings to light the paradoxes and contradictions inherent in celebrating the dead merely through public praise—without the "dark grief" that shows us we are human.

NOTES

1. Barnard 1991; see also Barnard 1978 for her remarks on Anyte.

2. See Arthur 1980, Gutzwiller 1997, Skinner 1989, 1991a, 1991b.

3. See Wright 1923. And Wilamowitz (1924, 136) asserted that Anyte's poetry lacks any "personal" or "womanly" qualities. More recently, Skinner (1991b, 21) expresses agreement with Wilamowitz's view and remarks that Anyte's epigrams show "how conventional such verse could be, even when composed by a woman."

4. See Snyder 1989; Barnard 1991; Gutzwiller 1998, 54–74.

5. See Barnard 1978 and 1991. Barnard argues that there is nothing in Anyte's poetry that indicates she would not have accepted the role of wife and mother, and thus Barnard fails to acknowledge what Gutzwiller (1998, 54) calls Anyte's "high degree of poetic self-consciousness."

6. See Snyder 1989, 67–77, on Anyte's importance in the pastoral tradition and on her freshness and originality in handling "stock" epigrammatic themes.

7. It is widely assumed that Anyte was a native of Tegea in the region of the Peloponnese called Arcadia. In *The Histories* (4.20–21), Polybius discusses how music—the practice of dancing and celebrating gods and heroes through song—was a necessary component of Arcadian life. In particular, Polybius suggests that the Arcadians incorporated music into their whole public life as a way to make the harsh conditions of Arcadia more tolerable. It is possible that Anyte's use of Homer may be linked to an Arcadian "song culture" similar to what we find in the Homeric poems.

8. Scholars are divided as to whether Hellenistic epigrams represent actual inscriptions on gravestones or are purely literary imitations of such inscriptions. While Snyder (1989, 70), for example, appears undecided as to whether Anyte's epigrams are "real or epideictic," she does assert that Anyte "was probably among the earliest Hellenistic poets to experiment with the traditional genre of the epigram." On the whole, Snyder's readings of Anyte's poems point to a view of them as literary exercises rather than as actual inscriptions. Gutzwiller (1998, 54) argues persuasively that Anyte's epigrams were issued in a book format and that her sophisticated, ingenious use of language reveals a "high degree of poetic self-consciousness," indicating that her poems are no longer epigrams in the "original sense of an inscription" but are representations of such epigrams. I believe that Anyte's sophisticated language and innovative use of literary tradition strongly support Gutzwiller's view. My own readings of Anyte's epigrams will be based on the assumption that her poems ought to be read as literary imitations rather than as "real" inscriptions. As Gutzwiller points out, the numerous voices and forms of address we hear in Anyte's epigrams often make it difficult to ascertain the source of the speaking voices in her poems—especially in light of the absence of any inscriptional setting. My interest here is not to try to identify who is speaking in any realistic sense, but to examine how Anyte uses the convention of the epigram to dramatize a dialogue between traditional forms of women's lament and the more public (masculine) forms of praise and lament for the dead. That Anyte takes on different voices in her epigrams, in my view, seems to suit very well her intertwining of public and private forms of discourse.

9. A continuous tradition of women's lament—from ancient to modern—has been well documented in the work of Margaret Alexiou 1974, Gail Holst-Warhaft 1992, and Anna Caraveli 1986.

10. See Alexiou 1974; Caraveli 1986; Holst-Warhaft 1992.

11. See Nagy's 1979 extensive discussion of the importance of the notion of *kleos* in the Homeric poems—particularly his analysis of the ways in which *kleos* is a remedy for *penthos* (94–106).

12. See Murnaghan 1999 on this point.

13. I use Lattimore's 1962 translation of *The Iliad* here as elsewhere.

14. Holst-Warhaft 1992, 110–15. See also Murnaghan (1999, 204) for her discussion of the role of women's lament in the Homeric epics, where she observes that "laments are the medium by which a female perspective on epic action makes its way into these male-centered texts . . . . these public opportunities become testaments of what it is like to be a woman in a world focused on male interests and values."

15. As Gutzwiller (1998, 1–14) points out, objectivity is the hallmark of the epigrammatic style. But as literary epigrams were collected into books, the presence of a persona could be revealed through thematic repetition and formal cohesiveness. Anyte seems to maintain a tension between the "objective" voice associated with traditional inscription and a more personal voice attendant on being the creator of a book. She also draws on other genres, such as epic, public funerary speech, and women's lament, thereby heightening the vacillation throughout her epigrams between traditionally masculine and feminine forms of expression.

16. See for example the translations of Snyder 1989, Balmer 1996, and Gutzwiller 1998.

17. See *Odyssey* 20.70–71:

Ἥρη δ' αὐτῇσιν περὶ πασέων δῶκε γυναικῶν
εἶδος καὶ πινυτήν, μῆκος δ' ἔπορ' Ἄρτεμις ἁγνή

And Hera granted to them, beyond all women,
beauty and good sense, and chaste Artemis gave them stature.

18. Ironically, καλός and πινυτή are the virtues Penelope is most associated with in the *Odyssey*.

19. In *Odyssey* 20, see line 76.

20. See Alexiou 1974, 55–122. See Caraveli 1986 on the lament as social protest; also Foley 1993 for an analysis of the ways in which women's lamentations in Greek tragedy often express a form of "political or social resistance."

21. Anyte's epigrams often seem to reflect the "double consciousness" Winkler 1990 attributes to Sappho—that is, an ability to speak in the languages of both the male public arena and the excluded female minority.

22. For discussions of the strict controls and restrictions placed on women in Attic death rituals, see Alexiou 1974, 14–23; Garland 1985, ch. 3, and 1989; Holst-Warhaft 1992, 114–24; Foley 1993; and Seaford 1994, 74–143.

23. See Loraux 1986, 42–56, for a discussion of the opposition between Athenian funerary oration and lament. Loraux emphasizes that, in the classical period, lament became the prerogative of women.

24. Plutarch (in Holst-Warhaft 1992, 26 n. 29).

25. Lysias writes that "Nature desires us to weep over them as mortals but their valor demands that we sing them as immortal" (ibis., 121 n. 78).

26. See Barnard 1991 for a discussion of pet epitaphs in Anyte and in other Hellenistic epigrammatists; also Snyder 1989, 70–72, and Gutzwiller 1998, 60–66. *The Palatine Anthology* has several epigrams with marked similarities to Anyte's animal epigrams, especially Nicias (*AP* 7.200) and Mnasalces (*AP* 7.212). It would be interesting to compare Nicias' and Mnasalces' versions of pet epitaphs with those of Anyte, but that is beyond the scope of this paper.

27. Gow and Page (1965) acknowledge that the point of the phrase cannot be determined. They conjecture that other dead animals may have been commemorated in neighboring poems or monuments. Geoghegan argues that the point of the phrase lies in its allusive nature, namely, that Homeric animals used a θάμνος to find a violent death (Geoghegan 1979, 106). The phrase is usually translated as "you too (perished)," but it may just as easily be translated as "even you perished."

28. See Hesiod (*Op.* 203) and Alcaeus (345.2 *PLF*). Gutzwiller 1998, 64 suggests that the word may connote "both the sparkle of its scales and the speed of its movement."

29. Although I refer to the speaker here as a "she," I do not think that the poem itself provides enough evidence to be certain of the speaker's gender. Scholars imagine that the speaker is a woman primarily because they assume that only women in Greek society could feel strong attachments to pets. Such an assumption is not only entirely too speculative but may reflect gender biases that are unsupportable.

30. I thank Kathryn Gutzwiller for pointing this out to me and for her comments on this paper in general. In the *Anthology*, see especially 7.33, 123, 342, 438, 725.

31. See Loraux 1986 for conventions of Athenian funeral oration.

32. I thank Marilyn Skinner for suggesting to me that epigram 4 provides an interesting example of gender inversion.

33. The text of the first line of the poem is uncertain and has given rise to a number of different versions. Scholars seem to agree that the first line contains a reference to a parent either grieving or being grieved, and that would certainly be in line with Anyte's theme of parents lamenting their children. With Gow and Page, Snyder (1989, 69) interprets the first line to mean that the deceased brings grief to the mother Pheidia, while Gutzwiller (1998, 58), prints the readings of Stadtmüller. I have used Geoghegan's text here. Geoghegan (1979, 59) argues that ματρός in line 1 is an objective genitive and cites a number of parallels for the double genitive to support his argument. I am equally convinced by Geoghegan's point that the understood object of ἔθου in line 2 is ἥβα in line 1. Geoghegan's reading takes Pheidias to be the name of the deceased captain and includes a simile that compares the grief of his fellow soldiers to the grief of children for their mother. The comparison of a soldier to a mother is consistent with the reminiscences of Homer throughout Anyte's epigrams. As mentioned earlier, the allusion to Achilles in epigram 5 recalls the simile comparing Achilles to Patroklos' mother, for example, and more specifically at *Iliad* 8 (271f.), Homer describes Teucer running toward Ajax's shield like "a child to his mother's skirts." Moreover, Geoghegan's text is in line with the ways Anyte constantly mixes up categories of both gender and genre throughout her epigrams.

34. See Barnard (1991, 172) for her comments on this poem.

35. I acknowledge that the phrase παίδων ἅτε ματρός in line 1 is ambiguous. Grammatically, the phrase can be translated as either "like children for their mother" or "like a mother for her children." But given that my reading of the poem (in accord with Geoghegan's text) concerns the death of a captain mourned by his soldiers, it makes more sense to compare the captain to a mother and the children to his soldiers.

36. Gutzwiller (1998, 59) argues that Anyte's human laments suggest "a world of female grief that stands as a counterpart to the predominantly male perception of death we find in the corpus of earlier epitaphs." I agree that Anyte's laments often concern the lives of women. But as I argue here, Anyte's laments frequently dissolve the boundaries of public and private spheres and of what may be considered strictly masculine or feminine experiences of grief and perceptions of death.

Sulpicia and the Art of Literary Allusion

[Tibullus] 3.13

Carol U. Merriam

In the past two decades, the amount of critical discussion of the short elegies of Sulpicia, contained in the third book of the Tibullan corpus, has increased greatly, especially when we consider that Sulpicia's body of work comprises fewer than fifty lines.[1] Most of the work on Sulpicia has concentrated on her poems as personal expressions of Sulpicia's feelings for Cerinthus, although recently N. Holzberg has raised again the question of Sulpicia's very existence. While Holzberg's theory—that "the *liber tertius* of the *Corpus Tibullianum* is supposed to make its readers believe that they are looking at Tibullus' early work" (1999, 178) and that all the poems of this book were written by one (male) author—is interesting and has its merits, it does not yet seem necessary that "the only Roman poetess that the handbooks of ancient literature have been able to cite as the author of a complete extant text must be banished to the realm of fiction" (1999, 188–189). For the purposes of the current study, I will continue to refer to Sulpicia as a distinct, probably female author, especially since the female persona is clearly intended by the author of the poems.

Generally, this persona has been accepted by scholars, and the poems have been treated as expressions of a girl's emotions, rather than as literature. So allusions to literary figures and tropes in the six short elegies of Sulpicia have been largely ignored in scholarly discussion of the poems. Indeed, it has generally been suggested that this poet makes no literary or mythic allusions in her short poems. H. Traenkle 1990, in his commentary on the *Appendix Tibulliana,* claims that Sulpicia shows little sign of the influence or awareness of other poets; M. S. Santirocco (1999, 237) calls her poems "unallusive, short, without mythological adornment," while C. Davies (1973, 26) dismisses the elegies as "personal and non-universalised" and "in no way academic." Most recently J. R. Bradley (1995, online) has described Sulpicia's elegies as "lacking any display of erudition." G. Luck (1982, 116) at least believes that "she must have read some of the authors prescribed by Ovid, and she handles language and metre well" but never ventures to identify any literary allusion in the poems. Even Sarah Pomeroy, a noted feminist Classicist, has declared that Sulpicia "is not a brilliant artist: her poems are of interest only because the author is female."

Fortunately for Sulpicia's reputation, this treatment of her began to change in the 1990s, partly because of the influence of feminism on the study of ancient literature. She is treated very differently by D. Roessel 1990, for example, who believes that her choice of Cerinthus as the pseudonym of her beloved is a conscious allusion to the connections of bees and honey with poetry in earlier Greek poets such as Erinna and Anacreon. A. Keith 1997, also, gives Sulpicia some credit for literary skills and knowledge, and Keith's is one of the most balanced and sensible interpretations of Sulpicia to date, giving the poet credit for both originality and literary sophistication. J. F. Gaertner 1999 goes too far in the opposite direction, presenting numerous parallels and antecedents for every phrase in [Tib.] 3.13, and thus seeming to indicate that Sulpicia's work is simply a pastiche constructed from what she has read. In general, though, Sulpicia is dismissed as unskilled in such literary arts as allusion, and the term "amateurish" that Gaertner uses of her in his title sums up the received critical opinion of the poet.[2]

This appraisal of Sulpicia's poetry, as unallusive, lacking in technical skill and literary artistry, and generally amateurish is the sort of appraisal that would commonly be given to the poetry of a young dilettante, writing solely for his or her own pleasure, with no thought of publication. With no intention of publication, the poet has no need to work at making the poetry in any way "literary": the emotion is enough, and skill and artistry are unnecessary. This seems to have been the accepted view of Sulpicia and her work for many years. It was assumed that her few short poems survived simply because she was the niece of Messalla, a prominent and important literary patron, and her efforts were for this reason included, with some other poems by members of Messalla's coterie, at the end of the collected works of Tibullus.

We have no reason to assume that Sulpicia did not write for some kind of broadcast or publication, however. Why would she, alone of all the Roman poets whose works have survived, have written solely for her own amusement?[3]

If, as we know, Sulpicia was part of, or at least attached to, the discriminating literary coterie of Messalla, and if she intended her work to be read by members of this circle and the wider public, why would she not avail herself of all the literary technique and sophistication possible? It can be argued that, in fact, she does.

Mythological allusion, one of the most common literary devices of Roman lyric and elegiac poets, is clearly present in Sulpicia's work. In the first of the poems as they appear in the Tibullan corpus, [Tib.] 3.13, the poet introduces the figures of Venus and the Muses and uses the mythological allusion thus made to express both her own allegiance to the goddess of love and the attitudes that both she and her beloved Cerinthus hold:

Tandem venit amor, qualem texisse pudori
    quam nudasse alicui sit mihi fama magis.
Exorata meis illum Cytherea Camenis
    attulit in nostrum deposuitque sinum.
Exsolvet promissa Venus: mea gaudia narret,
    dicetur si quis non habuisse sua.
Non ego signatis quicquam mandare tabellis,
    ne legat id nemo quam meus ante, velim,
sed peccasse iuvat, vultus componere famae
    taedet: cum digno digna fuisse ferar.

Finally love has come, and the report that I've covered it up
    would shame me more than to have laid it bare.
Begged by my Muses, Cytherea has lifted him up and deposited
    him in my lap.
Venus has fulfilled her promises; let him recount my joys who is
    said to lack his own.
I would not entrust anything to sealed tablets, to prevent anyone
    reading it before my beloved.
For it delights to have sinned, and bores me to compose a face for
    Rumor's sake.
Let me, a worthy woman, be said to have been with a worthy man.

                                                   ([Tib.] 3.13)

In this poem, Venus has deposited Cerinthus in Sulpicia's lap (lines 3–4), that is, in a place of safety. If Sulpicia were judged by the standards applied to other classical poets, and especially other Latin love elegists (whose allusions are well studied and commented upon), scholars would say the poet obviously intends to bring to mind other times when this particular goddess has performed this or a similar act. If we apply the same standards to the female poet, then in these lines Sulpicia is clearly alluding to the scenes in the *Iliad* when Aphrodite snatches her favorites up from the battlefield and deposits them in a place of safety. It is possible that Sulpicia also means to recall instances in poetry when things appear in people's laps, such as the lover's gift on the girl's lap in Catullus 65.19–24, or Callimachus' tablets, which are always on his knees in *Aetia* 1 fr.1.21–22.[4] But Venus' specific actions recalled here point us toward other sources. Rather than simply recalling poetic instances of things on people's laps, Sulpicia uses this image to express her admiration for the power of Venus, and her joy in receiving the benefits of the goddess's beneficence. Keith 1997 identified in this first poem a definite allusion to Vergil's *Aeneid*, and especially the Dido episode. My only disagreement with Keith's premise is that it requires the acceptance of a fairly tight chronological relation. While it is likely that Messalla and his circle of poets, and thus Sulpicia, were aware of Vergil's *Aeneid* while it was being written, this is not certain. It seems, rather, that Sulpicia is referring to scenes in Homer's *Iliad*— and we can be sure that Sulpicia, like all the other poets of her age, had read the *Iliad*.

Aphrodite is famous for this type of direct personal intervention in the lives of her favorites in the *Iliad*. At *Iliad* 5.311*sqq*, Aphrodite intervenes in the battle in order to snatch her son, Aeneas, from danger:

Καί νύ κεν ἔνθ' ἀπόλοιτο ἄνδρ'ν Αἰνείας
εἰ μὴ ἄρ'ὀξὺ νόησε Διὸς θυγάτηρ ᾽Αφροδίτη,
μήτηρ . . .

. . .

ἀμφὶ δ'ἑὸν φίλον υἱὸν ἐχεύατο πήχεε λευκώ

And at this time Aeneas, lord of men, would have perished
except that Aphrodite, daughter of Zeus, his mother
noticed . . .

. . .

and she wrapped her white arms around her dear son.

(*Iliad* 5.311–14)

Again, at *Iliad* 3.382, Aphrodite demonstrates her power by rescuing Paris from Menelaus in their duel. She has already saved her favorite from certain death by breaking the chinstrap of his helmet when Menelaus grabbed it:

καί νύ κεν εἴρυσσέν τε καὶ ἄσπετον ἤρατο κῦδος
εἰ μὴ ἄρ᾽ ὀξὺ νόησε Διὸς θυγάτηρ ᾽Αφροδίτη,
ἥ οἱ ῥῆξεν ἱμάντα βοὸς ἶφι κταμένοιο

Now he would have dragged him away and won everlasting glory
except that Aphrodite, the daughter of Zeus, noticed
and broke the oxhide chinstrap.   (*Iliad* 3.373–75)

After displaying her power in this way, Aphrodite goes on to rescue Paris from the battle altogether, by snatching him from the battle-field and depositing him in his own chamber:

. . . τὸν δ᾽ ἐξήρπαξ᾽ ᾽Αφροδίτηὺ
ῥεῖα μάλ᾽ ὥς τε θεός, κάλυψε δ᾽ ἄρ᾽ ἠέρι πολλῇ
κὰδ δ᾽ εἷς ἐν θαλάμῳ εὐώδεί κηώεντι.

. . . And Aphrodite snatched him up,
with ease, since she is a god, and wrapped him in a thick cloud
and deposited him in his own sweet-smelling chamber.
(*Iliad* 3.380–82)

Based on these well-known demonstrations of the goddess's power when she intervenes in mortal affairs, Venus' interference in Sulpicia's life identifies Sulpicia and Cerinthus in general with the favorites of Aphrodite, and identifies Cerinthus in particular with Paris and Aeneas, whom Aphrodite rescues from danger in the *Iliad*. But since, in all of her extant corpus, Sulpicia is especially concerned with the responses of the characters involved to the situation in which Venus has placed them, it is beneficial to consider the responses of the Homeric characters, as well, to the situation created by Aphrodite there. We can thus find that the attitudes of Paris and Helen are also reflected in Sulpicia's body of poems.

Helen's response to Aphrodite's actions is an inappropriate reaction to the favor that the goddess has shown her, in that she attempts to resist the goddess's power and the lures of Paris:

κεῖσε δ᾽ ἐγὼν οὐκ εἶμι — νεμεσσητὸν δέ κεν εἴη —
κείνου πορσανέουσα λέχος· Τρῳαὶ δέ μ᾽ ὀπίσσω
πᾶσαι μωμήσονται· ἔχω δ᾽ ἄχε᾽ ἄκριτα θυμῷ

> I will not go to that man — it would be too shameful —
> I will not lie in his bed, because all the Trojan women
> will forever blame me, and my heart is already bewildered.
>
> (*Iliad* 3.410–12)

This seems a polar opposite to Sulpicia's tone, where she demonstrates such joy and eagerness to partake of the joys of Venus, for in [Tib.] 3.13, when celebrating the fulfilment of her passion for Cerinthus, Sulpicia exults that love has finally come to her (*tandem venit amor*, 1), and that she plans to announce this to the world. This poem is a celebration of the victory of her love and the power of the only divinity whom she acknowledges in her poetry. In it she expresses an admiring and trusting attitude toward Venus, saying that *extoluit promissa Venus.* (Venus has carried out what she promised, 5). Sulpicia obviously believes in the power of Venus and accepts her as a beneficent god, who will do good for her favorites.

Sulpicia's attitude toward Venus in 3.13 is reminiscent of that of Sappho, who repeatedly makes requests of Aphrodite and confidently expects their fulfilment.[5] Sappho prays to the goddess in the first of her poems that we have (fr. 1.1–2): Ποικιλόθρην' ἀθάνατ'' Αφρόδιτα, παῖ Διος δολόπλοκα, λίσσομαί σε: (Splendid-throned, immortal Aphrodite, clever child of Zeus, I pray to you). She expects positive results from this prayer, because she has always had them before (fr. 1.13–15): σὺ δ', ὦ μάκαιπα, μειδιάσαισ' ἀθανάτῳ προσώπῳ ἤρε' ὅττι δηῦτε πέπονθα (you, blessed goddess, smiling with your immortal face, asked me from what I was again suffering).[6] Sappho's attitude toward Aphrodite is summed up in the last lines of this poem (fr. 1.27–28): σὺ δ' αὔτα σύμμαχος ἔσσο (you be my ally in battle).[7] In fragment 2, when she enjoins the goddess to come from Crete, Sappho again seems confident that the goddess will comply. And repeatedly in the remaining fragments of Sappho's poetry we find the beginnings of poems addressed to Aphrodite, seeming to express the poet's trust in the goddess's goodwill. Sulpicia, in her request of Venus and confident expectation that it will be fulfilled, seems to hold the same attitude and may be consciously alluding to Sappho. The possible allusion is emphasized in Sulpicia's reference to Venus as Cytherea, a mode of address commonly used by Sappho, as in fr. 86 and fr.140a: κατθνα[ί]σκει, Κυθέρη', ἄβρος" Αδωνις (O Cytherea, delicate Adonis is dying).[8]

This common view of the goddess shared by the two poets is interesting, and a couple of possible interpretations present themselves.

One is that Sulpicia may have consciously taken Sappho as a model in her writing. For in the Augustan era, at least, Sappho was apparently considered the prime model for women aspiring to poetry. Perilla, of whom Ovid writes in *Tristia* 3.7.19–20, aspires to emulate the achievements of Sappho in her own writing: *ergo si remanent ignes tibi pectoris idem, sola tuum vates Lesbia vincet opus* (thus, if the same fires remain in your heart, only the Lesbian bard will surpass your work). Perhaps Sulpicia is indeed conscious of a nascnet feminine literary heritage and seeks to place herself within it.[9]

Another possible interpretation is that, to the Roman love poets, Venus was a goddess who helped and favored women. Horace certainly thought this to be true. For he pictures Venus as rather frightening toward himself, if appeasible. He (*Odes* 1.19.1) calls her *mater saeva Cupidinum* (Savage mother of Loves), and pictures her (1.19.9–10) having fallen upon him (*in me tota ruens Venus Cyprum deseruit*). Then he asks his slaves to build an altar for the goddess, so that she will be appeased and look upon him favorably:

> Hic vivum mihi caespitem, hic
> Verbenas pueri, ponite turaque
> Bimi cum patera meri:
> mactat veniet lenior hostia.

> Here place living sod, boys, here
> Place branches and incense
> And bowls of pure wine:
> She will come more kindly with a
> Sacrifice having been slain.   (*Odes* 1.19.13–16)

Glycera's altar, however, is to be favored by Venus, descending enthusiastically from the heavens; nor must the woman herself make the sacrifice. Incense will do for her:

> O Venus, regina Cnidi Paphique,
> sperne dilectam Cypron et vocantis
> ture te multo Glycerae decoram
>   transfer in aedem.

> Fervidus tecum puer et solutis
> Gratiae zonis properentque Nymphae
> Et parum comis sine te Iuventas
>   Mercuriusque.

O Venus, queen of Cnidos and Paphos,
Leave esteemed Cyprus and betake yourself
To the altar of Glycera, decorated with much incense.

Let the eager boy hurry with you,
and the Graces with their girdles loosened,
and Nymphs,
And Youth not gracious enough without you
and Mercury. (*Odes* 1.30.1–8)

The tone here, again, is reminiscent of Sappho's confidence that
Aphrodite will hurry to her aid. Horace believes that Venus will hurry
to the aid of any woman in love.

The expectation that Venus will not help men is clearly present
in the expressed attitudes of some of the male elegists toward
Venus, whom they consider a vindictive and capricious goddess.
Propertius, (1.1.33), especially, fears the goddess's anger, and even
at the best of times she gives him bitter nights: *in me nostra Venus
noctes exercet amaras.* And in the second and third books of his elegies, Propertius demonstrates that he really expects no help from
Venus, even when he prays to her directly for assistance. Upon hearing that his rival has returned from Illyria, Propertius (2.16.13–14)
prays that the praetor will burst from lust: *at tu nunc nostro, Venus,
o succurre dolori, rumpat ut assiduis membra libidinibus.* But he
does not really expect this to happen and goes on to pray to other
gods for help, and to pray for impossible things, such as all wealth
vanishing from Rome so that even the leader himself would live in a
straw hut (2.16.19–20). In elegy 2.21 Propertius again prays to
Venus for help against an enemy, Panthus, but again he holds no
expectation of help. Finally, in elegy 3.16, the love poet depends on
the love goddess's help to save him from danger when he traverses
the streets of Rome after dark, but immediately after stating that
Venus protects lovers (3.16.20), *exclusis fit comes ipsa Venus,* he
begins to plan his funeral! It seems that, in the eyes of love poets,
Venus is a goddess who will help women, without extending the
same protection to men. Propertius really expects no help, whereas
Sappho, and now Sulpicia, confidently expect that Venus will protect and help them in their love affairs.

This welcoming of, and confidence in, Venus seems to extend
to her son, as well, in Sulpicia's opening, *tandem venit amor*
(3.13.1). For *amor* here can refer to either love, the love affair, or
the god who governs them both. But if Sulpicia is welcoming

Amor, then her attitude is the opposite of that expressed by the male elegists, who fear the god (Flaschenriem 1999). Propertius (1.1.14) opens his corpus with a depiction of Amor as a cruel captor: *caput impositis pressit Amor pedibus* (Love pressed my head with his feet placed upon it). Ovid expands upon the image throughout his *Amores*: in 1.2 Amor celebrates a triumph, and in 1.9 he is pictured as a conquering general. Finally, Ovid (3.9.5) reverses Propertius' original image and pictures himself as victor: *vicimus et domitum pedibus calcamus Amorem* (I have won and stomp on conquered Cupid with my feet). For those elegists, *amor* is a force to be feared rather than welcomed; only Sulpicia welcomes *Amor* and expects good things, just as she does of Venus.

Despite the confidence she expresses in the goddess's benefi-cence, Sulpicia does actually initially express some reluctance to give in to the works of Venus; she does echo Helen's initial resistance to the works of Aphrodite, as they are found in the *Iliad* passage.[10] In 3.18 (5–6), Sulpicia says that she is indeed embarrassed and con-cerned about having people know about her passion for Cerinthus: *hesterna quam te solum quod nocte reliqui, ardorem cupiens dissimulare meum* (Last night I left you alone, wishing to conceal my passion for you). Sulpicia has had the same concerns about shame and repu-tation as Helen has in *Iliad* 3 but has resolved her problems and, in 3.13, is no longer ashamed. The major point of 3.13 (9–10) is that she is no longer ashamed in front of the world because of her passion for Cerinthus: *vultus componere famae taedet* (to compose a false face for Rumor wearies me). Her original response to the prompt-ings of love was the same as that of Helen in *Iliad* 3, but she has recovered from this reluctance. She is, in 3.13, eager to enjoy the blessings of Venus.[11] And we should note that even Helen overcame her reluctance to some extent, as she ended up going to be with Paris at the end of Homer's scene (*Iliad* 3.447): Ἦ ῥα, καὶ ἄρχε λέχοσδε κιών· ἅμα δ᾽ εἵπετ᾽ ἄκοιτις (And so he went to bed, and his wife went along with him).

Paris' response in *Iliad* 3 to Aphrodite's interference is also sig-nificant for Sulpicia's purposes. Having been rescued from the battlefield by Aphrodite and deposited in the bedroom, with Helen before him, Paris is more than willing to enjoy the plans the goddess has for them. He quickly dismisses the recent battle from his mind and concentrates on essentials: ἀλλ᾽ ἄγε δὴ φιλότητι τραπείομεν εὐνηθέντε (Come, then, let us go to bed and to lovemaking, 441) and ὥς σεο ωῦω ἔραμαι καί με γλυκὺς ἵμερος αἱρεῖ (Not even then, as now, did I love you and did sweet desire seize me, 446). Paris' response to the presence of Helen and the promptings of Aphrodite is appropriate to Sulpicia's situation, as it is exactly the response she wishes Cerinthus to have. Throughout her short collection of poems, Sulpicia wishes that Cerinthus would have the same eagerness for her as Paris shows for Helen. This is a reason for her distress in 3.16, when she complains of his interest in some other woman of lower rank; it is also the cause for her very great dismay in 3.17, when Cerinthus apparently displays no concern whatsoever for her illness.[12] In Sulpicia's dream of the perfect love affair, Cerinthus should be overwhelmingly eager to make love with her and to love her almost beyond reason due to the promptings of Aphrodite.

The echo of *Iliad* 3 in Sulpicia's poem is not a mere coincidence, or a simple "resonance." Rather, it presents Sulpicia's view of how the love affair should progress: under the promptings of Venus, whom she considers a powerful and benevolent goddess, Sulpicia should turn from Helen's reluctance and shame to the eagerness and joy she displays in poem 3.13, while Cerinthus displays all the enthusiasm for her that Paris has for Helen when he is rescued from battle and deposited in the bedroom. And in using the figure of Venus and her actions in this way, Sulpicia demonstrates that she is indeed conversant with the art of allusion and is in no way technically inferior to the contemporary elegists.

NOTES

1. Parker, 1994 has recently argued that two of the poems attributed to the *auctor de Sulpicia* were really Sulpicia's own work; this would almost double the size of her surviving corpus.

2. The dismissal of Sulpicia as an author goes further than this, and Lowe (1988, 193) speaks of it feelingly: "The case could easily be made that Sulpicia, more perhaps even than Sappho, has found her poems condemned by accident of gender to a century and a half of condescension, disregard and wilful misconstruction to accommodate the inelastic sexual politics of elderly male philologists."

3. As Hemelrijk (1999, 152) notes, "that Sulpicia wrote for publication is now generally accepted."

4. It is possible to detect a recollection of Callimachus' tablets later in Sulpicia's poem, in line 7: *non ego signatis quicquam mandare tabellis* (I would not entrust anything to sealed tablets), but in this context the line calls to mind more the tablets with which other love poets, such as Ovid, send messages to the beloved (Ovid, *Amores* 1.11, 12).

5. Even Traenkle, who does not like to admit that Sulpicia read or was influenced by anyone at all, acknowledges in his commentary on 3.13 (1990) that this is an imitation of the Sappho poem. Robbins (1995, 229) writes that "[Sappho's] poetry burns with the sense of a woman who lives easily and confidently with her goddess."

6. Page (1955, 13–14) believes that Aphrodite is actually tiring of Sappho and her constant demands, and that the effectiveness of these demands is waning. Cameron (1949, 7) also noted Aphrodite's tone of "friendly impatience."

7. Cameron (1949) followed the trail of literary allusion still further back, demonstrating that Sappho, from opening prayer formula to the god's smile, to the σύμμαχος expression, is following Homeric formulae. Thus, in essence, Sulpicia alludes to Sappho alluding to Homer.

8. The force of "Cytherea" as Sapphic in intent is strengthened by its rarity in other archaic Greek sources. It appears only twice in Homer's works (*Odyssey* 8.288 and 18.193) and five times in the *Homeric Hymns* (Hainsworth 1998).

9. Gaertner (1999, 198) has suggested that "Sulpicia . . . places herself clearly into a literary tradition of female poetry."

10. Robbins (1995, 236) believes that Sappho, too, identified with Helen.

11. This progression from reluctance to eagerness is not as apparent in the present ordering of the poems but becomes very clear if we accept the rearrangement of the poems I suggested in Merriam 1990, in which 3.18 is taken as the first poem in the narrative sequence, with 3.13 as the final moment in the affair. Bradley (1995, online) accepts the conventional arrangement of the poems but also notes the framing qualities of 3.13 and 3.18: "Thus, in the final poem of the collection, as in the first, the poet affirms the shame of concealing a worthy love, whether from others or from the beloved himself." Santirocco (1979, 235) also sees no need to rearrange the poems: "There is a certain literary logic to their order as it stands"

12. Yardley 1990 attributes Sulpicia's displeasure to the fact that Cerinthus has actually committed a grave social error: as an *amicus*, Cerinthus is expected to perform the *beneficium* of visiting the sick friend. By not reciprocating Sulpicia's *beneficia* in the expected way, Cerinthus is once again placing Sulpicia in the position of a social inferior, perhaps even a slave, whose *ministeria* are expected but need not be reciprocated. (This concept is also discussed by Gibson 1995).

9   Sulpicia and the Rhetoric of Disclosure

Barbara L. Flaschenriem

An anecdote about the Greek painter Zeuxis, as Cicero adapts it, shows how certain kinds of narrative decorum may efface the "presence" of women in a text. In his youthful handbook on rhetoric, *De Inventione,* Cicero relates how the citizens of Croton once engaged Zeuxis, the most illustrious painter of his time, to decorate their temple of Hera ("Juno").[1] The artist decided to include a portrait of Helen among these commissioned works, and when he asked the townspeople if there were any young women in the city who could serve as his models, the citizens "immediately" conducted him to the *palaestra,* where the boys of the town were exercising nude. The painter was struck by the physical beauty of the youths ("puerorum . . . formas et corpora"), and the townsmen assured him that the boys' sisters were equally comely (*Inv. Rhet.* 2.1.2): "You can guess at the girls' merit from these boys" (qua sint illae dignitate, potes ex his suspicari). Here, by directing our gazes toward the unclothed youths, Cicero temporarily suppresses a slightly indecorous feature of the story—namely, that these respectable young girls ("sorores . . . virgines") will also be exposed to the artist's gaze as he paints his "Helen." Like Zeuxis at the wrestling school, Cicero's readers first "see" the girls of Croton only as they are reflected in and through male proxies, their brothers.

The decorum that attempts to shield the girls of Croton from our view in Cicero's text may serve elsewhere to mute the female voice, to render inaudible its particular timbres and concerns. In Roman works that treat women's conduct in the public sphere, propriety of speech is often equated with propriety of dress. Valerius Maximus' discussion of women orators (8.3.1–3), which has been perceptively analyzed by Judith Hallett (1989), illustrates this tendency very neatly. The discussion begins, in fact, with a sartorial metaphor: the three women speakers whom Valerius proposes to treat were, as he puts it, inhibited neither by their sex nor by the "modesty of the stola" (verecundia stolae) from pleading their cases before the public. But though Valerius is highly ambivalent about such incursions by women into the public sphere, as Hallett (1989, 66) points out, and though he has particularly harsh things to say about Gaia Afrania, he nonetheless reserves high praise for a speech given by Hortensia, the daughter of the jurist Quintus Hortensius. Hortensia's speech (8.3.3), he asserts, not only displayed her father's gift with language, ("patris facundia"); it also brought him figuratively back to life: "Quintus Hortensius lived again . . . in his female offspring and inspired his daughter's words" (Revixit . . . muliebri stirpe Q. Hortensius verbisque filiae aspiravit). Hallett (1989, 66, 67) observes that Valerius' respect for Hortensia's oratorical skill "was inseparable from his esteem for that of her late father," and that their close familial bond helped to "legitimate" her potentially transgressive participation in an activity normally reserved for men. If we are obliged to see women "through" male proxies in Cicero's handbook, Valerius Maximus strongly encourages us to view Hortensia as an extension—or a female likeness—of Hortensius, to see her "as" her famous parent.[2] Or, to invoke Valerius' sartorial metaphor, we might say that he makes Hortensia's public speaking more respectable by clothing her in the discourse, the verba and facundia, of her father.

As a norm of conduct, then, Valerius' verecundia stolae signifies a socially approved aversion to public display, whether of the body or through the act of asserting oneself in speech. For a Roman woman, to be reticent in the public realm was to be decently attired, whereas to speak freely was to risk being exposed to ridicule or censure. Hence when the elegiac poet Sulpicia (Corpus Tibull. 3.13.2) uses an image of disrobing to describe the act of writing her love poetry, "[amorem] nudasse," the verbal gesture is both daring and rich in implication:[3]

> Tandem venit amor, qualem texisse pudori
>   quam nudasse alicui sit mihi fama magis.

exorata meis illum Cytherea Camenis
    attulit in nostrum deposuitque sinum.
exsolvit promissa Venus: mea gaudia narret,   5
    dicetur si quis non habuisse sua.
non ego signatis quicquam mandare tabellis,
    ne legat id nemo quam meus ante, velim,
sed peccasse iuvat, vultus componere famae
    taedet: cum digno digna fuisse ferar.[4]   10

At last love has come, and the rumor that I've concealed it
    would shame me more than to have laid it bare.
Persuaded by my Muses, the goddess of Cythera
    has brought him and placed him in my embrace.
Venus has fulfilled her promises; let anyone recount my joys   5
    who is said to have lacked his own.
I wouldn't want to consign anything to sealed tablets,
    so that no one could read it before my lover.
No, my lapse delights me, and I'm tired of playing a role for rumor:
    let it be said that I, a worthy woman, have been with a man
                                        worthy of me.[5]   10

When she states at 1–2 that it would be more shameful to hide a
love like hers than to "lay it bare," the narrator insists on being
"seen" and heard, on making visible the passion that she presents as
her own. Significantly, however, her choice of metaphor is also at
least partially determined by the conventions of genre. Her assertion
of candor deftly reworks a recurrent structuring image in Roman
elegy—that of the partially or provocatively clothed woman. In the
work of Ovid and Propertius, for instance, as recent scholarship has
shown, the beloved's features and attire may serve as metaphors for
the poet's literary allegiances and "writing practices."[6] The ideal
mistress and the exemplary elegiac poem share similar attributes
and attract the same vocabulary of praise: both are refined, tender,
seductive. The fictions of erotic elegy—including its programmatic
fictions—are organized around a carefully regulated display of the
female body. Sulpicia alludes to this convention in the opening couplet
of 3.13, but she subverts its procedures, translating the image of the
unclothed *puella* into a figure of speech. What will be revealed here
is not a woman's body, but the story of her love.

    In her opening declaration, then, the speaker proposes to strip
away disguises, and to reveal what modesty or discretion might well

counsel her to hide; she emphatically refuses to dissimulate. But despite her daring posture, the metaphor of disrobing suggests a certain unease about exposing herself to the commentary of others, and about how the apparent disclosures of her poetry will be received. Moreover, this unease makes itself felt in the rhetorical disposition of the poem, as well as in its governing metaphor.[7] Although she openly celebrates her love, the narrator does not altogether eschew the protection of certain kinds of linguistic reserve. The gnarled diction that we encounter in lines 1–2 may comprise another, and more subtle, form of reticence.[8] In this couplet, the speaker appears only in a subordinate clause, entering the text in the *mihi* of line 2, a pronoun that is both rhetorically unmarked and metrically unemphatic, providing the two short syllables of a dactyl. Here, it is as if the narrator is attempting to claim a public voice, and yet remain partially hidden, preserving a kind of privacy. The impulse to assert herself is checked by an opposing impulse, a need to devise rhetorical and prosodic strategies of self-protection.

Critics of Sulpicia have pointed to the double sense of *fama* in 3.13, where it signifies both the "rumor" of idle talk and gossip, and the "fame" of literary reputation. Even as she aspires to poetic *fama,* the speaker must find means of controlling the potentially harmful effects of ungoverned talk.[9] Yet for the female narrator, the project of controlling *fama* entails more than subverting the "vocabulary of Roman propriety," or choosing, however boldly, to commemorate her love affair "on her own terms in her own poem" (Lowe 1988, 205, 204). For, as I have tried to suggest, Sulpicia was also obliged to modify elegiac idiom, to find ways of mastering the anxieties occasioned by her literary role, when she adopts the self-revelatory postures of the elegiac lover.

Indeed poem 3.13 opens with what might be called an enabling fiction, one that justifies the narrator's provocative breach of modesty, her need to let others know about her love affair. The speaker exultantly welcomes love, "At last love has come" (1), and the very phrasing of her declaration testifies rhetorically to the force of this new emotion: *amor,* and not a human agent, is the subject of the first couplet and presides over its verbal action. Love impels the narrator to speak, much as *Amor* subdues the Propertian lover and forces his complaint in the first poem of the *Monobiblos.*[10] While it is not surprising that two elegiac poets should indicate *amor* as a source of discourse, the topos of speech inspired or constrained by love does not serve the same ends in Sulpicia's text as it does in that of her male counterpart. For in Propertius' elegy, love is invoked in order to "explain" the speaker's subservience to a woman, and his persistence in an unmanly and scandalously idle way of life. Sulpicia, in contrast, proclaims the object of her passion—and hence the passion itself—worthy of herself and her poetry (digno, 10), but uses *amor* to justify an act of speech that could be deemed immodest if not transgressive for a woman. The same trope accounts for distinct (and gender specific) sorts of impropriety and provides their fictive rationale.

Like the Propertian elegy, however, 3.13 is a text that demonstrates an acute sensitivity to its possible reception: each of its five couplets responds in a perceptibly different way to the imagined presence of a listener or reader. The daring avowal of the first couplet yields to the literary fantasy of the two following lines, where Sulpicia mythologizes an exchange in which poetic utterance proves wholly efficacious and achieves its intended effect on the addressee. Whereas the first couplet informs us about the occasion of the poem, providing a context for its enunciation, the second depicts, in an almost allegorical fashion, the auspicious beginning of the poet's love affair and the speech act that inaugurated it. Moved by her eloquence, Venus has conveyed Sulpicia's beloved to her embrace, like a welcome gift. Sulpicia's tone is playful here, and the motif of seduction through song is conventional in elegiac poetry.[11] But in the context of her poem, the implications of the motif are more complex than one might expect. When she suggests that she won her beloved through the power of her verse, Sulpicia presents herself explicitly as a love poet, the protégée of Venus (Cytherea) and the Muses.[12] Significantly, however, this familiar motif also calls attention to the fictionality—the "constructedness"—of Sulpicia's literary posture. Through it, she implies that her poetic persona need not be too rigidly identified with its author, and thus she mitigates the impropriety of celebrating ostensibly personal joys and pleasures in verse. Finally, in pairing Venus with the Camenae (3), Sulpicia completes an elegant programmatic maneuver. She gives Venus a Greek cult title, Cytherea, which occurs in erotic poetry as early as that of Sappho, but aligns the goddess with Roman deities of song, the Camenae, as if to impute to herself the authority of two poetic traditions.[13] Frank as they may appear, the assertions of the first two couplets also direct the reader and point to ways of responding to her poem.

As lines 1–4 clearly demonstrate, Sulpicia's attempts to anticipate and guide the reader can be extremely artful. In the following couplet (5–6), however, she seems deliberately to relinquish a measure of her authorial control, and to allow other speakers to participate in her story: "mea gaudia narret,/ dicetur si quis non habuisse sua" (let anyone recount my joys/ who is said to have lacked his own). By so pointedly defying what other people might say, Sulpicia reveals her awareness of a power that confronts her in the realm of genre, as well as in the sphere of social relations. In the governing fictions of elegy, the female lover is constituted for the most part not as a subject of discourse in her own right, but as its eroticized (or reviled) object. She is "spoken" by others, and we generally apprehend her through the discourse of a male narrator.[14] Yet Sulpicia also alludes here, I think, to the pleasures of responding to a text, for the indefinite pronoun *quis* of line 6 is not limited to the purveyor of gossip; it encompasses the listener or reader as well. "Anyone" who lacks *gaudia* of his (or her) own is welcome to recount those of the elegiac poet, or to participate in them vicariously.[15] Here, in addition to giving her "private" joys a literary form, Sulpicia also affirms their representative power. In her deft way, she reverses the decorum that governs elegiac writing and that encourages us, like Cicero's anecdote about Zeuxis, to "see" women through men. By means of the inclusive *quis,* the narrator of 3.13 claims implicitly to speak for men as well as for women, sketching the outlines of a plot in which both sexes may find their experience represented.[16]

As if to emphasize the inclusive nature of her poetic *amores,* Sulpicia declares in the next couplet (7–8) that she would rather not be obliged to seal her "letters," and thereby keep her exchanges with her lover strictly private. She imagines a setting in which her text might circulate freely, and in which her lover is not necessarily her first or her only reader. In lines 7–8, then, the language of disclosure takes a more sophisticated form: the imagery of being seen and talked about modulates into that of being read, and the unclothed body is replaced by the open tablets. Furthermore, when she describes her poetry as communication that the author may choose to seal, she borrows from the vocabulary of the *sphragis* (poetic seal), though in a curiously refracted way. For Sulpicia does not employ the *sphragis* in order to assert a proprietary claim upon her text, as Theognis does, for example, in his famous manifesto (19–23), nor does she attempt at this point to endow the poem with a definitive authorial "signature" or stamp.[17] Indeed elegy 3.13 gives us very little in the way of specific information about the two lovers: neither is even mentioned by name (Snyder 1989, 130–31).[18]

Sulpicia's "open" *tabellae* invite comparison with the unsealed tablets of Propertius, whose loss (or "death") the narrator mourns in elegy 3.23.[19] Like Sulpicia, Propertius uses the motif as a means of imagining the fate of his poetry and its treatment by future readers (Prop. 3.23.1–6):

> Ergo tam doctae nobis periere tabellae,
>> scripta quibus pariter tot periere bona!
> has quondam nostris manibus detriverat usus,
>> qui non signatas iussit habere fidem.
> illae iam sine me norant placare puellas   5
>> et quaedam sine me verba diserta loqui.

> So my skilled tablets are lost,
>> and all the fine things written on them are lost as well!
> My hands had previously worn them down through use,
>> which made them recognizable when they were left unsealed.
> They knew how to appease women now without me,   5
>> and without me how to utter eloquent words.

Even without the imprint of his signet ring, the narrator claims, his *doctae tabellae* have proved their authenticity. In his correspondence with various women, they remained faithful to his intentions, "speaking" eloquently for him in his place, "sine me" (5, 6). Nor did they belie their origins: worn and smoothed by his hands, the tablets retained the impress of the poet, the signs of his aesthetic labors. To the discerning reader, the author's stamp was always visible even in his "unsigned" texts (Putnam 1982, 217; cf. Fedeli 1985, 663): his tablets kept their sealing power.

But despite the speaker's insistence on the fidelity of his *tabellae*, the fact that he composes a fiction about their loss suggests, of course, a fear that they are somehow "vulnerable," just as the allusion to sealing implies a desire to protect their content from tampering or alteration.[20] The fictions of Propertius' poem, like those of Sulpicia's, are in some measure compensatory. In each poem, the speaker confronts—and partially allays—anxieties induced by the prospect of the text's entering the public realm and circulating more widely. Thus, at the same time as it acknowledges the hazards of transmission, Propertius 3.23 also develops (beginning at line 11) a fantasy about the poet's continuing control over his text, his ability to recover what has been alienated or lost. Although he has lost his means of communication with his mistress and the letter that she wrote in reply to his, the poet-lover manages to reconstruct the message that she inscribed on the lost tablets. He attributes two alternative responses to his beloved, both of which are extremely flattering to himself. The missing letter either expressed her anger, chiding him for his disloyalty and indifference, or else it summoned him to a night of love (3.23.11–18). In either case, its alleged content betrays her desire for him and testifies to his undiminished power in his erotic and epistolary exchanges with her.

This fantasy of control extends, moreover, to spheres of communication beyond the purely erotic. Beginning at line 19, the speaker imagines that his writing tablets have fallen into the hands of a supremely incompetent reader of amatory texts, an *avarus,* who has effaced the lovers' tender correspondence and pressed the *tabellae* into service as account books (Prop. 3.23.19–20):

> me miserum, his aliquis rationem scribit avaru<s>
>   et ponit duras inter ephemeridas!

> Poor me! Some stingy businessman is writing his gains
>   and losses on them,
>   and placing them among his callous account books.

Here the erotic rivalry that is so characteristic of elegiac fiction has been replaced by a clash of idioms. As a hoarder, the *avarus* has disrupted the cycle of amatory exchange, obscuring the words of the two lovers with the banal and tedious language of the commercial world. Threatened by this rival discourse, the poet-lover responds by expressing its sentiments in elegiac terms, and judging it according to elegiac systems of value.[21] Thus at line 20, he gives an exotic coloring to the stolid account books of the *avarus,* referring to them with the Greek synonym *ephemeridas,* while marking their distance from his own tender verses by deeming their content "harsh" and "unfeeling" (*duras*).[22] In addition, he subjects the account books to a strikingly Alexandrian refinement, and one that we encounter frequently in Propertius' first book of elegies, for in their new, elegiac guise, the businessman's *ephemerides* make up the five concluding syllables of a "long pentameter."[23] When he employs this Alexandrian metrical device and describes the businessman's records in language favored by elegiac poets, the narrator suggests, by contrast, how far removed the language and the values of his rival are from those of the elegiac world. Here, moreover, elegiac idiom expands to accommodate a less refined mode of discourse: the narrator incorporates the records of the *avarus* into a new poem and in so doing regains possession, as it were, of the writings that seemed to be permanently lost to him. In the wish-fulfillment scenario of 3.23, the elegiac text can never be wholly estranged from its authorial source: it can always be at least partially reclaimed or reconstructed.

To summarize the point I am making about Propertius 3.23, then, both this poem and Sulpicia's imagine the encounter between the text and its future audience and reflect a need to anticipate and control this encounter through the vehicle of fiction. But though both poets use the motif of unsealed or "open" tablets, they respond in different ways to the prospect of entering the public domain. Their fictions arise, I think, from related but not identical sorts of tension, and the motif serves different purposes in their texts. While Propertius' "lost" or "perished" tablets reflect uncertainty about the survival of his poetry, and about the forces that might impede or curtail its transmission, Sulpicia appears to be more concerned with the immediate circumstances of her text's reception.[24] The narrator of 3.13 both courts visibility and expresses unease about its consequences. In the metaphor of disrobing, she alludes to her own exposed and vulnerable self but then directs attention away from it, to the tablets that she longs to leave open for anyone who might care to see them. Just as the lover yearns to share her secret, so the poet yearns to make her writings public. Thus, while Propertius tries to assure himself that even his "unsigned" texts retain a kind of sealing power and can be made to refer back again to their authorial source, for the narrator of Sulpicia's poem, sealing her tablets is ultimately less attractive than leaving them unclosed. The motif signifies her intention to abandon reticence and to claim a literary identity.[25]

In her final couplet (9–10), Sulpicia restates her desire to assume a literary identity when she declares: "vultus componere famae/ taedet: cum digno digna fuisse ferar" (I'm tired of playing a role for rumor:/ let it be said that I, a worthy woman, have been with a man worthy of me). Here, of course, the speaker also rejects the attention to reputation expected of a woman, and the pretense that such deference to *fama* would now require of her. Yet her choice of words is suggestive, since in elegiac poetry, the verb *componere* is frequently used to describe the act of literary composition or creation.[26] Her rejection of one literary role, one way of defining or "composing" a public persona, implies the creation of another. As I have tried to suggest, Sulpicia's poetic confession is mediated by various literary strategies. Her refusal to dissimulate—what we might call her rhetoric of disclosure—entails a new and more artful presentation of the self.

After a series of partial disclosures, Sulpicia concludes her poem by announcing the consummation of her love. In Roman erotic idiom, of course, the expression "to be with" (*esse cum*) is a euphemism for "to make love," and in 3.13 the statement "cum digno digna fuisse ferar" amplifies and glosses the poet's earlier declaration, *sed pecasse iuvat* (my lapse delights me, 9).[27] The narrator's so-called lapse pleases her, because she has found a man who is worthy of her trust and love. Yet the exultant and challenging tone of the statement "cum digno digna fuisse ferar" is not its most remarkable feature; the assertion is striking too for its epitaphic quality, and for the way in which it appeals covertly to the reader. Like an epitaph, which summarizes the meaning of a life and endows it with significance, this closing declaration presents the nascent love affair in a retrospective light. It attempts to give an official and memorable form to what people say, pronouncing favorable judgment on the relationship in advance.

Indeed the pointed diction of the line calls to mind the literary epitaphs that are so prominent a feature of elegiac discourse. In its syntactic structure, it is particularly close to the epitaph that Cornelia envisions for herself at Propertius 4.11.36: "in lapide hoc uni nupta fuisse legar" (On this stone I shall be read as having been married to one man only). Like many surviving epitaphs of Roman women, Cornelia's sepulchral verse announces her status as *univira*, commemorating her lifelong devotion to a single husband.[28] Cornelia's *fides*, her publicly acknowledged reputation for chastity, becomes the defining feature of her life, while the private emotions that her husband feels for her are left unrecorded. Sulpicia's "epitaph," in contrast, is far less reticent and one-sided, for it gives almost equal weight and prominence to the responses of the man. Sulpicia's declaration celebrates the virtually equivalent stature of lover and beloved, at least within the charmed circle of the erotic relationship (cf. Tschiedel 1992, 95). The adjective *dignus* is applied to each of the two lovers in succession, while *digno* and *digna* mirror one another in the pentameter, balanced on either side of the diaeresis. Metrically and rhetorically, the collocation *digno digna* underscores the mutuality of the love relationship.[29] The speaker's beloved is "worthy" because his passion equals her own.

In a sense, then, poem 3.13 attempts to imagine the love affair in its entirety, from its inception, "Tandem venit amor," to the retrospective view implicit in the final line. In poem 3.16, by contrast, the erotic narrative takes a very different course from the one intimated in 3.13. There, instead of celebrating the rapport that she and her beloved share, Sulpicia bitterly rebukes him for his apparent breach of faith (*Corpus Tibull.* 3.16):

> Gratum est, securus multum quod iam tibi de me
> > permittis, subito ne male inepta cadam.
> sit tibi cura togae potior pressumque quasillo
> > scortum quam Servi filia Sulpicia:
> solliciti sunt pro nobis, quibus illa dolori est,   5
> > ne cedam ignoto, maxima causa, toro.

> I'm grateful that you in your assurance now presume so much
> > > where I'm concerned,
> > so that I don't without warning foolishly take a fall.
> Let your passion for a toga-clad whore, burdened by her
> > > spinning,
> > be preferred to Servius' daughter Sulpicia!
> There are others who worry about me, to whom this
> > > is the greatest source of distress—   5
> > that I may yield to a low-born mistress.

Here the estrangement between Sulpicia and her beloved punctuates the love story, delineating one of its phases or chapters, the movement from the glow of infatuation to the suspicion or disillusionment of betrayal. It marks a turning point in the elegiac narrative, a juncture at which the love story might well conclude. Although a quarrel can be followed by reconciliation, it always raises the possibility of a lasting rift. Futhermore, in elegiac fiction, being in love is a precondition for the writing of amatory verse: love inspires the poet-lover's *amores,* while the end of a love affair also implies the cessation of the erotic discourse that it had inspired. On generic grounds, then, it makes sense that Sulpicia should "seal" this elegy with her proper name. The poem bears some of the rhetorical hallmarks of the *renuntiatio amoris* (farewell to love), and it could easily be the final text in an amatory cycle.[30]

In addition to formal pressures, however, emotional forces also seem to underlie the speaker's need to inscribe her signature in her poem. For the narrator of 3.16, (as I shall argue more fully below), the act of signing her text counters—or "heals"—the kinds of division within the self precipitated both by her love and by the act of writing. The problem of the divided self haunts Sulpicia's poetry as it does the love poetry of Catullus, and even in the small corpus of her work that still remains for us, she returns to it again and again. We have seen already how in poem 3.13, the narrator is torn between the impulse to celebrate her love openly and the need to devise a self-protective rhetoric. And in the next poem of the corpus, 3.14, she dramatizes the division of the self in spatial terms. Obliged to accompany her kinsman Messalla to Arretium, and to spend her birthday there without her beloved, Sulpicia declares that her mind and emotions remain at Rome, although she is "taken away" to the countryside against her will: "hic animum sensusque meos abducta relinquo" (3.14.7). In 3.16, however, this division of the self is not induced by social constraints, which forbade even an aristocratic woman like Sulpicia to manage her affairs, as she puts it (3.14.8), in the way that she sees fit, "arbitrio . . . meo." Here rather, it is Sulpicia's own desire that divides her against herself.

Yet poem 3.16 communicates more than a straightforward *odi et amo,* despite its epigrammatic brevity: the range of emotional tones in the elegy is surprisingly rich. In the scant six lines of Sulpicia's poem, rage at being taken for granted by her lover and pain at his betrayal vie with her own lingering passion. In a perceptive study, S. Hinds 1987 has suggested that the tonal richness of the poem is matched by the complexity of its play with elegiac modes of representation. Sulpicia's presentation of herself here both as poet and as lover is intriguingly fluid, embracing contradictions instead of fully resolving them, and even her depiction of her rival is charged with considerable ambiguity. Not surprisingly, Sulpicia directs the full force of her anger and outrage at her beloved's new *amica* along with Cerinthus himself. She calls attention to the wide social gulf that separates her, the daughter of Servius Sulpicius, from the prostitute ("scortum," 4; "ignoto . . . toro," 6) who has now apparently become Cerinthus' mistress, emphasizing the disparity in their rank through her bitingly terse allusions to the other woman's toga and wool basket.[31] As an indicator of female status, the prostitute's toga inevitably brings to mind its sartorial opposite, the *stola* that Sulpicia will be privileged to wear as a freeborn matron. The garment makes the sexual availability of Sulpicia's rival all too evident, while the phrase "pressum . . . quasillo" (burdened by her wool basket, 3) points, with devastating economy, to her humble social position.[32] A mere spinning-girl (*quasillaria*), she is oppressed by day-to-day toil, the monotonous and "unremunerative" task of working wool.[33]

But though Sulpicia draws attention to her own impeccable pedigree as Servius' daughter, the gulf between her and her rival is not as absolute as it might at first appear, and in fact the text of 3.16 establishes a kind of kinship, an area of rapprochement, between the two female figures, where social and generic distinctions cease to hold so rigidly. In the erotic sphere, of course, Sulpicia and the *quasillaria* are linked by their involvement with the same man. As Girard 1966 reminds us, the conditions of rivalry may themselves produce a heightened awareness of, or even a fascination with, one's rival, fostering a bond that can be as powerful and compelling, in its way, as that which ties lover and beloved. Although the poet's beloved is the addressee of the elegy, the *scortum* is essential to its strategies of representation. She serves as the "other" in contrast to whom Sulpicia attempts to characterize herself, yet she is also a kind of shadow self, as the rival often is in fictions that center upon erotic competition.

The fluid identity that marks the speaker in the erotic scenario of 3.16 is also evident in the realm of genre. If the prostitute's male garment makes her marginal social position immediately visible, Sulpicia's own position, at least in literary terms, is no less insecure. Sulpicia may likewise be said (figuratively) to wear male garb, since she has claimed the role of speaker in a genre in which woman is a privileged, though generally silent, object of men's desire, (as Hinds 1987, 45, has suggested), and in a genre whose erotic fictions frequently address topics to which a female speaker had relatively limited access, including "warfare, politics, patronage," and "the rejection of public life" (Wyke 1995, 114). Furthermore, her sexual experience—the fact that she has made herself available to Cerinthus—is not simply a condition that Sulpicia shares with her rival; it is also generically significant. In erotic elegy, the ideal woman interlocutor or reader is generally imagined as being both cultured (*docta*) and of an amorous disposition. She is a responsive addressee, fully able to appreciate the amatory verse that she inspires, and she may be celebrated as a skillful composer of love poetry in her own right.[34] We might say that the speaker of poem 3.16 is simultaneously disguised in male garb and clothed in the provocative attire of the elegiac *puella*. Her literary persona combines features that, in the texts of her fellow elegists, serve to distinguish or individuate the male and female protagonists or that receive special emphasis in the case of one sex.[35] The very act of writing, of modifying the codes of elegiac representation and speaking "through" them, engenders a division–or fragmentation–of the narrator's poetic self.

Despite the generic constraints with which she grapples, however, and despite her own tumultuous emotions, the speaker in Sulpicia's poem finds a kind of equilibrium both in the act of "signing" her text and in the act of representation in general. The *sphragis* of 3.16 effaces divisions in the speaker's self, subsuming the disparate and sometimes contradictory aspects of her persona under a single name: Servi filia Sulpicia. When she signs her text, the narrator aspires to a kind of discursive wholeness: her signature provides the illusion of coherence, of a unified authorial persona. Like epitaphic discourse, moreover, the *sphragis* attempts to resist the pressures of change and loss, and to impose a stable identity on an oeuvre or on the self that the poet has "chose[n] to perpetuate."[36] It is significant, however, that Sulpicia commemorates herself here not in her elegiac role as the lover of Cerinthus, but in her public guise as the daughter of Servius Sulpicius. It is as if she retreats, if only for the moment, from the love affair: her fluid identity and her ability to adopt different positions as a speaker prove to be a strength as well as a source of tension within the poem. Instead of being wholly vulnerable to the whims or changing feelings of her beloved, she adopts the position of an outside observer, aligning herself with her unnamed well-wishers, and reminding Cerinthus of her formidable connections in the public world: unlike her rival, she is not the sort of woman who might be obliged to endure an insult meekly. Her authority as speaker and observer is sustained by a social milieu, by the network of friends, admirers, and relatives who share her values and modes of engaging with the world. At the poem's close, the private grief and chagrin of the elegiac lover are replaced by the collective distress of those who have her best interests at heart (Santirocco 1979, 233).

In 3.16, then, representation—both of the self and of others— becomes a means of self-mastery, as Sulpicia the unguardedly passionate ("male inepta," 2) lover finds refuge in her familial identity, and in the official and public designation of a name. Moreover, the specificity with which she identifies herself in this text contrasts sharply with her treatment of her lover. Refusing to see herself as the slighted object of a man's waning desire, the speaker now takes the initiative, requiting her lover's affront by denying him a concrete presence in the text. While she gives her signature a prominent place in the poem, rhetorically "framing" it by embedding it in the central couplet, she pointedly refuses to call her beloved by name (as she does in 3.14 and 3.17), even in a context of dismissal. Likewise, while she claims the "invisible" authority that inheres in the narratorial voice, she objectifies her rival, reducing her to a metonymic series of objects: toga, wool basket, and most witheringly of all, a "lowly" bed ("ignoto . . . toro," 6).[37] Here, the expression *ignoto . . . toro* is more than a final, unkind jibe at the other woman; the phrase is also self-reflexive and helps the speaker to define her own emotional posture. It simultaneously justifies her fury and serves as a kind of consolation. Through the adjective *ignoto,* Sulpicia points once again to the disparity in status between herself and her rival, and hence to the personal insult implicit in Cerinthus' choice of mistress, but she closes her verse-letter with the vivid yet dismissive *toro,* as if to emphasize the purely sexual nature of the new relationship, its limited and partial character. If (as I suggested at the beginning of this paragraph) the poet's self-presentation can offer a rhetorical means of self-mastery, this construction of a poetic self is always governed by certain imaginary scenarios: it is linked to the representation of others.

In his analysis of love as it is represented in Greek and Roman literature, D. Konstan (1994, 159) has described what he calls the "master plot" of Roman elegy as one that ultimately finds its "denouement" in the rejection of the beloved "on grounds of inconstancy." Although Konstan's model fits the course of the erotic narratives implicit in the oeuvres of the male elegists (particularly those of Ovid's *Amores* and of Propertius books 1–3), the elegiac "cycle" of Sulpicia—at least as the manuscripts have transmitted it to us—follows a different trajectory. Whereas the amatory narratives of the male elegists tend to close with the *amator* deploring his beloved's infidelity, or proclaiming his release from the abasement and self-deception imposed by his desire, the narrative implicit in Sulpicia's poems 3.13–18 ends with the woman lover fully claiming a voice. To a large extent, I think, Sulpicia's cycle assumes a distinct and individual shape because she does not ask the same questions in her fictions as her male colleagues do: her erotic narratives and theirs issue from different kinds of imaginative inquiry. If, in the erotic narratives of Tibullus, Propertius, and Ovid, the poet-lover repeatedly, indeed almost obsessively, seems to pose the question "How do I assuage my desire?", Sulpicia's most searching poems imply a question of a different sort.[38] In texts such as 3.13 and 3.18, she seems rather to ask, "How do I fully articulate my desire?"

Critics of Sulpicia are fond of observing that her six elegies, as they are arranged in the manuscripts, begin with a declaration of her love to a general public (3.13), and conclude with the narrator's private disclosure of her passion to her beloved (*Corpus Tibull.* 3.18):

> Ne tibi sim, mea lux, aeque iam fervida cura
>   ac videor paucos ante fuisse dies,
> si quicquam tota commisi stulta iuventa,
>   cuius me fatear paenituisse magis,
> hesterna quam te solum quod nocte reliqui,   5
>   ardorem cupiens dissimulare meum.

> Let me no longer be, my light, as fiery a passion to you
>   as I seem to have been a few days ago,
> if I've foolishly done anything my whole youth long
>   which I would admit that I've regretted more,
> than the fact that I left you alone last night,   5
>   because I longed to hide my own fervent desire.

With its dense and rather complicated syntax, poem 3.18 gives the impression, like 3.13 and 3.16, of being a statement articulated against tremendous inner resistance, though it is less haunted by the imagined presence of others than are its companion texts. The world encompassed by the author's poetry contracts from one that contains the many observers implied in the previous two elegies, to a world in which only the lover and her beloved seem to matter: the scandalmongers and gossips of 3.13 have vanished, along with the concerned watchers of the love affair whom the narrator invokes in 3.16. But whereas 3.13 ends with a glance toward the future ("cum digno digna fuisse ferar," 10), in 3.18 the speaker turns to the recent past ("paucos ante . . . dies," 2; "hesterna . . . nocte," 5), in an attempt to reconcile "then" and "now," "last night" and the moment of the poem's enunciation.[39]

Despite its brevity, this final poem in the sequence completes a surprising number of verbal gestures at once. Structured by the formal rhetoric of the oath ("let x occur, if y is not the case"), the elegy is simultaneously avowal, apology, and confession as well as a dramatically enacted revision of the past. When Sulpicia apologizes to Cerinthus for leaving him alone the night before—an act occasioned, she suggests, by her inexperience and youth (Smith 1913,

516)—she describes her action in such a way as to rectify her previous failure of nerve. The line that recounts her departure now attempts, at least rhetorically, to undo it. As the one, protracted sentence that comprises the poem unfolds, it embraces Cerinthus syntactically, placing him, "te solum," at the center of its measured and heavily spondaic final hexameter: "hesterna quam te solum quod nocte reliqui" (5).[40] In her closing line, moreover, the narrator completes the admission that she was afraid to make before, when she was alone with her beloved. Sulpicia openly avows her love, which is a passionate one ("ardorem," 6), yet this avowal is not articulated in its entirety until the final word of the elegy. Here, it is almost as if she restages, in the rhetorical organization of the poem, her former hesitation—her impulse to hide her ardor—but then firmly renounces such concealment and evasion. With the possessive adjective "meum," emphatically positioned as the final word both in its line and in the poem as a whole, the speaker's interior and public selves—what she feels and what she aspires to communicate—finally seem to coalesce, as she lays claim explicitly to her own desire ("ardorem . . . meum," 6).

Closing the cycle like the clasp on a necklace, poem 3.18 thus brings the narrative implicit in the sequence 3.13–3.18 "full circle."[41] With its celebration of mutuality, 3.18 looks back to the quasi-epitaphic conclusion of poem 3.13; like that text, this final poem in the sequence insists on the commensurability of the lovers' feelings. The "burning love" (fervida cura) of the male addressee (3.18.1) finds its response in the narrator's own equally fiery passion. Like the two previous elegies examined here, 3.18 thematizes the narrator's struggle to attain full discursive and erotic selfhood, and to define her own position as a subject of speech, desire, and writing. Here, however, the narrator seems to enter the realm of concrete verbal action with increasing assurance. N. J. Lowe has observed that, "of the 27 verbs" in her oeuvre "of which Sulpicia herself is the subject," a mere four are in the indicative, "while no fewer than 24 verbs are used impersonally or with abstract or hypothetical subjects."[42] Intriguingly, three of these four indicatives occur in elegy 3.18: "videor" (2), "commisi" (3), "reliqui" (5). Sulpicia's reluctance elsewhere to present herself as the subject of an indicative may well be another strategy for veiling herself rhetorically, but it is a strategy that the imaginative scenario of 3.18 enables her to forgo. The poem presents itself as intensely private communication, which involves only the poet and her beloved. Within this fictive setting, the poet-lover can fully acknowledge her agency because she reveals it to her beloved alone, and not to the potentially censorious public world: an imagined context of "privacy" allows her to make this literary confession.

Even the order in which the indicatives appear in poem 3.18 is suggestive, since as a series they mark the speaker's shift from self-contemplation (*videor*) to the action implied by the active voice (*commisi, reliqui*), and from a "specular" mode to one of narration.[43] Thus at 3.18.1–2, Sulpicia regards herself, as it were, from an external vantage, assuming what she imagines was her lover's prior point of view, and picturing herself as the object of his desire: "Ne tibi sim . . . aeque iam fervida cura/ ac videor . . . fuisse" (Let me no longer be . . . as fiery a passion to you/ as I seem to have been). Yet this passage, where the narrator apprehends herself indirectly and through a perspective ascribed to another person, yields to one in which she becomes an active participant in the story she creates: she moves, in short, from being "seen" to claiming agency and voice.

In this respect, 3.18 follows a trajectory similar to that of 3.13, although the admissions that the poet-lover makes here are more intimate even than those of its companion elegy. To be sure, in 3.13 the narrator celebrates the joys of an avowedly sexual relationship, yet she is as concerned in that text with how others will respond to the affair as she is with exploring her private experience of love. In 3.18 the intensity of the speaker's ardor makes her uneasy, and she seems to struggle with the temptation to hide it not only from her lover, but even in some ways from herself. In fact she begins this poetic confession of her love not by speaking about her own emotions, but by alluding to the "fiery passion" of her beloved. Yet the endearment with which she opens the poem ("mea lux," 1), and the accumulation of expressions that denote passionate desire ("fervida cura"; "ardorem . . . meum"; "cupiens"), all hint at the depth of her feelings, even before she acknowledges them explicitly. Sulpicia's highly charged diction works in counterpoint to her syntax, which attempts to postpone full disclosure until the final, unequivocal "meum." Here, it is as if the speaker protects herself from the intensity of her own desire through her delaying tactics, through the gradual unfolding of the poem's one sentence; the elegy betrays her contradictory impulses. In this, the most forthright "confession" of her oeuvre, the poet-lover claims her passion frankly, but she does so by means of syntax that seems, paradoxically, to retain a trace of the reserve she now rejects.

In 3.18 as elsewhere in her poetry, then, Sulpicia grapples with the unease occasioned by her literary stance, in which she adopts the self-dramatizing and highly "visible" postures of the elegiac lover. At key points in the oeuvre, she takes pains to distinguish her authorial self from her poetic persona. In all three of the texts examined here, moreover, she modifies the generic materials of elegy—its topoi, idioms, and amatory mises-en-scène—creating fictions that explain and justify her literary revelations, which thus mitigate the impropriety of writing verse that claims to be based on her own erotic life. In Sulpicia's poetry, anxieties that arise from the prospect of being observed and talked about yield to the exigencies of being read. She develops an authoritative elegiac rhetoric, yet one that allows her to preserve a kind of privacy, and even propriety, within her scenarios of disclosure.

NOTES

This article previously appeared as B. L. Flaschenriem, "Sulpicia and the Rhetoric of Disclosure," in *Classical Philology* 94(1999): 36–54. © 1999 by the University of Chicago. I would like to thank the Univeristy of Chicago Press for granting permission ro reprint this article. I would also like to thank the editors of *Classical Philology*. For a recent and comprehensive bibliography of scholarship on the Sulpicia poems, see Mathilde Skoie, *Reading Sulpicia: Commentaries 1475-1990* (Oxford: Oxford University Press, 2002).

1. *Inv. Rhet.* 2.1.1–2.5. The Latin text of Cicero is that of Achard 1994. Unless otherwise noted, citations of Sulpicia and Propertius follow Traenkle 1990 and Fedeli 1994, respectively; those of Valerius Maximus follow Faranda 1971. All other quotations from the Latin or Greek are taken from the Oxford Series of Classical Texts.

2. Or, to use Hallett's terminology, this passage represents woman as being the "Same" as her male kin. It is interesting, too, that Valerius Maximus alludes only in passing to the occasion and content of Hortensia's speech; he is less interested in what she purportedly said than in the phenomenon of the woman orator.

3. Hinds 1987, 44; Keith 1997, 301. See also Tschiedel 1992, 92, who contrasts Sulpicia's desire to celebrate her love openly with the tendency of the male elegists to characterize their liaisons as stolen or clandestine. On the attribution of the poems collected in the *Corpus Tibullianum*, and for the history of scholarship on the corpus, see Lowe's concise and extremely useful discussion (1988, 193-97), as well as Traenkle 1990, 9–12. Scholars and editors now generally concur in attributing poems 3.13–18 of the Tibullan corpus to Sulpicia and elegies 3.8–12 to the so-called *auctor de Sulpicia,* though opinions on the authorship and ascription of the poems are not unanimous. (See, e.g., Parker 1994 for a dissenting voice on the attribution of poems 3.9 and 3.11.) In an

influential paper published in 1871, and collected in his *Opuscula*, Haupt ([1876] 1967, 502–503) argued that Sulpicia was the daughter of Valeria, a sister of Messalla, and Servius Sulpicius, son of the celebrated jurist and consul of 51 BCE, Servius Sulpicius Rufus. On the elegist's father, the younger Servius Sulpicius, see Syme 1981.

4. At line 1, I read *pudori* with Postgate 1915, Lenz and Galinsky 1971, and Luck 1988.

5. The translations of Sulpicia are adapted, often freely, from Goold and Postgate 1988 and Snyder 1989. On the translation and interpretation of Sulpicia's sometimes challenging text, I have benefited from the commentaries of Smith 1913, Traenkle 1990, and Yardley 1992, and the discussion of Bréguet 1946.

6. See, for example, Wyke 1987a, 1989a, 1989b; cf. DeBrohun 1994. See also Richlin 1992, 57–80, on Roman invective and satire in general; and Hallett 1996 on Catullus, Martial, and the *Carmina Priapea*, where the body in question is that of the aggressively phallic male. Later versions of the articles by Wyke cited in this paper are now collected in Maria Wyke, *The Roman Mistress* (Oxford: Oxford University Press, 2002).

7. On the narrator's acute sensitivity to *fama* (rumor, fame, reputation) and to the effects of discourse, see esp. Santirocco 1979, 234–35; cf. Hinds 1987, 43–44, and Hallett 1989, 71.

8. Kammer 1979 identifies similar forms of verbal "camouflage" in the work of Emily Dickinson and of the modernist poets Marianne Moore and H. D.

9. See esp. Santirocco 1979, 234–35, on the tension between the two kinds of *fama*; cf. Lowe 1988, 203–205, on the speaker's attempts to make *fama* "subject to refinement and to control."

10. "tum mihi constantis deiecit lumina fastus/ et caput impositis pressit Amor pedibus,/ donec me docuit castas odisse puellas/ improbus, et nullo vivere consilio" (Then shameless Love brought down my gaze of resolute pride;/ he placed his feet on my head and trampled it down,/ until he taught me to despise chaste girls,/ and to live with no thought for the future, Prop. 1.1.3–6). Cf. Ovid's parody of the trope in *Amores* 1.1.

11. See, for example, Prop. 1.8.39–40: "hanc ego non auro, non Indis flectere conchis,/ sed potui blandi carminis obsequio" (I could not sway her with gold, nor with pearls from India,/ but rather with the service of my seductive song); also Prop. 2.13a.3–7. Cf. also Ov. *Am.* 2.1.33–34: "at facie tenerae laudata saepe puellae/ ad vatem, pretium carminis, ipsa venit" (But when a tender girl's beauty has been lauded, often/ she herself comes to the bard, a reward for his poetry).

12. Cf., for example, Santirocco 1979, 234; Snyder 1989, 130. Here Sulpicia claims authority as a writer of *amores* and creates a scenario of fulfillment and control: control over the desire personified in Venus, over her beloved, and over the persuasive powers of language.

13. For Cytherea as an epithet of Aphrodite-Venus, see, for example, Sappho fr. 86, 90 in Lobel and Page; cf. the fragment of Sappho's lament for the dying Adonis (140a L-P); Prop. 2.14. 25; Hor. *Carm.* 1.4.5, 3.12.4; Verg. *Aen.* 1.257; Ov. *Am.* 1.3.4, *Her.* 17.241, *Met.* 10.717. Cytherea is also an epithet of Aphrodite in Greek epic (*Od.* 8.288; 18.193). For additional citations, see Bréguet 1946, 46. In Roman texts, the Camenae appear, for example, at Verg. *Ecl.* 3.59; Hor. *Carm.* 3.4.21, *Epist.* 1.19.5; and Prop. 3.10.1. See also Keith 1997, 301, on Virgilian echoes in the second couplet of poem 3.13.

14. In recent years, critics have been particularly attentive to this feature of elegiac discourse; see, for example, Hinds 1987, 40, 43–44 (on Sulpicia); Wyke 1987a, 1989a, and Gold 1993 (on Propertian elegy). Wyke (1995, 115) cogently observes that the "female speaker of the Sulpician corpus both controls and struggles not to be controlled by the strategies of elegy's erotics and poetics." Ultimately, of course, every speaker or writer must grapple with language, with modes of discourse and representation that preexist him or her. The struggle is, however, especially difficult for the female author working in a male tradition, since its literary idioms and generic conventions may not readily accommodate her particular interests and concerns.

15. Cf. Hallett 1990, 192. As Hinds (1987, 42) wittily observes, at least one poet, the *auctor de Sulpicia*, might appear to have taken Sulpicia's assertion as a programmatic "cue."

16. Most (1981, 16) discerns a similar poetic gesture in Sappho 16 L-P. He points out that, when the speaker of Sappho's lyric describes Helen as surpassing all mortals (ἀνθρώπων) in loveliness rather than all women (γυναίκων), she expands her "sphere of reference beyond women alone to . . . human beings" as a totality.

17. The passage from Theognis runs as follows: Κύρνε . . . μὲν . . . σφρηγὶς ἐπικείσθω/ τοῖσδ' ἔπεσιν—λήσει δ' οὔποτε κλεπτόμενα,/ οὐδέ τις ἀλλάξει κάκιον τοὐσθλοῦ παρεόντος,/ ὧδε δὲ πᾶς τις ἐρεῖ· "Θεύγνιδός ἐστιν ἔπη/ τοῦ Μεγαρέως" (Cyrnus . . . let a seal be placed/ on these words, and they will never be stolen secretly,/ and no one will exchange what is inferior for the good that is present,/ but everyone will say, "They are the words of Theognis/ the Megarian," *Theognidea* 19-23).

18. We might compare Sulpicia's poem to the first elegy in the short Lygdamus cycle (*Corpus Tibull.* 3.1–6), which introduces the poet's beloved, Neaera, by name. Tibullus similarly identifies Delia in the opening elegy of book 1, while the name of Propertius' mistress, Cynthia, is the first word of his entire oeuvre.

19. See Hubbard 1975, 90–91, and Putnam 1982, 217, on the double sense of *periere*, and on the echoes of funeral lament in the poem. Both Hubbard and Putnam observe that the poet-lover speaks of the *tabellae* as if they were faithful go-betweens or slaves.

20. The vulnerability of the poet's text extends, of course, to the physical materials on which it is preserved and transmitted, as Putnam (1982, 217) has observed.

21. I would like to thank the anonymous referee of *Classical Philology* for suggestions that helped me refine the argument of this paragraph.

22. Given the highly programmatic character of Prop. 3.23, which has been well examined by Cairns 1972, 78–79, I favor reading *duras* at line 20 rather than the alternative *diras*.

23. With the term "long pentameter," I am referring to a pentameter that ends in a word of more than two syllables. Pentameters concluding with words of three or more syllables are common in the *Monobiblos*, but rare in book 3, where Propertius' use of the device calls attention to itself. See, for example, Wilkinson 1963, 123, and the statistics that Goold (1989, 118 n. 30) supplies. More than a third (36.3 percent) of the pentameters in the *Monobiblos* end with words of three or more syllables, but the percentage of such endings drops precipitously in book

3 (2.4 percent). Fedeli (1977, 80 and 1994, 286) notes that, while there are nine five-syllable pentameters in book 1 and seven in book 2, books 3 and 4 contain only one each (at 3.23.20 and 4.5.28).

24. For a more detailed discussion of literary anxiety in Propertius, see Flaschenriem 1997, 259–67.

25. See Hinds 1987, 42, on 3.13 as a statement of Sulpicia's "intent to publish her love."

26. Both Propertius and Ovid use *componere* to denote the writing of elegiac or erotic verse; see, for example, Prop. 1.7.19; Ov. *Am.* 2.1.1, *Tr.* 5.12.60. In his elegy 1.11, Propertius punningly describes Cynthia, reclining on the beach at Baiae, as *molliter . . . compositam* (14): she is both "comfortably settled" and "composed in a tender (elegiac) manner." The latter passage is briefly but insightfully treated by Commager 1974, 11–12.

27. On *esse cum*, see, for example, Pierrugues [1826] 1965, 197; Smith 1913, 508; Adams 1982, 177.

28. On Roman women's epitaphs, see Williams 1958, 23–25, and the examples that Lattimore (1962, 295–99) collects.

29. Smith 1913, 508. Traenkle (1990, 306) points out that Sulpicia's "cum digno digna" evokes the proverbial expression *digna dignis;* Traenkle cites Plautus *Poen.* 1270 and an inscription (recorded by the elder Pliny, *HN* 35.115) that honored Marcus Plautius, the artist who painted the temple of Juno at Ardea. Along with Traenkle, Probst and Probst (1992, 29) observe that in Sulpicia's text the phrase "cum digno digna" implies that "Sulpicia's beloved has earned her devotion."

30. On the characteristics of the *renuntiatio amoris*, see Cairns 1972, 79–82. In elegy, the rejected or disenchanted lover may have recourse to the procedures of satire, as the Propertian *amator* does, for example, in poems 3.24–25.

31. See Santirocco 1979, 233, who comments on the way these "concrete representations" of her rival's low social status "forcefully" convey "class consciousness."

32. Cf. Snyder 1989, 133–34, on the phrase *pressum . . . quasillo.*

33. Smith 1913, 514; Currie 1983, 1763-64; Traenkle 1990, 316–17. Both Smith and Traenkle cite Petronius *Sat.* 132.3, which associates the *quasillaria* with the most lowly (or disreputable) members of the household: "convocat omnes quasillarias familiaeque sordidissimam partem" (She calls together all the spinning-girls and the basest portion of the household). For the legal and social status of the prostitute in Rome, see Gardner 1986, 132–34, 250–53.

34. Propertius (3.2.2) makes the connection between sexual experience (or an amorous disposition) and the appreciation of elegiac verse explicit in poem 3.2, when he refers to the female reader of his poetry: "gaudeat in solito tacta puella sono" (Let my girl be touched and delight in the sound she's accustomed to). Here, in its context, the word "tacta" bears a second implication, suggesting that the *puella* is sexually experienced and not a virgin (*intacta*). Cf. also Ovid's programmatic *Amores* 2.1.5, where the responsive temperament of the woman reader is stressed: "me legat in sponsi facie non frigida virgo" (Let the ardent young girl read me in the presence of her fiancé). The Propertian narrator alludes to his mistress's gifts as a poet at 1.2.30, 2.1.9–10, and 2.3.19–22. For a blurring of different women's roles and identities similar to that of Sulpicia's poem, see Lange 1979 and Wyke 1987b, 173, on book 4 of

Propertius, where the demimondaine, Cynthia (4.7), and the aristocratic matron, Cornelia (4.11), are made to share traits in common. I borrow the notion of the responsive addressee or reader from Hallett 1996.

35. Hinds 1987, 45; Hallett 1989, 70–71; Wyke 1995, 114–15.

36. To use a phrase that Brooks (1993, 182) employs in another context.

37. Here the word *torus* is a metonym for "sexual partner" or "mistress"; see Smith 1913 ad loc.

38. Cf. Conte 1994, 41, who states that "the elegiac poet's characteristic gesture is his (vain) attempt to free himself from . . . [his] painful slavery" to love. Following this line of argumentation, one might say that erotic elegy repeatedly stages the question How do I free myself from the compulsion of *amor*? This way of formulating the question, however, does not fully account for the variety of elegiac scenarios that turn upon the problematics of desire.

39. On the complex schemes of time in poem 3.18, see Lowe 1988, 199.

40. As Santirocco (1979, 234) points out, poem 3.18 is the only elegy of the Sulpician cycle that is structured as one sentence. Unlike this final poem in the cycle, poems 3.13–3.17 are organized in self-contained units of a couplet.

41. As Keith (1997, 307) points out, though her discussion of the relationship between 3.18 and 3.13 differs in emphasis from my own.

42. Lowe 1988, 202 n. 36. Lowe speculates that this may be "[o]ne 'feminine' effect in the poems' cumulative texture," but he does not take this suggestive observation any further. The other indicative of which Sulpicia is the subject is "relinquo" at 3.14.7; Lowe seems to lean toward construing "ferar" at 3.13.10 as a subjunctive, though he concedes it might be a future indicative (205). In any case, the narrator's claim to agency is less fully enacted here than in poem 3.18, with its indicatives in the active voice.

43. The expression is that of Brooks 1993, 254.

Appendix   Greek and Roman Women Writers

Below is a list and brief description of nearly all the women writers in Greece and Rome whose works, often extremely fragmentary, span a period from the seventh century BCE to the sixth century ACE. Although we know the names of approximately one hundred Greek and Roman women writers, fragments of about fifty of these women authors remain. For commentary and translation on these women writers, see I. M. Plant's comprehensive anthology, *Women Writers of Ancient Greece and Rome*, (University of Oklahoma Press, 2004). Plant's complete list of attested women writers of the Greco-Roman world is extremely useful. See also Jane McIntosh Snyder's very helpful introduction to these authors: *The Woman and the Lyre: Women Writers in Classical Greece and Rome*, (Southern Illinois University Press, 1989). I have included in the list below the authors whose works either survive or are considered significant because of references to them in major ancient sources.

Aesara: Third-century BCE Greek author of a philosophical work *On Human Nature*, quoted in part by Stobaeus, Greek author of an anthology of poets and prose writers (early fifth century ACE).

Anyte: Greek Hellenistic poet (generally dated between 310 and 290 BCE), writer of epigrams, twenty-one of which have survived.

Boeo: Greek author whom Pausanias discusses in reference to a short fragment of hers about the oracle of Delphi.

Caecilia Trebulla: Roman writer who composed three epigrams around 130 ACE.

Cleobulina: Greek writer probably from sixth century BCE, composer of riddles. Only three of those riddles remain.

Cleopatra: Greek physician who wrote a treatise called *Cosmetics*, possibly around 64 ACE or later. She is not to be confused with the famous Egyptian queen.

Cleopatra the Alchemist: Greek alchemical writer whose works date anywhere from the first to the third centuries ACE. Her work, The *Chrysopeia* (gold-manufacture) survives only in a diagram (see Plant 2004).

Corinna: Well known, highly regarded Greek poet, probably from fifth century BCE, although some scholars believe her to be from third century BCE. Two main fragments, and a few very short fragments, survive.

Cornelia: Prominent late-Republican Roman woman (second century BCE) who wrote letters that were much admired.

Demo: Greek writer of one short epigram, (Plant 2004, 157), dated to approximately 196 ACE or later.

Dionysia: Greek epigram writer from around 122 ACE. Only one short epigram survives.

Egeria: Roman writer of a religious pilgrimage to Jerusalem, probably from early fifth century ACE. Her account of her pilgrimage, the *Itinerarium*, was discovered in 1884.

Elephantis: Roman author of erotica, "popular at the end of the first century BCE" (Plant 2004, 118).

Erinna: Greek Hellenistic poet probably from around the middle of the fourth century BCE. She was praised in antiquity for her poem *The Distaff,* which still remains in a fragmentary form along with a few fragmentary epigrams.

Eucheria: Roman poet from late fifth or early sixth centuries ACE. One of her poems has survived.

Eudocia: Greek epic poet who wrote on Christian themes, in fifth century ACE. A number of her works survive.

Eurydice: Greek epigram writer from fifth century BCE.

Fabulla: Roman medical writer from first century ACE.

Hedyle: Greek poet who probably lived in second half of fourth century BCE. One fragment of hers, quoted by Athenaeus, has survived.

Hortensia: Roman orator around 44 BCE, whose famous speech in the Forum was cited by Valerius Maximus, (Roman writer of a handbook consisting of illustrative examples of memorable deeds and sayings), in the first century ACE.

Julia Balbilla: Roman poet from first century ACE. Four of her poems survive, all inscribed on the colossal statue of Memnon in Egypt.

Lais: Greek prostitute (fifth century BCE), famous in antiquity. Pliny (Roman writer, first century ACE) refers to a work on menstruation attributed to Lais. As Plant 2004 notes, we do not have enough evidence to judge the authenticity of Lais' writings.

Maria: Greek first century ACE (or earlier) alchemical writer, quoted by the Greek historian Zosimus of Panopolis in third or fourth centuries ACE. Eight fragments of her work remain.

Melinno: Greek poet, probably early second century BCE. Stobaeus, a Greek writer in the fifth century ACE, quotes one short poem by her.

Melissa: Greek philosophical writer from approximately third century BCE.

Moero: Greek poet from third century BCE. The *Suda*, a historical encyclopedia compiled in the tenth century ACE, says that Moero was the author of epic and lyric poetry. Three short fragments of hers have survived.

Myia: Greek philosophical writer probably from third or second century ACE.

Myrtis: Greek lyric poet possibly from late sixth century BCE. Reputed to be a teacher of both Pindar and Corinna, two of the most highly regarded Greek lyric poets. None of Myrtis' work survives, only a paraphrase of one of her poems in Plutarch (Greek writer, first century ACE).

Nicobule: Greek historical writer who lived sometime between third and first centuries ACE. Two fragments of her work survive.

Nossis: Greek writer of epigrams (inscriptional poems) who lived around 300 BCE. Twelve of her poems survive.

Pamphila: Roman historical writer who lived during Nero (54–68 ACE) in the first century ACE. Eleven of the thirty-three books of Pamphila's *Historical Commentu.* remain.

Perictione (I and II): Two Greek philosophical writers with the same name. The first lived in the late fourth or third century BCE and the second in the third or second century BCE. The work *On the Harmony of Women* is attributed to Perictione I, and the work *On Wisdom* to Perictione II.

Perpetua: Roman Christian martyr, arrested in Carthage during a persecution of Christians in 202–203 ACE. The diary of a female Christian martyr, *The Martyrdom*, is attributed by some to Perpetua.

Philinna: Greek author of an incantation to cure a headache, dated to the first century BCE.

Phintys: Greek writer of a treatise on the correct behavior for women. Scholars differ as to whether her work is authentic. Two fragments from her treatise remain. Plant 2004 dates her work to the third century BCE, but her date is controversial.

Praxilla: Fifth-century BCE Greek lyric poet. Eight fragments of her work have survived. She wrote drinking songs, hymns, and choral odes performed at festivals dedicated to the god Dionysus.

Proba: Christian author from fourth century ACE. She wrote a 690-line poem, using lines or half-lines from Virgil's *Aeneid*, *Georgics*, and *Eclogues*, to weave a biblical narrative. Proba is the first Christian writer that we know was a woman.

Ptolemais: Greek musical theorist, possibly from the first century ACE. She is known to us through a reference by the Greek scholar and philosopher (234–305 ACE) Porphyry to her work *The Pythagorean Principles of Music*. Porphyry quotes Ptolemais' work in its entirety.

Salpe: Greek author of a medical treatise, mentioned by Pliny. Pliny paraphrases six of Salpe's remedies.

Sappho: Greek poet from the island of Lesbos who lived during the seventh century BCE. She was the most famous woman writer in antiquity and continues to be the most well known by far.

Although it is thought that she wrote many books of poetry, only two hundred fragments have survived, many of them consisting of only several words.

Sulpicia: Roman writer of love poems who lived during the reign of Augustus Caesar (31 BCE–14 ACE). Her poems are the only surviving lyric poems written in Latin by a woman. Only six of her poems have survived.

Telesilla: Greek lyric poet from fifth century BCE. She was admired in antiquity and a number of references indicate she was very highly regarded. Only one fragment survives.

Terentia: Roman poet of first century ACE. Her only known work is an epitaph composed for her brother. We have six lines of the poem, though it might have been longer.

Theosebeia: Greek writer of epigrams. One epitaph attributed to her has survived in the *Greek Anthology,* an ancient compilation of epigrams.

List of Abbreviations Used throughout the Text, Notes, and Bibliography

AJAH   *American Journal of Ancient History*
AJP   *American Journal of Philology*
ANRW   *Aufstieg und Niedergang der römischen Welt*
Anth. Pal. or *AP*   The Palatine Anthology. *Anthologia graeca epigrammatum palatina cum planudea* (Stadmüller 1894-1906). For the anthology in English, see Cameron 1993, Gow and Page 1965, or Paton 1918; in French, Waltz 1928-1957; in German, Beckby 1965.
AU   *Der altsprachliche Unterricht*
BCH   *Bulletin de correspondance hellenique*
BICS   *Bulletin of the Institute of Classical Studies*
BSAA   *Bulletin. Société Archeologique d'Alexandrie*
CJ   *Classical Journal*
Cl. Ant. *Classical Antiquity*
CP   *Classical Philology*
CQ   *Classical Quarterly*
CW   *Classical World*
EC   *Études Classiques*
fr.   fragment
GB   *Grazer Beitrage*
G-P   Gow and Page 1965

GLP	*Greek Lyric Poetry* (Bowra 1961)
GRBS	*Greek Roman and Byzantine Studies*
IG	*Inscriptiones graecae*
JHS	*Journal of Hellenic Studies*
JRS	*Journal of Roman Studies*
L-P	Lobel and Page 1963
LSJ	Liddell, Scott, and Jones 1869
PCPhS	*Proceedings of the Cambridge Philological Society*
PLF	*Poetarum lesbiorum fragmenta* (Lobel and Page 1963)
PLRE	*The Prosopography of the Later Roman Empire* (Martindale 1980)
PMG	*Poetae melici graeci* (Page 1962)
PSI	Vitelli, G. et al., Papiri della Societa Italiana (1912–1932)
RE	*Pauly-Wissoa, Real-Encyclopädie der classischen Altertumswissenschaft*
SE	*The Standard Edition of the Complete Psychological Works of Sigmund Freud* (Freud 1953-1973)
SEG	*Supplementum epigraphicum Graecum*
SH	*Supplementum Hellenisticum* (Lloyd-Jones and Parsons 1983)
SIG	*Sylloge Inscriptionum Graecarum* (Dittenberger 1915–1924)
SLG	*Supplementum lyricis graecis* (Page 1974)
TAPA	*Transactions of the American Philological Association*
ZPE	*Zeitschrift für Papyrologie und Epigraphik*

Bibliography

Achard, G., ed. and trans. 1994. *Cicéron: De l'invention*. Paris: Belles Lettres.

Adams, J. N. 1982. *The Latin Sexual Vocabulary*. Baltimore: Johns Hopkins University Press.

Alexiou, M. 1974. *The Ritual Lament in Greek Tradition*. Cambridge: Cambridge University Press.

Allen, A., and J. Frel. 1972. "A Date for Corinna." *CJ* 68:26–30.

Amigues, S. 1993. *Théophraste: Recherches sur les plantes*. Vol. 3. Paris: Belles Lettres.

Andreadis, H. 1996. "Sappho in Early Modern England: A Study in Sexual Reputation." In Greene 1996b, 105–21.

Andrewes, A. 1963. *The Greek Tyrants*. New York: Harper and Row.

Arthur, M. B. 1973. "Early Greece: The Origins of the Western Attitude toward Women." *Arethusa* 6:7–58. Reprinted in *Women in the Ancient World: The Arethusa Papers,* ed. J. Peradotto and J. P. Sullivan, 7–58. Albany: State University of New York Press, 1984.

———. 1980. "The Tortoise and the Mirror: Erinna *PSI* 1090." *CW* 74:53–65.

———. 1982. "Cultural Strategies in Hesiod's *Theogony*: Law, Family, Society." *Arethusa* 15:63–82.

Avagianou, A. 1991. *Sacred Marriage in the Rituals of Greek Religion*. Bern: Peter Lang.

Baale, M. J. 1903. *Studia in Anytes poetriae vitam et carminum reliquias*. Haarlem: Kleynenberg.

Bakker, E. 2002. "Remembering the God's Arrival." *Arethusa* 35:63-81.

Balmer, J. 1996. *Classical Women Poets*. Newcastle upon Tyne: Bloodaxe Books.

Barnard, S. 1978. "Hellenistic Women Poets." *CJ* 73:204–13.

———. 1991. "Anyte: Poet of Children and Animals." In De Martino, 163–76.

Bartol, K. 1992. "Where Was Iambic Poetry Performed? Some Evidence from the Fourth Century." *CQ* 42:65–71.

Beckby, H., ed. 1965. *Anthologia graeca: Griechische-Deutsch*. Munich: E. Heimran.

Beissinger, M., J. Tylus, and S. Wofford, eds. 1999. *Epic Traditions in the Contemporary World: The Poetics of Community*. Berkeley, Los Angeles, and London: University of California Press.

Bing, P. 1988. *The Well-Read Muse. Hypomnemata; Heft 90*. Göttingen: Vandenhoeck und Ruprecht.

Boll, Fr., and H. Gundel. 1937. "Sternbilder, Sternglaube und Sternsymbolik bei Griechen und Römern." In W. H. Roscher, *Ausführliches Lexikon der griechischen und römischen Mythologie*, vol. 6, ed. K. Ziegler, 867–1071. Berlin and Leipzig: Teubner.

Bolling, G. M. 1956. "Notes on Corinna." *AJP* 282–87.

Bowie, E. L. 1986. "Early Greek Elegy, Symposium, and Public Festival." *JHS* 106:13–35.

Bowman, L. 1998. "Nossis, Sappho and Hellenistic Poetry." *Ramus* 27:39–59.

Bowra, C. 1936. "Erinna's Lament for Baucis." In *Greek Poetry and Life*, eds. C. Bailey, E. A. Barber, C. Bowra, J. Denniston, and D. Page, 325–42. Oxford: Clarendon Press.

———. 1953a. "The Daughters of Asopus." In *Problems in Greek Poetry*, 54–65. Oxford: Clarendon Press.

———. 1953b. "Erinna's Lament for Baucis." In *Problems in Greek Poetry*, 151–68. Oxford: Clarendon Press.

———. 1961. *Greek Lyric Poetry from Alcman to Simonides*. 2nd rev. ed. Oxford: Clarendon Press.

———. 1979. "Corinna." In *The Oxford Classical Dictionary*, 2nd edition, ed. N. G. L. Hammond and H. H. Scullard, 290. 2nd ed. Oxford: Oxford University Press.

Bradley, J. R. 1995. "The Elegies of Sulpicia: An Introduction and Commentary." *New England Classical Journal* 22:159–64.

Bréguet, E. 1946. *Le Roman de Sulpicia: Elégies IV, 2–12 du "Corpus tibullianum."* Geneva: Georg et Cie.

Brooks, P. 1993. *Body Work: Objects of Desire in Modern Narrative*. Cambridge: Harvard University Press.

Burn, A. R. 1960. *The Lyric Age of Greece*. London: Edward Arnold.

Burnett, A. P. 1979. "Desire and Memory (Sappho Frag. 94)." *CP* 74:16–27.

————. 1983. *Three Archaic Poets: Archilochus, Alcaeus, Sappho*. Cambridge: Harvard University Press.

————. 1985. *The Art of Bacchylides*. Cambridge: Harvard University Press.

Burzacchini, G. 1990. "Corinna e i Plateesi: In margine al certame di Elicone e Citerone." *Eikasmos* 1:31–36.

————. 1991. "Corinniana." *Eikasmos* 2:39–90.

————. 1992. "Corinna in Roma." *Eikasmos* 3:47–65.

Cagiano de Azevedo, M. 1958-1966. "Encausto." In *Enciclopedia de'arte antica, classica, e orientale*, 3:331–35.

Cairns, F. 1972. *Generic Composition in Greek and Roman Poetry*. Edinburgh: Edinburgh University Press.

Calame, C. 1977. *Choeurs de jeunes filles in Grèce archaïque*. Roma: Edizioni dell'Ateneo e Bizzarri. Translated by D. Collins and J. Orion as *Choruses of Young Women in Ancient Greece: Their Morphology, Religious Role, and Social Functions*. Lanham: Rowman and Littlefield, 1997. Revised translated edition by D. Collins and J. Orion. Lanham: Rowman and Littlefield, 2001.

————. 1996. "Sappho's Group: An Initiation into Womanhood." In Greene 1996a, 115–24.

Cameron, A. 1949. "Sappho's Prayer to Aphrodite." *Harvard Theological Review* 32:1–17.

————. 1993. *The Greek Anthology from Meleager to Planudes*. Oxford: Clarendon Press.

————. 1995. *Callimachus and His Critics*. Princeton, N.J.: Princeton University Press.

Cameron, A., and A. Cameron. 1969. "Erinna's *Distaff*." *CQ* 19:285–88.

Campbell, D. A. 1967. *Greek Lyric Poetry: A Selection of Early Greek Lyric, Elegiac, and Iambic Poetry*. London: Macmillan.

————. 1982. *Greek Lyric*. Vol. 1, Sappho, Alcaeus. Cambridge: Harvard University Press.

————. 1983. *The Golden Lyre: The Themes of the Greek Lyric Poets*. London: Duckworth.

————. 1992. *Greek Lyric*. Vol. 4. *Bacchylides, Corinna, and Others*. Loeb Classical Library. Cambridge: Harvard University Press.

Cancik, H., H. Schneider, M. Landfester, eds. 2002–2004. *Der Neue Pauly: Enzyklopädie der Antike*. 13 vols. Stuttgart: J. B. Metzler.

Cantarella, E. 1987. *Pandora's Daughters: The Role and Status of Women in Greek and Roman Antiquity*. Baltimore: Johns Hopkins University Press.

Caraveli, A. 1986. "The Bitter Wounding: The Lament as Social Protest in Rural Greece." In *Gender and Power in Rural Greece*, ed. J. Dubisch, 169–94. Princeton, N.J.: Princeton University Press.

Carey, C. 1981. *A Commentary on Five Odes of Pindar, Pythian 2, Pythian 9, Nemean 1, Nemean 7, Isthmian 8*. Salem, N.H.: Arno Press.

Carson, A. 1982. "Wedding at Noon in Pindar's *Ninth Pythian*." *GRBS* 23:121–28.

———. 1986. *Eros the Bittersweet*. Princeton, N.J.: Princeton University Press.

Cazzaniga, I. 1970. "Critica testuale ed esegesi a Nosside *AP* VII 718." *Parola del Passato* 25:431–45.

———. 1972. "Nosside, nome aristocratico per la poetessa di Locri?" *Annali della Scuola Normale Superiore di Pisa* 3a, ser. 2, 173–76.

Chantraine, P. 1968–1980. *Dictionnaire étymologique de la langue grecque, histoire des mots*. 4 vols. Paris: Klincksieck.

Cixous, H. 1986. "The Laugh of the Medusa." In *Critical Theory since 1965*, ed. H. Adams and L. Searle, 308–20. Tallahassee: University Presses of Florida. Originally in *Signs* 1 (1976): 875–93, trans. K. Cohen and P. Cohen of a revised version of "Le Rire de la Méduse," *L'Arc* 61 (1975): 39–54; and frequently reprinted.

Clark, I. 1998. "The Gamos of Hera: Myth and Ritual." In *The Sacred and the Feminine in Ancient Greece*, ed. S. Blundell and M. Williamson, 13–26. London: Routledge.

Clayman, D. L. 1976. "Callimachus' Thirteenth *Iamb*: The Last Word." *Hermes* 104:29–35.

———. 1993. "Corinna and Pindar." In *Nomodeiktes: Greek Studies in Honor of Martin Ostwald*, ed. R. M. Rosen and J. Farrell, 633–42. Ann Arbor: University of Michigan Press.

Cole, S. G. 1981. "Could Greek Women Read and Write?" In Foley 1981, 219–45.

Commager, S. 1974. *A Prolegomenon to Propertius*. Lectures in Memory of Louise Taft Semple, 3rd ser. Norman: University of Oklahoma Press.

Consbruch, M., ed. 1906. *Hephaestionis* Enchiridion *cum commentariis veteribus*. Leipzig: Teubner.

Conte, G. B. 1994. *Genres and Readers: Lucretius, Love Elegy, Pliny's Encyclopedia*. Translated by G. W. Most. Baltimore: Johns Hopkins University Press.

Crusius, O. 1892. *Untersuchungen zu den Mimiamben des Herondas*. Leipzig: Teubner.

Cunningham, I. C. 1964. "Herodas 6 and 7." *CQ* 14:32–35.

———. 1971. *Herodas: Mimiambi*. Oxford: Clarendon Press.

Currie, H. 1983. "The Poems of Sulpicia." *ANRW* 2.30.3:1751–64.

Davies, C. 1973. "Poetry in the 'Circle' of Massalla." *Greece and Rome* 20:25–35.

Debrohun, J. B. 1994. "Redressing Elegy's *Puella*: Propertius IV and the Rhetoric of Fashion." *JRS* 84:41–63.

Degani, E. 1981. "Nosside." *Giornale Filologico Ferrarese* 4:43–52.

DeJean, J. E. 1989. *Fictions of Sappho, 1546–1937*. Chicago: University of Chicago Press.

————. 1996. "Sex and Philology: Sappho and the Rise of German Nationalism." In Greene 1996b, 122–45.

Demand, N. 1982. *Thebes in the Fifth Century: Heracles Resurgent*. London: Routledge.

De Martino, F., ed. 1991. *Rose de Pieria*. Bari: Levante Editori.

Denniston, J. D. 1950. *The Greek Particles*. 1934. 2nd ed. Oxford: Clarendon Press.

Detienne, M. 1977. *The Gardens of Adonis*. Atlantic Highlands, N.J.: Humanities Press. Translation by J. Lloyd of *Les Jardins d'Adonis*. Paris: Editions Gallimard, 1972.

Devereux, G. 1970. "The Nature of Sappho's Seizure in fr. 31 as Evidence of Her Inversion." *CQ* 20:17–31.

Diehl, J. F. 1978. "'Come Slowly—Eden': An Exploration of Women Poets and Their Muse." *Signs* 3:572–87.

Dittenberger, W. 1915–1924. *Sylloge Inscriptionum Graecarum* (SIG). 3rd edition. Lipsiae: S. Hirzelium.

Dover, K. J. 1978. *Greek Homosexuality*. London: Duckworth. Updated and with new postscript. Cambridge: Harvard University Press, 1989.

Downey, G. 1959. "Ekphrasis." In *Reallexicon für Antike und Christentum*, 4:921–44. Stuttgart: Anton Hiersemann.

DuBois, P. 1995. *Sappho Is Burning*. Chicago: University of Chicago Press.

Dunbabin, T. J. 1948. *The Western Greeks*. Oxford: Clarendon Press.

Ebert, J. 1978. "Zu Corinnas Gedicht vom Wettstreit zwischen Helikon und Kithairon." *ZPE* 30:5–12.

Edmonds, J. M. 1938. "Erinna P.S.I. 1090." *Mnemosyne* 6:195–203.

Ender, E., ed. 1993. *"Reading Otherwise?" La critique des femmes*. New York: Peter Lang. Originally the inaugural issue of *Compar(a)ison: An International Journal of Comparative Literature*.

Fantham, E. 1975. "Sex, Status, and Survival in Hellenistic Athens: A Study of Women in New Comedy." *Phoenix* 29:44–74.

Fantham, E., et al. 1994. *Women in the Classical World: Image and Text*. New York: Oxford University Press.

Faranda, R., ed. and trans. 1971. *Detti e fatti memorabili de Valerio Massimo*. Turin: Unione tipografico-editrice torinese.

Fedeli, P. 1977. "Properzio 1,15: Arte allusiva e interpretazione." In *Colloquium propertianum*, ed. M. Bigaroni and F. Santucci, 73–99. Assisi: Accademia properziana del Subasio.

————, ed. and trans. 1985. *Properzio: Il libro terzo delle Elegie*. Bari: Adriatica Editrice.

————, ed. 1994 (editio correctior). *Sexti properti elegiarum libri IV*. Stuttgart and Leipzig: Teubner.

Feldstein, R., and J. Roof, eds. 1989. *Feminism and Psychoanalysis*. Ithaca and London: Cornell University Press.

Felman, S., ed. 1982. *Literature and Psychoanalysis: The Question of Reading Otherwise.* Baltimore: Johns Hopkins University Press.

Flaschenriem, B. L. 1997. "Loss, Desire, and Writing in Propertius 1.19 and 2.15." *Classical Antiquity* 16:259–77.

———. 1999. "Sulpicia and the Rhetoric of Disclosure." *CP* 94:36–54.

Foley, H. P., ed. 1981. *Reflections of Women in Antiquity.* New York: Gordon and Breach.

Foley, H. P. 1993. "The Politics of Tragic Lamentation." In *Tragedy, Comedy, and the Polis,* ed. A. Sommerstein, S. Halliwell, J. Henderson, and B. Zimmerman, 101–43. Bari: Levante Editori.

———, ed. 1994. *The Homeric Hymn to Demeter: Translation, Commentary, and Interpretive Essays.* Princeton, N.J.: Princeton University Press.

Forbes, C. 1952. "Crime and Punishment in Greek Athletics." *CJ* 47:169–74.

Fordyce, C. J. 1961. *Catullus.* Oxford: Clarendon Press.

Fraenkel, E. 1952–1953. "Zur griechischen Wortbildung." *Glotta* 32:16–33.

Fränkel. H. 1973. *Early Greek Poetry and Philosophy.* New York: Harcourt Brace Jovanovich. Translation by M. Hadas and J. Willis of *Dichtung und Philosophie des frühen Greichentums.* Munich: Beck, 1962.

Frazer, J. G., ed. 1973. *Publius ovidius naso, fastorum libri sex.* Vol. 4, *Commentary on Books 5 and 6.* London: Macmillan, 1923; rpt. Hildesheim: Helms.

Frazer, P. M. 1972. *Ptolemaic Alexandria.* 3 vols. Oxford: Clarendon Press.

Freud, S. 1953–1973. *The Standard Edition of the Complete Psychological Works of Sigmund Freud.* Edited by J. Strachey. 24 vols. London: Hogarth Press. (*SE*)

Friedman, S. 1975. "Who Buried H. D.? A Poet, Her Critics, and Her Place in 'The Literary Tradition.'" *College English* 37:801–14.

Furiani, P. L. 1991. "Intimità e socialità in Nosside di Locri." In De Martino, 177–95.

Furley, W. D. 1981. *Studies in the Use of Fire in Ancient Greek Religion.* New York: Arno Press.

Gaertner, J. F. 1999. "The Literary Background of an Amateurish Poetess: On [Tib.] 3.13." *Parola del Passato* 306:198–200.

Gallavotti, C. 1953. "Auctarium Oxyrhynchium." *Aegyptus* 33:159–71.

Gantz, T. 1993. *Early Greek Myth: A Guide to Literary and Artistic Sources.* Baltimore: Johns Hopkins University Press.

Gardner, J. F. 1986. *Women in Roman Law and Society.* Bloomington: Indiana University Press.

Garland, R. 1985. *The Greek Way of Death.* Ithaca: Cornell University Press.

———. 1989. "The Well-Ordered Corpse: An Investigation into the Motives behind Greek Funerary Legislation." *BICS* 36:1–15.

Geffcken, J. 1932. "Moiro." *RE* 15.2:2512–13.

Gentili, B. 1984. *Poesia e pubblico nella Grecia antica: da Omero al V secolo.* Roma: Laterza. 2nd Italian edition, 1995. Translated by A. T. Cole as

Poetry and Its Public in Ancient Greece. Baltimore: Johns Hopkins University Press, 1988.

Geoghegan, D., ed. and comm. 1979. *Anyte: The Epigrams.* Testi e commenti 4. Roma: Edizioni dell'Ateneo e Bizzarri.

Gerber, D. E. 1997. *A Companion to the Greek Lyric Poets. Mnemosyne Suppl. 173.* Leiden and New York: Brill.

Giangrande, G. 1969. "An Epigram of Erinna." *Classical Review,* n.s., 19:1–3.

————. 1980. "Sappho and the "λισβος." *Emerita* 40:249–50.

Gibson, R. 1995. "How to Win Girlfriends and Influence Them: *Amicitia* in Roman Love Elegy." *PCPhS* 41:62–82.

Gigante, M. 1074. "Nosside." *Parola del Passato* 29:22–39.

————. 1981. "Il manifesto poetico di Nosside." In *Letterature comparate: problemi e metodo,* ed. V. Ussani et al., 1:243–45. Bologna: Pàtron Editore.

Gilbert, S. M., and S. Gubar. 1979. *The Madwoman in the Attic.* New Haven: Yale University Press.

Ginsberg, A. 1961. *Kaddish and Other Poems.* San Francisco: City Lights Books.

Girard, R. 1966. *Deceit, Desire, and the Novel: Self and Other in Literary Structure.* Translated by Y. Freccero. Baltimore: Johns Hopkins University Press.

Gold, B. K. 1993. "'But Ariadne Was Never There in the First Place': Finding the Female in Roman Poetry." In Rabinowitz and Richlin, 75–101.

Gomme, A. W. 1957. "Interpretations of Some Poems of Alkaios and Sappho." *JHS* 77:255–66.

Goold, G. P. 1989. "Problems in Editing Propertius." In *Editing Greek and Latin Texts,* ed. J. N. Grant, 97–119. New York: AMS Press.

Goold, G. P, ed., and J. P. Postgate, trans. 1988. *Tibullus.* 2nd ed. Cambridge: Harvard University Press.

Gow, A. S. F. 1952. *Theocritus.* 2 vols. Cambridge: Cambridge University Press.

Gow, A. S. F., and D. L. Page, eds. 1965. *The Greek Anthology: Hellenistic Epigrams.* 2 vols. Cambridge: Cambridge University Press. (G-P)

Greene, E. 1994. "Apostrophe and Women's Erotics in the Poetry of Sappho." *TAPA* 124:41–56.

————, ed. 1996a. *Reading Sappho: Contemporary Approaches.* Berkeley, Los Angeles, and London: University of California Press.

————, ed. 1996b. *Re-Reading Sappho: Reception and Transmission.* Berkeley and Los Angeles: University of California Press.

Greene, E. 1996c. "Sappho, Foucault, and Women's Erotics." *Arethusa* 29:1–14.

————. 2000. "Playing with Tradition: Gender and Innovation in the Epigrams of Anyte." *Helios* 27:15–32.

————. 2002. "Subjects, Objects, and Erotic Symmetry in Sappho's Fragments." In Rabinowitz and Auanger, 85–105.

Greer, G. 1995. *Slip-Shod Sibyls: Recognition, Rejection, and the Woman Poet.* London: Viking.

Griffith, R. D., and G. D. Griffith. 1991. "Il Gioco della Chelichelone." *Maia* 43:83–87.

Griffiths, F. T. 1981. "Home before Lunch: The Emancipated Woman in Theocritus." In Foley 1981, 247–73.

Gronewald, M. 1974. "Fragmente aus einem Sappho-Kommentar." *ZPE* 14:114–18.

Guarino, A. 1981. "Professorenerotismus." *Labeo* 27:439–40.

Guillon, P. 1948. *La Béotie antique.* Paris: Belles Lettres.

———. 1958. "Corinne et les oracles béotiens: la consultation d'Asopos." *BCH* 82:47–60.

Gundel, H. 1924. "Kynosura." *RE* 12.1:37–41.

Gutzwiller, K. J. 1992. "Anyte's Epigram Book." *Syllecta Classica* 4:71–89.

———. 1997. "Genre Development and Gendered Voices in Erinna and Nossis." In Prins and Shreiber 1997, 202–22.

———. 1998. *Poetic Garlands: Hellenistic Epigrams in Context.* Berkeley, Los Angeles, and London: University of California Press.

Hallett, J. P. 1979. "Sappho and Her Social Context: Sense and Sensuality." *Signs* 4:447–71.

———. 1989. "Women as *Same* and *Other* in Classical Roman Elite." *Helios* 16:59–78.

———. 1990. "Contextualizing the Text: The Journey to Ovid." *Helios* 17:187–95.

———. 1996. "*Nec castrare velis meos libellos*: Sexual and Poetic *lusus* in Catullus, Martial, and the *Carmina priapea*." In *Satura lanx: Festschrift für Werner A. Krenkel zum 70. Geburtstag,* ed. C. Klodt, 321–44. Hildesheim: Olms.

Hamm, E. M. V. 1957. *Grammatik zu Sappho und Alkaios.* Abhandlungen der Deutschen Akademie der Wissenschaften zu Berlin, Klasse für Sprachen, Literatur und Kunst. Jahrg. 1951, Nr. 2. Berlin: Akademie-Verlag.

Hartmann, H. 1964. *Essays on Ego Psychology: Selected Problems in Psychoanalytic Theory.* New York: International Universities Press.

Harvey, A. E. 1957. "Homeric Epithets in Greek Lyric Poetry." *CQ* 7:206–23.

Haupt, M. 1967. *Opuscula.* Vol. 3. Leipzig, 1867; rpt. Hildesheim: Olms.

Heath, M., and M. Lefkowitz. 1991. "Epinician Performance." *CP* 86: 173–91.

Hemelrijk, E. 1999. *Matrona docta: Educated Women in the Roman Elite from Cornelia to Julia Domna.* London: Routledge.

Henderson, J. 1991. *The Maculate Muse: Obscene Language in Attic Comedy.* 2nd ed. New York: Oxford University Press.

Henderson, W. J. 1989. "Criteria in the Greek Lyric Contests." *Mnemosyne* 42:24–40.

———. 1995. "Corinna of Tanagra on Poetry." *Acta Classica* 38:29–41.

Henry, M. M. 1985. *Menander's Courtesans and the Greek Comic Tradition.* Frankfurt am Main: Peter Lang.

Herington, C. J. 1985. *Poetry into Drama: Early Tragedy and the Greek Poetic Tradition.* Berkeley and Los Angeles: University of California Press.

Herrlinger, G. 1930. *Totenklage um Tiere in der antiken Dichtung.* Stuttgart: W. Kohlhammer.

Heubeck, A., S. West, J. B. Hainsworth, eds. 1988. In *A Commentary on Homer's Odyssey,* vol. 1 of 3. Oxford: Clarendon Press.

Hinds, S. 1987. "The Poetess and the Reader: Further Steps towards Sulpicia." *Hermathena* 143:29–46.

Holst-Warhaft, G. 1992. *Dangerous Voices: Women's Laments and Greek Literature.* London and New York: Routledge.

Holzberg, N. 1998–1999. "Four Poets and a Poetess, or A Portrait of the Poet as a Young Man? Thoughts on Book 3 of the *Corpus tibullianum.*" *CJ* 94:169–91.

Howie, J. G. 1983. "The Revision of Myth in Pindar Olympian One: The Death and Revival of Pelops." *Papers of the Liverpool Latin Seminar* 4:277–313.

Hubbard, M. 1975. *Propertius.* New York: Scribner's Sons.

Hubbard, T. K. 1988. *The Pindaric Mind. Mnemosyne Suppl. 85.* Leiden: Brill.

Huys, M., ed. 1991. *Le Poème élégiaque hellénistique P. Brux. Inv. E. 8934 et P. Sorb. Inv. 2254.* Papyri Bruxellenses Graecae, 2:22. Brussels: Latomus.

Instone, S. 1996. *Pindar: Selected Odes.* Warminster: Aris and Phillips.

Johnston, S. I. 1999. *Restless Dead: Encounters between the Living and the Dead in Ancient Greece.* Berkeley and Los Angeles: University of California Press.

Jones, A. R. 1985. "Writing the Body: Toward an Understanding of *l'écriture féminine.*" In Showalter 1985, 361–75. Originally in *Feminist Studies* 7 (1981) and frequently reprinted.

Kammer, J. 1979. "The Art of Silence and the Forms of Women's Poetry." In *Shakespeare's Sisters: Feminist Essays on Women Poets,* ed. S. M. Gilbert and S. Gubar, 153–64. Bloomington: Indiana University Press.

Keith, A. 1997. "*Tandem venit Amor:* A Roman Woman Speaks of Love," In *Roman Sexualities,* ed. J. P. Hallett and M. B. Skinner, 295–310. Princeton, N.J.: Princeton University Press.

Kirkwood, G. M. 1974. *Early Greek Monody: The History of a Poetic Type.* Ithaca and London: Cornell University Press.

———. 1982. *Selections from Pindar.* APA Textbook Series 7. Chico, Calif.: Scholars Press.

Klaitch, D. 1974. *Woman + Woman: Attitudes towards Lesbianism.* New York: Morrow.

Klinck, A. L. 1994. "Lyric Voice and the Feminine in Some Ancient and Medieval *Frauenlieder.*" *Florilegium* 13:13–36.

Kock, Th. 1976. *Comicorum atticorum fragmenta.* Vol. 2. Utrecht: Hes.

Kohnken, A. 1985. "'Meilichos orga': Liebesthematik und aktueller Sieg in der neunten pythischen Ode Pindars." *Entretiens Hardt* 31:71–110.

Kolodny, A. 1980. "A Map for Rereading, or, Gender and the Interpretation of Literary Texts." *New Literary History* 11:451–67.

Konstan, D. 1994. *Sexual Symmetry: Love in the Ancient Novel and Related Genres.* Princeton, N.J.: Princeton University Press.

Kranz, W. 1961. "*SPHRAGIS*: Ichform und Namensiegel als Eingangs- und Schlussmotiv antiker Dichtung." *Rheinisches Museum* 104:3–46, 97–124.

Kurke, L. 1991. *The Traffic in Praise: Pindar and the Poetics of Social Economy.* Ithaca: Cornell University Press.

Lacan, J. 1988. *The Seminar of Jacques Lacan, Book 2.* Translated from the French by S. Tomaselli and J. Forrester. New York: W. W. Norton.

Lacey, W. K. 1968. *The Family in Classical Greece.* Ithaca: Cornell University Press.

Lange, D. K. 1979. "Cynthia and Cornelia: Two Voices from the Grave." In *Studies in Latin Literature and Roman History,* vol. 1, ed. C. Deroux, 335–42. Collection Latomus 164. Brussels: Latomus.

Lardinois, A. 1994. "Subject and Circumstance in Sappho's Poetry." *TAPA* 124:57–84.

———. 1996. "Who Sang Sappho's Songs?" In Greene 1996a, 150–72.

———. 2001. "Keening Sappho: Female Speech Genres in Sappho's Poetry." In Lardinois and McClure 2001, 75–92.

Lardinois, A., and L. McClure, eds. 2001. *Making Silence Speak: Women's Voices in Greek Literature and Society.* Princeton, N.J.: Princeton University Press.

Larmour, D. H. J. 1999. *Stage and Stadium: Drama and Athletics in Ancient Greece.* Nikephoros Beihefte 4. Hildesheim: Weidmann.

Larson, J. 2001. *Greek Nymphs: Myth, Cult, Lore.* Oxford: Oxford University Press.

Lasserre, F. 1966. *Die Fragmente des Eudoxos von Knidos.* Berlin: Walter de Gruyter.

Latte, K. 1953. "Erinna." *Nachr. Ges. der Wiss. zu Göttingen, Phil-hist. Kl.* 3:79–94.

Lattimore, R. 1962. *Themes in Greek and Latin Epitaphs.* Urbana: University of Illinois Press.

Lear, J. 1990. *Love and Its Place in Nature: A Philosophical Interpretation of Freudian Psychoanalysis.* New Haven and London: Yale University Press.

Lefkowitz, M. R. 1973. "Critical Stereotypes and the Poetry of Sappho." *GRBS* 14:113–23. Reprinted in *Heroines and Hysterics,* (New York: St Martin's Press, 1981), 59–68; and in Greene 1996a, 26–34.

———. 1981. *The Lives of the Greek Poets.* Baltimore: Johns Hopkins University Press.

Lenz, F. W., and G. K. Galinsky, eds. 1971. *Albii tibulli aliorumque carminum libri tres.* 3rd ed. Leiden: E. J. Brill.

Lerner, G. 1986. *The Creation of Patriarchy*. New York and Oxford: Oxford University Press.

Levin, D. N. 1962. "Quaestiones Erinneanae." *Harvard Studies in Classical Philology* 66:193–204.

Liddell, H. G., R. Scott, and H. S. Jones. 1869. *A Greek–English Lexicon* (LSJ). Oxford: Clarendon Press [Citations possibly to 9th rev. ed., 1996].

Lidov, J. B. 2002. "Sappho, Herodotus, ad the *Hetaira*." *CP* 97:203–37.

Lightfoot, J. L., ed. 1999. *Parthenius of Nicaea*. Oxford: Clarendon Press.

Lilja, S. 1972. *The Treatment of Odours in the Poetry of Antiquity*. Commentationes Humanarum Litterarum 49. Helsinki: Societas Scientiarum Fenica.

Linders, T. 1972. *Studies in the Treasure Records of Artemis Brauronia Found in Athens*. Stockholm: Svenska Institutet i Athen.

Lipking, L. 1983. "Aristotle's Sister: A Poetics of Abandonment." *Critical Inquiry* 10:61–81.

Lloyd-Jones, H. 1963. "The Seal of Posidippus." *JHS* 83:75–99.

Lloyd-Jones, H., and P. Parsons, eds. 1983. *Supplementum Hellenisticum*. Berlin: Walter de Gruyter. (*SH*)

Lobel, E., and D. Page. 1963. *Poetarum lesbiorum fragmenta*. Oxford: Oxford University Press. (L-P) (PLF).

Loewald, H. 1980. *Papers on Psychoanalysis*. New Haven: Yale University Press.

Loraux, N. 1986. *The Invention of Athens: The Funeral Oration in the Classical City*. Cambridge: Harvard University Press.

———. 1987. *Tragic Ways of Killing a Woman*. Translated from the French by A. Forster. Cambridge and London: Harvard University Press.

Lowe, N. J. 1988. "Sulpicia's Syntax." *CQ*, n.s., 38:193–205.

Luck, G. 1954. "Die Dichterinnen der griechischen Anthologie." *Museum Helveticum* 11:170–87.

———. 1982. "Love Elegy." In *The Cambridge History of Classical Literature*, vol. 2, part 3, *The Age of Augustus*, ed. P. E. Easterling and E. J. Kenney. Cambridge: Cambridge University Press.

———, ed. 1988. *Albii tibulli aliorumque carmina*. Stuttgart: Teubner.

Maas, P. 1936. "Nossis." *RE* 17.1: cols. 1053–54.

MacLachlan, B. C. 1995. "Love, War, and the Goddess in Fifth-Century Locri." *Ancient World* 26.2:205–23.

Magrini, M. M. 1975. "Una nuova linea interpretativa della 'Conocchia' di Erinna." *Prometheus* 1:225–36.

Manitius, C., ed. 1844. *Hipparchi in Arati et Eudoxi* Phaenomena *commentariorum*. Leipzig: Teubner.

Marcovich, M. 1972. "Sappho Fr. 31: Anxiety Attack or Love Declaration?" *CQ* 22:19–32.

Martin, J. 1956. *Histoire du texte des* Phénomènes *d'Aratos*. Paris: C. Klincksieck.

Martindale, J. R. 1980. *The Prosopography of the Later Roman Empire.* Vol. 2. Cambridge: Cambridge University Press.

Mastromarco, G. 1984. *The Public of Herondas.* Amsterdam: J. C. Gieben.

McClure, L. 2003. *Courtesans at Table: Gender and Greek Literary Culture in Athenaeus.* New York and London: Routledge.

Merkelbach, R. 1958. "Literarische Texte mit Ausschluss der christlichen." *Archiv für Papyrusforchung* 16:82–129.

R. Merkelbach and M. L. West, eds. 1967. *Fragmenta Hesiodea.* Oxford: Clarendon Press.

Merriam, C. U. 1990. "Some Notes on the Sulpicia Elegies." *Latomus* 49:95–98.

Meyerhoff, D. 1984. *Traditioneller Stoff und individuelle Gestaltung: Untersuchungen zu Alkaios und Sappho.* Hildesheim: Olms-Weidmann.

Miller, A. M. 1982. "*Phthonos* and *Parphasis: Nemean* 8.19–34." *GRBS* 23:111–20.

Minogue, S. 1990. "Prescriptions and Proscriptions: Feminist Criticism and Contemporary Poetry." In *Problems for Feminist Criticism,* ed. S. Minogue, 179–236. London: Routledge.

Most, G. W. 1981. "Sappho Fr. 16.6-7 L-P." *CQ,* n.s., 31:11–17.

Murnaghan, S. 1999. "The Poetics of Loss in the Greek Epic." In Beissinger, Tylus, and Wofford 1999, 203–20.

Murray, O. 1993. *Early Greece.* 2nd ed. Cambridge: Harvard University Press.

Nagy, G. 1973. "Phaethon, Sappho's Phaon, and the White Rock of Leukas." *Harvard Studies in Classical Philology* 77:137–77.

———. 1979. *The Best of the Achaeans: Concepts of the Hero in Archaic Greek Poetry.* Baltimore: Johns Hopkins University Press.

———. 1990. *Pindar's Homer: The Lyric Possession of an Epic Past.* Baltimore and London: Johns Hopkins University Press.

Nauck, A. 1964. *Tragicorum graecorum fragmenta*[2]. Supp. B. Snell. Hildesheim: Olms.

Neri, C. 1996. *Studi sulle testimonianze di Erinna.* Bologna: Pàtron.

———. 1997. "Erinna a Ossirinco." *ZPE* 115:57–72.

———. 1998. "Baucide e le Bambole (Erinna: *SH* 401, 1–4, 19–22)." *Athenaeum* 86:165–78.

Nisetich, F. J. 1989. *Pindar and Homer.* APA Monographs in Classical Philology 4. Baltimore: Johns Hopkins University Press.

Olck, F. 1897. "Byssos." *RE* 3.1: cols. 1108–14.

Oldfather, W. A. 1927. "Lokroi." *RE* 13.2: cols. 1289–363.

Onians, J. 1979. *Art and Thought in the Hellenistic Age.* London: Thames and Hudson.

Ostriker, A. 1985. "The Thieves of Language: Women Poets and Revisionist Mythmaking." In Showalter 1985, 314–38. Originally in *Coming to Light: American Women Poets in the Twentieth Century,* ed. D. W. Middlebrook and M. Yalom, 256–99. Ann Arbor: University of Michigan Press, 1985.

Page, D. L. 1953. *Corinna*. London: Society for the Promotion of Hellenic Studies.

———. 1955. *Sappho and Alcaeus: An Introduction to the Study of Ancient Lesbian Poetry*. Oxford: Oxford University Press.

———. 1962. *Poetae melici graeci*. Oxford: Clarendon Press. (*PMG*)

———. 1974. *Supplementum lyricis graecis*. Oxford: Oxford University Press. (*SLG*)

———. 1975. *Epigrammata graeca*. Oxford: Clarendon Press.

Pardini, A. 1991. "Problemi dialettali Greci ed interpretazioni antiche e moderne: P.S.I. 1090 (Erinna); P. Oxy. 8 (Anonimo); P. Antinoë S.N. (Teocrito)." *ZPE* 85:1–7.

Parker, H. 1993. "Sappho Schoolmistress." *TAPA* 123:309–51.

———. 1994. "Sulpicia, the *Auctor de Sulpicia*, and the Authorship of 3.9 and 3.11 of the *Corpus tibullianum*." *Helios* 21:39–62.

———. 1996. "Sappho Schoolmistres." In Greene 1996b, 146–86.

Parsons, P. 1993. "Identities in Diversity." In *Images and Ideologies: Self-Definition in the Hellenistic World*, eds. A. W. Bulloch, et al., 152–70. Berkeley and Los Angeles: University of California Press.

Paton, W. R., trans. 1918. *The Greek Anthology*. 5 vols. Cambridge: Harvard University Press.

Pearson, L. 1987. *The Greek Historians of the West: Timaeus and His Predecessors*. Atlanta: Scholars Press.

Pembroke, S. 1970. "Locres et Tarante: le rôle des femmes dans la fondation de deux colonies grecques." *Annals E.S.C.* 25:1240–70.

Pfeiffer, R., ed. 1949–1951. *Callimachus*. Oxford: Oxford University Press.

Pfuhl, E. 1955. *Masterpieces of Greek Drawing and Painting*. Trans. J. D. Beazley. New York: Macmillan.

Phillips, A. 2001. *Promises, Promises: Essays on Psychoanalysis and Literature*. New York: Basic Books.

Pierrugues, P. 1965. *Glossarium eroticum linguae latinae*. Paris, 1826; rpt. Amsterdam: A. M. Hakkert.

Plant, I. M. 2004. *Women Writers of Ancient Greece and Rome*. Norman: University of Oklahoma Press.

Podlecki, A. J. 1984. *The Early Greek Poets and Their Times*. Vancouver: University of British Columbia Press.

Pollard, J. R. T. 1965. *Seers, Shrines, and Sirens: The Greek Religious Revolution in the Sixth Century B.C.* London: Allen and Unwin.

Pomeroy, S. B. 1975. *Goddesses, Whores, Wives, and Slaves: Women in Classical Antiquity*. New York: Schocken.

———. 1977. "*TECHNIKAI KAI MOUSIKAI*: The Education of Women in the Fourth Century and in the Hellenistic Period." *AJAH* 2:51–68.

———. 1978. "Supplementary Notes on Erinna." *ZPE* 32:17–22.

———, ed. 1991. *Women's History and Ancient History*. Chapel Hill and London: University of North Carolina Press.

Postgate, J. P., ed. 1915. *Tibulli aliorumque carminum libri tres*. 2nd ed. Oxford: Oxford University Press.

Powell, J. U. 1925. *Collectanea alexandrina*. Oxford: Clarendon Press.

Pratt, L. H. 1993. *Lying and Poetry from Homer to Pindar: Falsehood and Deception in Archaic Greek Poetics*. Ann Arbor: University of Michigan Press.

Prins, Y. 1999. *Victorian Sappho*. Princeton, N.J.: Princeton University Press.

Prins, Y., and M. Shreiber, eds. 1997. *Dwelling in Possibility: Women Poets and Critics on Poetry*. Ithaca and London: Cornell University Press.

Probst, S., and V. Probst. 1992. "Frauendichtung in Rom: Die Elegien der Sulpicia." *AU* 35.6:19–36.

Prückner, H. 1968. *Die lokrischen Tonreliefs*. Mainz am Rhein: Philipp von Zabern.

Putnam, M. C. J. 1982. *Essays on Latin Lyric, Elegy, and Epic*. Princeton, N.J.: Princeton University Press.

Rabinowitz, N., and A. Richlin, eds. 1993. *Feminist Theory and the Classics*. New York: Routledge.

Rabinowitz, N., and L. Auanger, eds. 2002. *Among Women: From the Homosocial to the Homoerotic in the Ancient World*. Austin: University of Texas Press.

Race, W. 1989. "Sappho, Fr. 16 L-P. and Alkaios, Fr. 42 L-P.: Romantic and Classical Strains in Lesbian Lyric." *CJ* 85:16–33.

Rachewiltz, S. de. 1987. *De Sirenibus: An Inquiry into Sirens from Homer to Shakespeare*. New York and London: Garland.

Ragland-Sullivan, E. 1989. "Seeking the Third Term: Desire, the Phallus, and the Materiality of Language." In Feldstein and Roof, 40–64.

Raubitschek, A. E. 1968. "Das Denkmal-Epigramm." In *L'Epigramme grecque*, 3–26. Entretiens sur l'Antiquité classique 14. Geneva: Vandoeuvres.

Rauk, J. 1989. "Erinna's *Distaff* and Sappho Fr. 94." *GRBS* 30:101–16.

Rayor, D. 1991. *Sappho's Lyre: Archaic Lyric and Women Poets of Ancient Greece*. Berkeley and Los Angeles: University of California Press.

———. 1993. "Korinna: Gender and the Narrative Tradition." *Arethusa* 26:219–31.

Redfield, J. M. 2004. *The Locrian Maidens: Love and Death in Greek Italy*. Princeton, N.J.: Princeton University Press.

Rehm, R. 1994. *Marriage to Death: The Conflation of Wedding and Funeral Rituals in Greek Tragedy*. Princeton, N.J.: Princeton University Press.

Reitzenstein, R. 1893. *Epigramm und Skolion: ein Beitrag zur Geschichte der alexandrinischen Dichtung*. Giessen: Ricker'sche Buchhandlung; rpt. Hildesheim and New York: Olms, 1970.

Richlin, A. 1992. *The Garden of Priapus: Sexuality and Aggression in Roman Humor*. Oxford: Oxford University Press.

Riedweg, C. 1994. "Reflexe hellenistischer Dichtungstheorie im griechischen Epigramm." *Illinois Classical Studies* 19:123–30.

Robbins, E. 1995. "Sappho, Aphrodite, and the Muses." *Ancient World* 26:225–39.

Roessel, D. 1990. "The Significance of the Name *Cerinthus* in the Poems of Sulpicia." *TAPA* 120:243–50.

Rösler, W. 1975. "Ein Gedicht und sein Publikum: Überlegungen zu Sappho Fr. 44 Lobel-Page." *Hermes* 103:275–85.

———. 1980. *Dichter und Gruppe: eine Untersuchung zu den Bedingungen und zur historischen Funktion früher griechischer Lyrik am Beispiel Alkaios*. Munich: W. Fink.

Rutherford, I. 2001. *Pindar's Paeans: A Reading of the Fragments with a Survey of the Genre*. Oxford: Oxford University Press.

Saake, H. 1971. *Zur Kunst Sapphos: Motiv-analytische und kompositionstechnichische Interpretationen*. Munich: Schöningh.

Sansone, D. 1988. *Greek Athletics and the Genesis of Sport*. Berkeley and Los Angeles: University of California Press.

Santirocco, M. S. 1979. "Sulpicia Reconsidered." *CJ* 74:229–39.

Scanlon, T. F. 2002. *Eros and Greek Athletics*. Oxford: Oxford University Press.

Schachter, A. 1981–1994. *Cults of Boeotia*. 4 vols. BICS Suppl. 38.1–4. London: Institute of Classical Studies.

Schadewaldt, W. 1950. *Sappho: Welt und Dichtung, Dasein in der Liebe*. Potsdam: Eduard Stichnote.

Scholz, U. W. 1973. "Erinna." *Antike und Abendland* 18:15–40.

Seaford, R. 1994. *Reciprocity and Ritual: Homer and Tragedy in the Developing City-State*. Oxford: Oxford University Press.

Segal, C. 1975. "Pebbles in Golden Urns: The Date and Style of Corinna." *Eranos* 73:1–8.

———. 1984. "Underreading and Intertextuality: Sappho, Simaetha, and Odysseus in Theocritus' Second Idyll." *Arethusa* 17:201–209.

———. 1986. *Pindar's Mythmaking: The Fourth Pythian Ode*. Princeton, N.J.: Princeton University Press.

Seremetakis, C. N. 1991. *The Last Word: Women, Death, and Divination in Inner Mani*. Chicago and London: University of Chicago Press.

Sharrock, A., and R. Ash. 2002. *Fifty Key Classical Authors*. London and New York: Routledge.

Showalter, E. 1977. *A Literature of Their Own: British Women Novelists from Brontë to Lessing*. Princeton, N.J.: Princeton University Press.

———. 1979. "Toward a Feminist Poetics." In *Women Writing and Writing about Women*, ed. M. Jacobus, 22–41. London: Croom Helm.

———. 1981. "Feminist Criticism in the Wilderness." *Critical Inquiry* 8: 179–205.

———, ed. 1985. *The New Feminist Criticism*. New York: Pantheon.

Skinner, M. B. 1982. "Briseis, the Trojan Women, and Erinna." *CW* 75: 265–69.

———. 1983. "Corinna of Tanagra and Her Audience." *Tulsa Studies in Women's Literature* 2:9–20.

———. 1987. "Greek Women and the Metronymic: A Note on an Epigram by Nossis." *Ancient History Bulletin* 1:39–42.

———. 1989. "Sapphic Nossis." *Arethusa* 22:5–18.

———. 1991a. "Aphrodite Garlanded: *Erôs* and Poetic Creativity in Sappho and Nossis." In De Martino 1991, 77–96.

———. 1991b. "Nossis *Thêlyglôssos*: The Private Text and the Public Book." In Pomeroy 1991, 20–47.

———. 1993a. "Perillus at Tomis." In *Tria Lustra,* ed. H. D. Jocelyn, 301–310. Liverpool Classical Papers no. 3. Liverpool: *Liverpool Classical Monthly.*

———. 1993b. "Woman and Language in Archaic Greece, or, Why Is Sappho a Woman?" In Rabinowitz and Richlin 1993, 125–44.

———. 2001. "Ladies' Day at the Art Institute: Theocritus, Herodas, and the Gendered Gaze." In Lardinois and McClure 2001, 201–22.

———. 2002. "Aphrodite Garlanded: Erôs and Poetic Creativity in Sappho and Nossis." In Rabinowitz and Auanger 2002, 60–81.

Smith, K. F., ed. 1913. *The Elegies of Albius Tibullus.* New York: American Book Company.

Snell, B. 1931. "Sapphos Gedicht *phainetai moi kenos*." Hermes 66:71–90.

———. 1953a. "Der Anfang eines äolischen Gedichts." *Hermes* 81:118–19.

———. 1953b. *The Discovery of the Mind.* Translated by T. G. Rosenmeyer. Cambridge: Cambridge University Press.

———. 1967. *Scenes from Greek Drama.* Berkeley and Los Angeles: University of California Press.

Snell, B., and H. Maehler, eds. 1987–88. *Pindari carmina cum fragments.* Leipzig: Teubner.

Snyder, J. M. 1984. "Korinna's Glorious Songs of Heroes." *Eranos* 82: 125–34.

———. 1989. *The Woman and the Lyre: Women Writers in Classical Greece and Rome.* Carbondale and Edwardsville: Southern Illinois University Press.

———. 1991. "Public Occasion and Private Passion in the Lyrics of Sappho of Lesbos." In Pomeroy 1991, 1–19. Most of this essay is included in a slightly different form in Snyder 1989.

———. 1997. *Lesbian Desire in the Lyrics of Sappho.* New York: Columbia University Press.

Solmsen, F., R. Merkelbach, and M. L. West, eds. 1983. *Hesiodi* Theogonia; Opera et dies; Scutum; *[and] fragmenta selecta.* 2nd ed. Oxford: Clarendon Press.

Sourvinou-Inwood, C. 1974. "The Votum of 477/6 B.C. and the Foundation Legend of Locri Epizephyrii." *CQ* 24:186–98.

———. 1978. "Persephone and Aphrodite at Locri: A Model for Personality Definitions in Greek Religion." *JHS* 98:101–21.

Sprengel, C. 1820. *Pedanii Dioscoridis Anazarbei* De materia medica *libri quinque.* Vol. 1. Leipzig: Car. Cnoblochius.

Stadtmüller, H., ed. 1894–1906. *Anthologia graeca epigrammatum palatina cum Planudea.* 3 vols. Leipzig: Teubner.

Stehle, E. 1981. "Sappho's Private World." In Foley 1981, 45–61.

———. 1997. *Performance and Gender in Ancient Greece: Nondramatic Poetry in Its Setting.* Princeton, N.J.: Princeton University Press.

———. 2001. "The Good Daughter: Mothers' Tutelage in Erinna's *Distaff* and Fourth-Century Epitaphs." In Lardinois and McClure 2001, 179–200.

Stern, J. 1979. "Herodas' *Mimiamb* 6." *GRBS* 20:247–54.

Swindler M. H. 1929. *Ancient Painting.* New Haven: Yale University Press.

Syme, R. 1981. " A Great Orator Mislaid." *CQ,* n.s., 31:421–27.

Taplin, O. 1993. *Comic Angels and Other Approaches to Greek Drama through Vase-Paintings.* Oxford: Clarendon Press.

Tarán, S. L. 1979. *The Art of Variation in the Hellenistic Epigram.* Leiden: Brill.

Tedesco, V. 1994. *Il canto delle sirene.* Castrovillari: Teda.

Traenkle, H. 1990. *Appendix tibulliana.* Berlin: Walter de Gruyter.

Treu, M. 1963. *Sappho.* Munich: Heimeran.

———. 1966. "Neues über Sappho und Alkaios (P. Ox. 2506)." *Quaderni Urbinati* 2:9–36.

Trump, J. 1973. "Über das Trinken in der Poesie der Alkaios." *ZPE* 12:139–60.

Tsagarakis, O. 1977. *Self-Expression in Early Greek Lyric, Elegiac, and Iambic.* Wiesbaden: Steiner.

Tschiedel, H. J. 1992. "Die Gedichte der Sulpicia (Tib. 3.13–18)—Frauenlyrik?" *GB* 18:87–102.

Tsomis, G. 2001. *Zusammenschau der frühgriechischen monodischen Melik: Alkaios.* Stuttgart: Franz Steiner.

Tyson, P., and R. L. Tyson. 1990. *Psychoanalytic Theories of Development: An Integration.* New Haven: Yale University Press.

Van der Valk, M., ed. 1971. *Eustathii archiepiscop, Thessalonicensis commentarii ad Homeri Iliadem pertinentes.* Vol. 1. Leiden: Brill.

Van Sickle, J. 1981. "Poetics of Opening and Closure in Meleager, Catullus, and Gallus." *CW* 75:64–75.

Vara Donado, J. 1972. "Notas sobre Erina." *EC* 16:67–86.

———. 1973. "Cronologia de Erinna." *Emerita* 41:349–76.

Vitelli, G. 1929. "Frammenti della 'Conocchia' di Erinna." *BSAA* 24:9–16.

Vivante, P. 1979. "Korinna's Singing Mountains." In *Teiresias,* Suppl. 2, Proceedings of the Second International Conference on Boeotian Antiquities, 1979, 83–86. Montreal: Department of Classics, McGill University.

Voigt, E. 1971. *Sappho et Alcaeus: Fragmenta.* Amsterdam: Athenaeum-Polak and Van Gennep.

Walker, J. 2000. *Rhetoric and Poetics in Antiquity*. Oxford: Oxford University Press.

Waltz, P. 1928–1957. *Anthologie grecque*. 7 vols. Paris: Société d'édition "Les Belles Lettres."

Watson, L. 1991. Arae: *The Curse Poetry of Antiquity*. Leeds: Francis Cairns.

Webster, T. B. L. 1967. *The Tragedies of Euripides*. London: Methuen.

Weiler, I. 1974. *Der Agon im Mythos: Zur Einstellung der Griechen zum Wettkampf*. Darmstadt: Wissenschaftliche Buchgesellschaft.

Wendel, C., ed. 1958. *Scholia in Apollonium Rhodium vetera*. 2nd ed. Berlin: Weidmannsche Verlagsbuchhandlung.

West, M. L. 1970a. "Burning Sappho." *Maia* 22:307–30.

———. 1970b. "Corinna." *CQ* 20:277–87.

———. 1977. "Erinna." *ZPE* 25:95–119.

———. 1985. *The Hesiodic Catalogue of Women: Its Nature, Structure, and Origins*. Oxford: Clarendon Press.

———. 1990. "Dating Corinna." *CQ* 40:553–57.

———. 1993. *Greek Lyric Poetry*. Oxford: Oxford University Press.

———. 1996a. *Die griechische Dichterin: Bild und Rolle*. Lectio Teubneriana 5. Stuttgart and Leipzig: Teubner.

———. 1996b. *Hesiod: Theogony*. Oxford: Oxford University Press.

White, H. 1980. "An Epigram by Moero." In *Essays in Hellenistic Poetry*, 21–25. London Studies in Classical Philology 5. Amsterdam and Uithoorn: J. C. Gieben.

Wilamowitz-Moellendorff, U. von. 1914. "Neue lesbische Lyrik." *Neue Jahrbücher für das klassische Altertum* 33:225–47. Reprinted in *Kleine Schriften* 1:384–414 (Berlin: Weidmann, 1935–1972).

———. 1924. *Hellenistische Dichtung in der Zeit des Kallimachos*. 2 vols. Berlin: Weidmannsche Buchhandlung.

Wilkinson, L. P. 1963. *Golden Latin Artistry*. Cambridge: Cambridge University Press.

Williams, G. 1958. "Some Aspects of Roman Marriage Ceremonies and Ideals." *JRS* 48:16–29.

Williamson, M. 1995. *Sappho's Immortal Daughters*. Cambridge and London: Harvard University Press.

———. 1996. "Sappho and the Other Woman." In Greene 1996a, 248–64.

Wilson, L. H. 1996. *Sappho's Sweetbitter Songs: Configurations of Female and Male in Ancient Greek Lyric*. New York: Routledge.

Winkler, J. J. 1981. "Gardens of Nymphs: Public and Private in Sappho's Lyrics." In Foley 1981, 63–89. Originally in *Women's Studies* 8 (1981), and a later version was published as "Double Consciousness in Sappho's Lyrics," in Winkler 1990, 162–87.

———. 1990. *The Constraints of Desire: The Anthropology of Sex and Gender in Ancient Greece*. New York and London: Routledge.

Winnicott, D. W. 1971. *Playing and Reality*. London: Tavistock.

Woodbury, L. 1978. "The Gratitude of the Locrian Maiden, *Pyth.* 2.18–20." *TAPA* 108:285–99.

Wright, F. A. 1923. "The Woman Poets of Greece." *Fortnightly Review*, n.s., 113:322–28.

Wyke, M. 1987a. "Written Women: Propertius' *Scripta Puella*." *JRS* 77: 47–61.

———. 1987b. "The Elegiac Woman at Rome." *PCPhS*, n.s., 33:153–78.

———. 1989a. "Mistress and Metaphor in Augustan Elegy." *Helios* 16:25–47.

———. 1989b. "Reading Female Flesh: *Amores* 3.1" In *History as Text: The Writing of Ancient History*, ed. A. Cameron, 111–43. London: Duckworth.

———. 1995. "Taking the Woman's Part: Engendering Roman Love Elegy." In *Roman Literature and Ideology: Ramus Essays for J. P. Sullivan*, ed. A. J. Boyle, 110–28. Bendigo: Aureal Publications.

Yardley, J. C. 1990. "Cerinthus: *Pia Cura* ([Tibullus] 3.17.1–2)." *CJ* 40:568–70.

———, ed. 1992. *Minor Authors of the Corpus tibullianum*. Bryn Mawr: Bryn Mawr College.

Zanker, G. 1987. *Realism in Alexandrian Poetry*. London: Croom Helm.

Zumthor, P. 1986. *Speaking of the Middle Ages*. Lincoln: University of Nebraska Press.

Notes on Contributors

Ellen Greene is Joseph Paxton Presidential Professor of Classics at the University of Oklahoma. She has published articles on gender and sexuality in the poetry of Sappho, Catullus, Propertius, and Ovid. She is the author of *The Erotics of Domination: Male Desire and the Mistress in Latin Love Poetry* (Johns Hopkins 1998), and the editor of *Reading Sappho: Contemporary Approaches* and *Re-reading Sappho: Reception and Transmission* (University of California 1997). The volume she edited with Ronnie Ancona, *Gendered Dynamics in Latin Love Poetry*, will be published in 2005 by Johns Hopkins University Press. She is currently at work on a book-length study of the relationship between gender and genre in Propertius Book 2.

Barbara L. Flaschenriem is Associate Professor of Classics at Grand Valley State University in Michigan. Her scholarly interests encompass Augustan poetry, Greek lyric and drama, and theories of gender. Her publications include "Speaking of Women: 'Female Voice' in Propertius" (*Helios* 25 [1998]: 49–64) and "Loss, Desire, and Writing in Propertius 1.19 and 2.15" (*Cl. Ant.* 16 [1997]: 259–77).

David H. J. Larmour is Professor of Classics at Texas Tech University and an editor of the comparative literature journal *Intertexts*. He is coauthor of an interpretative commentary on Lucian's *True Histories*

(1998) and author of *Stage and Stadium: Drama and Athletics in Ancient Greece* (1999). He is the editor of two collections of essays: *Rethinking Sexuality: Foucault and Classical Antiquity* (1998) and *Discourse and Ideology in Nabokov's Prose* (2002). He has also written articles on Euripides, Plutarch, Lucian, Ovid, and Nabokov.

Elizabeth Manwell is Assistant Professor of Classical Studies at Kalamazoo College. Her scholarly interests focus on the literature and culture of the Roman Republic. She is currently working on a study of oral behaviors in late Republican poetry and oratory.

Carol U. Merriam is Associate Professor and Chair of the Department of Classics at Brock University in St. Catharines, Ontario, Canada. She is the author of numerous articles on elegy, particularly on Sulpicia and Gallus, as well as on erotic madness in elegy and Parthians in Augustan poetry. She is the author of a book on the development of the epyllion, and a forthcoming book on Venus in the Latin Love Elegy. She is currently working on a study of Priapus in Latin poetry.

Holt Parker is Professor of Classics at the University of Cincinnati. He has been awarded the Rome Prize, the Women's Classical Caucus Prize for Scholarship, and a Fellowship from the National Endowment for the Humanities. He has published works on Sappho, Sulpicia, sexuality, slavery, sadism, and spectacles. *Olympia Morata: The Complete Writings of an Italian Heretic* (Chicago 2003) was given the Josephine Roberts Award by the Society for the Study of Early Modern Women. Some of his recent work focuses on ancient medicine. His edition of the *Gynecology* by Metrodora, the oldest surviving work by a woman doctor, is forthcoming in Brill's Studies in Ancient Medicine.

Diane J. Rayor is Professor and Chair of the Department of Classics at Grand Valley State University in Michigan. She has published four books of translations, including *The Homeric Hymns* (2004) and *Sappho's Lyre: Archaic Lyric and Women Poets of Ancient Greece* (1991). She is coeditor of *Latin Lyric and Elegiac Poetry* (1995) and *Callimachus: Hymns, Epigrams, Select Fragments* (1988).

Marilyn B. Skinner is Professor of Classics at the University of Arizona in Tucson. From 1995 to 2000 she served as the editor of

Transactions of the American Philological Association and is now American Philological Association Vice-President for Publications. Her primary research specialization is Roman literature of the Republican and Augustan eras. She has authored two monographs, *Catullus' Passer: The Arrangement of the Book of Polymetric Poems* (1981) and *Catullus in Verona* (2003). Her coedited collection of scholarly essays *Philodemus, Vergil, and the Augustans* appeared in 2004. Dr. Skinner is also well known for her work on sexuality and gender in antiquity; she coedited *Roman Sexualities* (1997) and has written the first comprehensive overview of ancient sexual mores, *Sexuality in Greek and Roman Culture*, published in 2005. She has also authored numerous articles on the Greek female poetic tradition dealing with Sappho and her successors Korinna, Erinna, Anyte, Moero, and Nossis.

Index